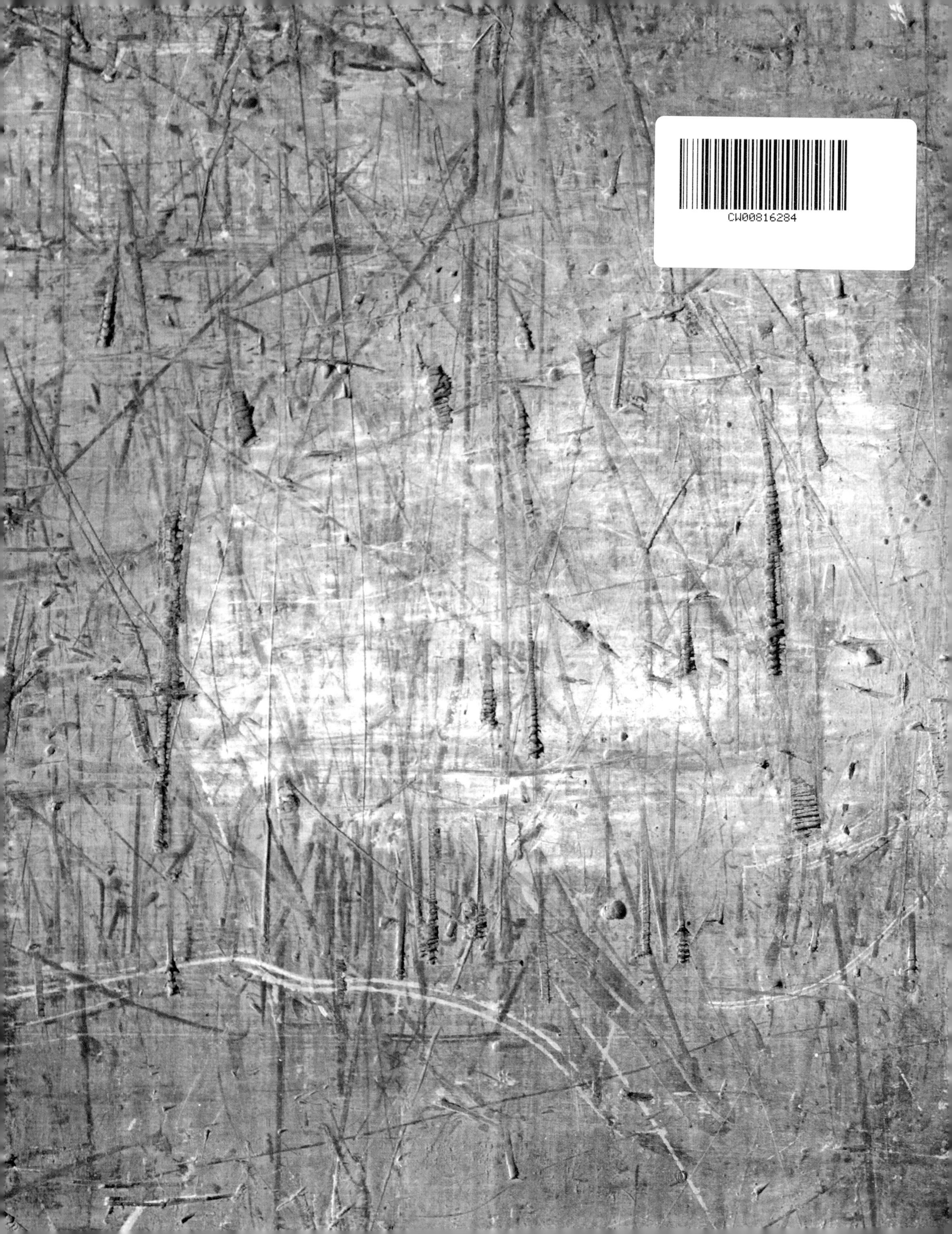
CW00816284

THERE ARE NO RULES ANYMORE. IT JUST HAS TO BE BLOODY TASTY.

SCOTT PICKETT

BISTRONOMY

FRENCH FOOD UNBOUND

KATRINA MEYNINK

MURDOCH BOOKS

SI
TU ME
ÇA
LA

FOR CHEFS. AND THE WAY THEY USE THEIR HEARTS, HANDS AND MINDS AS COOKS, CHEMISTS, PHYSICISTS AND CULTURAL HISTORIANS TO FEED OUR BELLIES AND OUR SOULS.

THANK YOU.

AMERICAN RANGE

ANATOMIE

THE ANATOMY OF BISTRONOMY

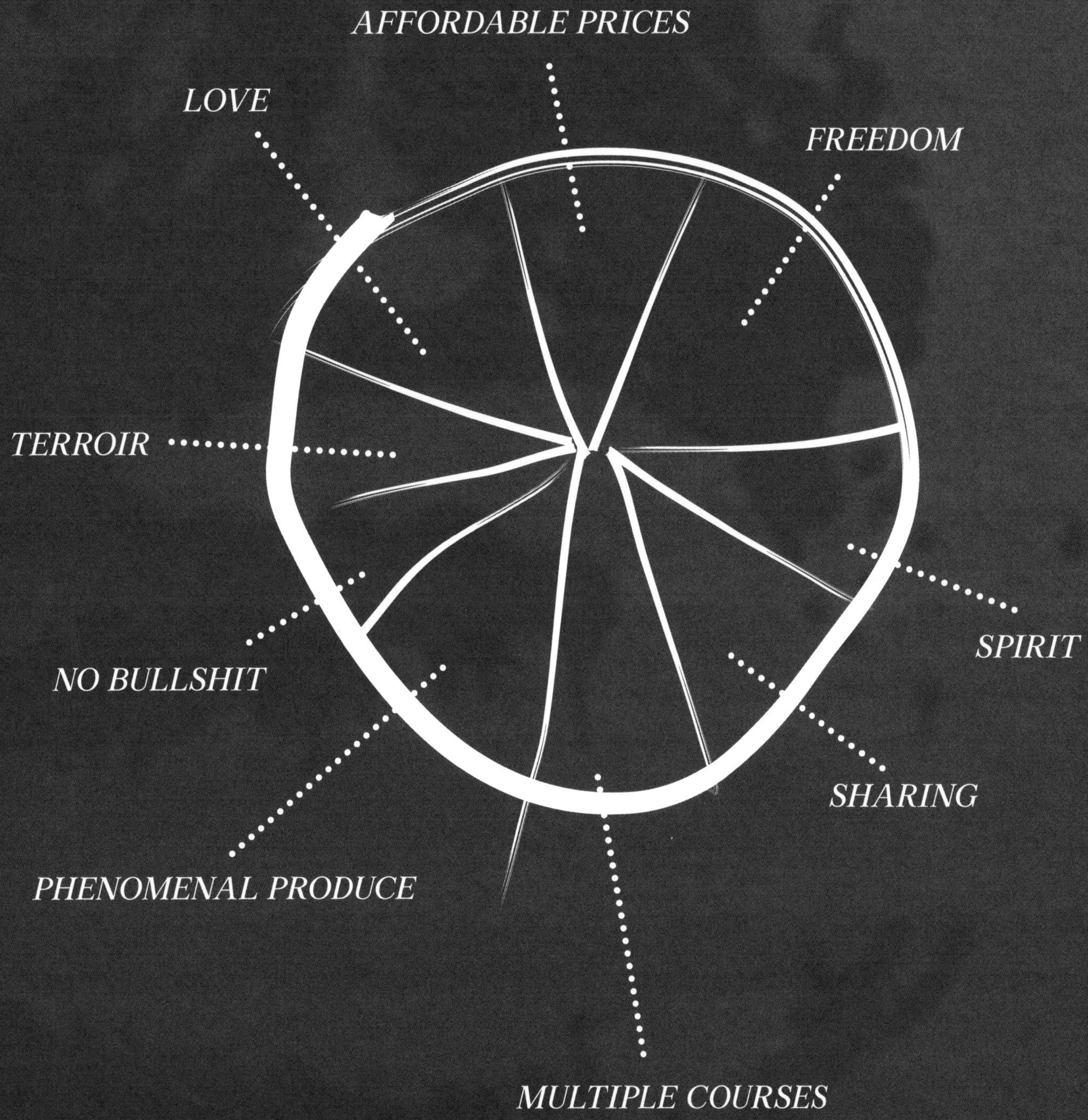

AFFORDABLE PRICES

LOVE

FREEDOM

TERROIR

SPIRIT

NO BULLSHIT

SHARING

PHENOMENAL PRODUCE

MULTIPLE COURSES

AMUSE-BOUCHE

This book lives because of Julia Child. And it breathes because of the generous chefs who inhabit its pages.

In 2012, I applied for a Julia Child grant through the Culinary Institute of America. I pondered the idea of bistronomy — that elusive partnership of gastronomic excellence in the comfortable, relaxed atmosphere of a bistro — and what it meant in terms of Julia's love of French gastronomy and her absolute ideals of sharing food around the table. Somewhere, somehow the culinary gods were on my side. I received the grant, packed my bags and headed to Paris. I ate, I talked to chefs, I discovered. Then I did it all again. And again, for good measure.

What fascinated me were the glimpses of wine bars in alleyways, forgotten corner shops turned restaurants, and the attraction of nameless locales as tiny hubs of food and wine. It wasn't dining in Paris. The formality, the sense of pomp and circumstance of eating in restaurants — the sort of constipated churches of *haute cuisine* where good conversations go to die — suddenly seemed peripheral to this new style of dining: top-notch cooking prepared with a *haute cuisine* touch and served in fun, relaxed surrounds. It was enthralling to feel the undercurrents of culinary revolt; that 'sticking it to the man' mentality that continues to bubble deliciously, and ever so subtly, under everything these chefs are doing.

The meals. Holy hell, the meals. They were so good. Gutsy. Honest. Often unexpected. Food that ranged from the beautifully sophisticated to dishes as homely as a dent in the couch. Dishes as decorative as modern art and as neckable as a packet of chips. And I could actually afford to eat them, even more than once. I cannot ever remember consuming food that prompted so many actual, physical responses. My face pursed like a cat's bum at the sharp kick of fresh, pungent horseradish grated over a gloriously marbled wagyu rump cooked on coal, or the unexpected sourness of a citrus sherbet and whey ice-cream dessert. There were groans of horny delight at a light-as-air waffle with artichoke-heart cream whipped into submission and topped with delicate shavings of jambon, before murmuring over and prodding a duck dish that was

earthy, piquant, meaty, wobbly, crunchy and fatty — all those textures in a few mere mouthfuls — all before eating the sort of thick, indulgent and creamy rice pudding that I had only ever dreamed of. To watch me was probably indecent, but here I was suddenly experiencing the holy grail of food in the city I'd read about as a culinary student and the city I'd dreamed about as a romantic waiting to be swept off my feet. I would never be full.

I immersed myself in the restaurants and wine bars, eating everything, picking dishes apart, making notes and taking photographs, trying to absorb as much of the culinary energy of these chefs and their spaces as I possibly could to share in this book. I turned my search further afield, and discovered more and more chefs and restaurants across the globe are embracing this way of cooking and eating.

Let's be clear: this tome is not about capturing a trend. It would be ignorant not to acknowledge that this style of dining has and still is returning France to the culinary map, after witnessing her decade of suffering as the rest of the gastronomically attuned world followed the foamista chefs to Spain, went foraging with the bearded boy scouts in the Nordic regions and digested everything nose-to-tail on Fergus Henderson's coat-tails through Britain.

This is first and foremost a celebration of food, of the people who grow it, the people who cook it and the people who eat it. Some of the chefs on the following pages are doing family-style food, some are doing super-high-end intellectual food while others are still very produce-and-tweezer driven. The collection of chefs and restaurants are those I feel tell the story of where excellence in bistronomy may be found. It is by no means an exhaustive survey. It is about who is interesting, who has a unique voice, and ultimately who is really owning what they are doing within a bistronomy-style setting.

This book is simply an attempt to capture the sensory light and shade of this elusive thing called bistronomy. So what you hold in your hands is a collection of moments, cleaved into parts, not an autopsy performed by some kind of culinary oracle, as I dare say there is plenty more to come in the bistronomy story ...

Katrina Meynink

TASTING NOTES

6 things I should point out ...

1. Cooking these recipes, like the bistronomy dining experience itself, can be rough, unrefined, beautiful and occasionally painful. The food is not designed by committee so it varies from the accessible to the aspirational.

2. This is not an attempt to answer the who, what, where, why, how and will it last mysteries of bistronomy: it is merely a few lucidly pointed fingers, signposts — if you will — to the phenomenal success of this style of dining and its greatest global ambassadors — the chefs, the producers, and you, the willing eater.

3. This book is a celebration of flavours. Off-the-wall combinations, reinterpretations of the classics, the joy found in the simple and the challenge of the complex. It is a chance to sniff out what these chefs are doing and how they make the food taste so amazing. The menus at bistronomy restaurants change. Constantly. So these recipes are, for the most part, fleeting tastes of what the chefs can do, and a chance for you to try them at home.

4. Sometimes, a restaurant, chef or recipe has been included within these pages that may not fit your perception of what bistronomy is; but sometimes there is food, an ambience, or a chef's spirit that defies description. It is for everyone, but it doesn't aim to please all comers.

5. Don't be afraid to cook. Ingredients and chefs like to misbehave, so they make epic bedfellows. The wonderful thing about cooking is that mistakes are usually very short lived. So enjoy your cooking, pass your pleasure to the table, and discover that the food is likely to be far less rebellious when accompanied by love and wine.

6. Veal tongue is surprisingly tasty.

J'ASSURE
EN CHAIR

CONTENTS

LIBERTÉ. ÉGALITÉ. FRUGALITÉ.

FREEDOM. EQUALITY. FRUGALITY.

Refined, focused, honest and humble

AIR-DRIED BEEF AND KIMCHI

SEAWEED AND TOFU BEIGNET, YUZUKOSHO AND LIME MAYONNAISE

PICKLED COCKLES

CARROTS, YOGHURT AND PRAWN FLOSS

DUCK CONFIT CROQUETTES

SAUSAGE, SMOKED HERRING ROE AND HORSERADISH MOUSSE

CRISP CHICKEN SKIN, ROSEMARY MASCARPONE AND BACON JAM

SALT AND VINEGAR CRISPS

PUFFED RICE, SASHIMI AND SMOKED BUTTER

STEAMED OYSTERS AND AGED APPLE CIDER EMULSION

MARINATED SARDINES, POACHED WHITE ASPARAGUS AND TRUFFLE

PRAWN, RED CAPSICUM AND LARDO DI COLONNATA

BARBECUED SCALLOPS WITH SEAWEED GREMOLATA

AIR-DRIED BEEF AND KIMCHI

CHEF: RYAN SQUIRES

SERVES 10-12

You will need to begin this recipe one day ahead.

500 g (1 lb 2 oz) marbled Scotch fillet (rib eye), sinew removed, trimmed
75 ml (2½ fl oz/⅓ cup) fish sauce

KIMCHI

65 g (2¼ oz/½ cup) sea salt
2 litres (70 fl oz/8 cups) water
½ large Chinese cabbage (wong bok), outer leaves and base removed
50 g (1¾ oz) salt
50 ml (1¾ fl oz) fish sauce
125 g (4½ oz) ginger, finely minced
90 g (3¼ oz) garlic, finely minced
100 g (3½ oz) caster (superfine) sugar
125 g (4½ oz) French shallots, peeled, finely minced
35 ml (1¼ fl oz) sesame oil
50 g (1¾ oz) sesame seeds, lightly toasted
30 g (1 oz) shichimi togarashi spice

Using your hands, mould the piece of Scotch fillet into a nice compact shape, wrap in plastic wrap and place in the freezer to harden.

For the kimchi, prepare a brine of the sea salt and water in a stockpot. Separate and wash the cabbage leaves, place in the brine solution and weigh down for 24 hours at room temperature. At this stage the cabbage should feel wilted. Rinse under gently running water and lay on clean cloths until completely dry.

Add the remaining kimchi ingredients to a small bowl and stir to combine. Pour the mixture over the dried cabbage leaves and agitate often to ensure they are well coated in the mixture. Taste and adjust the flavour if necessary – you should be looking for a pleasant, sweet, salty and spicy flavour profile.

Once the meat has frozen, remove from the freezer, allow it to thaw just slightly, and use a mandolin or rotary slicer to slice very thin slices across the grain, and place on a wire rack for drying. Use a clean spray bottle to mist a thin coating of fish sauce over the beef.

Place the cabbage leaves and beef slices in a dehydrator for 4–6 hours or a 50°C (120°F/Gas ¼) fan-forced oven until crisp. The beef will be ready when the fat is translucent and the meat has a crisp snap in the mouth. Similarly the leaves will be delicate but crisp.

SEAWEED AND TOFU BEIGNET, YUZUKOSHO AND LIME MAYONNAISE

CHEF: ARI TAYMOR

SERVES 12–16

½ cup dried seaweed
225 g (8 oz/1½ cups) plain (all-purpose) flour, sifted
1½ teaspoons bicarbonate of soda (baking soda)
2 teaspoons salt
1 large egg
85 g (3 oz) silken tofu
375 ml (13 fl oz/1½ cups) soda water
vegetable oil, for deep-frying
yuzukosho, green or red, to serve

LIME MAYONNAISE

3 egg yolks
1 eggwhite
3 limes, finely grated zest, juice
1½ tablespoons sea salt
750 ml (26 fl oz/3 cups) grapeseed oil

Place the seaweed in a small bowl and cover with warm water. Stand for 10 minutes until softened. Drain. Squeeze the seaweed to remove excess water and julienne. Whisk the flour, bicarbonate of soda and salt in a large bowl. Whisk in the seaweed, eggs and tofu. Gradually add the soda water, until a smooth batter forms: it should be the consistency of a thick pancake batter. Refrigerate the batter until ready to cook.

For the lime mayonnaise, process the egg yolks and eggwhite, lime and salt in a food processor on high speed until combined. While the food processor is still running, add the grapeseed oil in a thin stream and process until emulsified and the mixture is thick. Chill and reserve.

Heat the vegetable oil in a large, heavy-based saucepan to 175°C (345°F) or until a cube of bread dropped into the oil turns brown in 20 seconds. Deep-fry tablespoon-size portions of the batter, in batches, turning occasionally, until they are golden and puffed (2–3 minutes on each side), then drain on paper towel. Take care, as the hot oil will spit.

Dot a serving plate with the lime mayonnaise and, using a pastry brush, generously brush the beignets with yuzukosho. Serve immediately.

Note: Leftover mayonnaise can be stored in an airtight container in the refrigerator for up to one week.

PICKLED COCKLES

CHEF: SHAUN KELLY

SERVES 4–6

250 ml (9 fl oz/1 cup) water
250 ml (9 fl oz/1 cup) white wine vinegar
125 g (4½ oz) caster (superfine) sugar
pinch of saffron threads
1 bay leaf
1 thyme sprig
cracked black pepper
1 red onion, cut into petals, trimmings reserved
1 carrot, finely diced (brunoise), trimmings reserved
1 kg (2 lb 4 oz) cockles, washed
white wine, to coat
30 g (1 oz/1 bunch) chervil, leaves picked
olive oil, for drizzling

Make a pickling liquid by putting the water, vinegar, sugar, saffron, bay leaf, thyme and cracked black pepper in a medium saucepan. Add the reserved onion and carrot trimmings. Place over medium heat and simmer for 15 minutes for the flavours to infuse. Strain the mixture and return to the saucepan. Add the onion petals and carrot brunoise and simmer for 5 minutes or until the vegetables are just cooked. Set aside and cool. Season with salt and pepper to taste.

Place the cockles with enough wine to coat in a large saucepan over medium heat and steam open the cockles. Reserve the shells and put the cockle meat in the pickling mixture for at least 2 hours, preferably overnight.

Serve the cockles cold with the shells, scatter with the chervil and a healthy drizzle of olive oil.

CARROTS, YOGHURT AND PRAWN FLOSS

CHEF: PASI PETANEN
SERVES 4–8

- 100 g (3½ oz) green prawns, peeled and deveined
- 2 tablespoons anchovy juice or fish sauce
- vegetable oil, for deep-frying
- 8 baby carrots, washed, peeled, green tops reserved
- 50 g (1¾ oz) Greek-style yoghurt

Put the prawns in a bowl, cover with the anchovy juice and set aside for 30 minutes to marinate. Dry the prawns on paper towel and cut each prawn into 6 pieces.

Put a heavy-based saucepan over medium–high heat and heat the vegetable oil to 180°C (350°F) or until a cube of bread dropped into the oil turns brown in 15 seconds. Add the prawn pieces and fry for 4 minutes until golden brown (be careful as the hot oil will spit). Dry on paper towel. Cool the cooked prawns in the refrigerator for 30 minutes. Once cool, blend the cooked prawn pieces in a spice grinder until the fibres break up and the prawns take on a breadcrumb consistency. Set aside.

When ready to serve, brush each carrot with the yoghurt, making sure the carrots are evenly coated, then coat the carrots in the prawn floss and serve.

DUCK CONFIT CROQUETTES

CHEF: YVES CAMDEBORDE

SERVES 6–10

2 confit duck legs, approximately 600 g (1 lb 5 oz)
100 g (3½ oz) button mushrooms
2 teaspoons finely chopped French shallots
2 tablespoons olive oil
250 ml (9 fl oz/1 cup) whipped cream
1 teaspoon finely chopped chives
100 g (3½ oz) foie gras, chopped
2 eggs
plain (all-purpose) flour, for dusting
breadcrumbs, for coating
vegetable oil, for deep-frying

HERB MAYONNAISE

75 g (2½ oz/½ bunch) flat-leaf (Italian) parsley
45 g (1½ oz/½ bunch) coriander (cilantro)
25 g (1 oz/1 bunch) dill
2 egg yolks
2 tablespoons white wine vinegar
½ teaspoon dijon mustard
150 ml (5 fl oz) grapeseed oil
1 lime, juice and finely grated zest

Preheat the oven to 210°C (415°F/Gas 6–7). Warm the duck legs in the oven for 2–3 minutes. Remove the skin and finely julienne, then sweat in a small frying pan over medium heat, cooking until crisp. Remove and drain on a paper towel. Debone the legs and put the thigh meat with a small glass of water in the frying pan. Cook slowly over low heat until the liquid has evaporated. Shred the meat with a fork and set aside.

Wash and finely chop the mushrooms. Place the olive oil in the frying pan with the mushroom and shallot and cook until lightly golden. Season generously and add the cream. Cook for 2–3 minutes, then pour into a bowl and set aside. Add the shredded duck meat, skin, chives and foie gras to the mushroom mixture. Adjust seasoning to taste, cover and place in the refrigerator until cool.

Beat the eggs in a bowl. Lightly flour your hands then shape small amounts of the duck and mushroom mixture into croquettes by rolling between the palms of your hands. Coat in the egg then roll in the breadcrumbs. Coat again in egg and breadcrumbs. Place in the refrigerator.

To make the herb mayonnaise, blanch the herbs in boiling salted water until bright green (about 30 seconds), refresh in iced water, strain thoroughly and squeeze out excess water. Process the herbs, egg yolks, vinegar and mustard in a food processor until well combined, then, with the motor running, add the grapeseed oil in a thin steady stream until the mixture emulsifies. Season and adjust consistency with lime juice and zest. Set aside.

Heat the vegetable oil in a deep-fryer or large, heavy-based saucepan to 170°C (325°F) or until a cube of bread dropped into the oil turns brown in 20 seconds. Cook the croquettes in batches until brown and crisp. Place on paper towel to drain, then serve hot with the herb mayonnaise.

SAUSAGE, SMOKED HERRING ROE AND HORSERADISH MOUSSE

CHEF: YVES CAMDEBORDE

SERVES 4

- 2 gourmet pork sausages
- 250 ml (9 fl oz/1 cup) thickened (whipping) cream
- 1 teaspoon grated horseradish
- 4 teaspoons smoked herring roe

Slice the sausages into six pieces. Fry the sausage in a large frying pan over medium heat until cooked through and golden in colour. Remove the sausage, add the cream to the pan and bring to a simmer. Season generously, then add the horseradish. Process with a stick blender until foamy.

Serve the sausage with the horseradish mousse and top with the smoked herring roe.

CRISP CHICKEN SKIN, ROSEMARY MASCARPONE AND BACON JAM

CHEF: JAMES KNAPPETT

SERVES 6–8

skin of 2 chickens, excess fat and sinew scraped and removed

ROSEMARY MASCARPONE

2 teaspoons finely chopped rosemary leaves
100 g (3½ oz) mascarpone

BACON JAM

250 g (9 oz) bacon, diced
½ red onion, diced
250 g (9 oz) brown sugar
250 ml (9 fl oz/1 cup) red wine vinegar

Preheat the oven to 175°C (345°F/Gas 3–4). Generously season the chicken skin, lay it between two sheets of baking paper and sandwich it between two flat baking trays. Roast the chicken skin for 30–50 minutes or until crisp and golden brown. Remove from the oven and leave to cool, then break into large pieces and set aside.

Mix together the rosemary and mascarpone and season to taste. Refrigerate until ready to serve.

Sauté the bacon and red onion in a medium frying pan until soft. Strain off any excess oil. Add the brown sugar and red wine vinegar. Turn the heat to low and reduce for about 20 minutes until the mixture reaches the consistency of jam.

To assemble, bring the rosemary mascarpone to room temperature. Use a palette knife to spread the rosemary mascarpone on the chicken skin. Randomly place dabs of bacon jam on the top and serve.

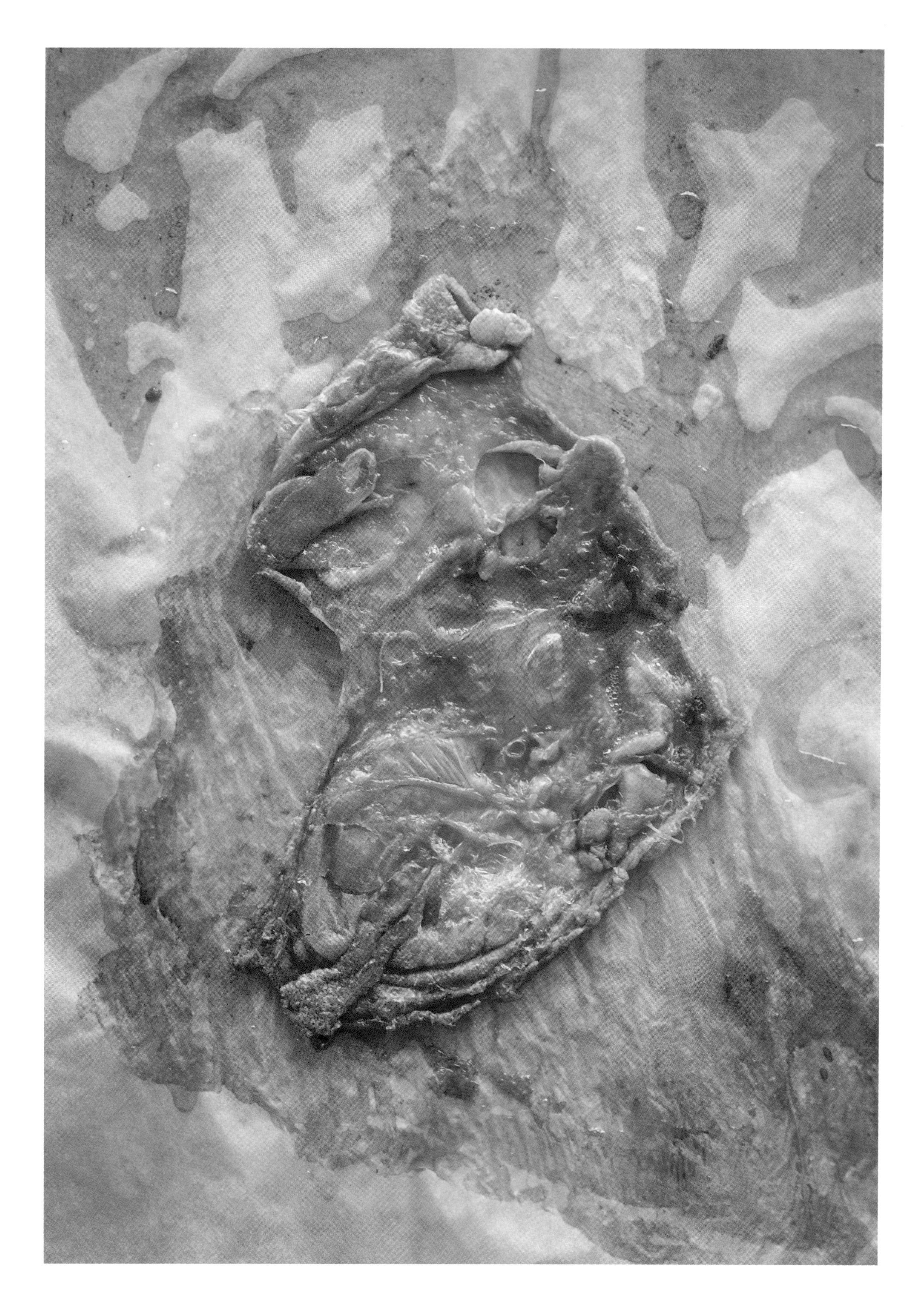

SALT AND VINEGAR CRISPS

CHEF: RYAN SQUIRES
SERVES 2-4

2 large kennebec potatoes, washed
1 litre (35 fl oz/4 cups) rice bran oil
1–2 teaspoons freeze-dried vinegar
1–2 teaspoons maltodextrin
white wine vinegar (optional) to spray

Using a mandolin, slice the potatoes into 1 mm (1/32 inch) slices and place on a clean tea towel (dish towel).

Heat the rice bran oil in a large saucepan or deep-fryer to 180°C (350°F) or until a cube of bread dropped into the oil turns brown in 15 seconds. Deep-fry the potato in small batches, stirring occasionally, for 2–3 minutes or until crisp and golden (be careful as hot oil will spit). Drain on paper towel. Combine the freeze-dried vinegar and maltodextrin in a large bowl, mixing well to combine. Add the chips and toss gently to coat then serve.

Note: If freeze-dried vinegar and maltodextrin are unavailable, season the chips generously with salt and spray with a mist of vinegar, using a spray bottle, before serving.

A RENEGADE AND A GENTLEMAN

In 1992 chef Yves Camdeborde purchased La Régalade, a small run-down bistro in the 14th arrondissement of Paris.

The move was deemed culinary suicide, but Yves sniffed out its unctuous potential. He looked beyond the battered and weary façade, the grubby lace curtains, the tiled floors with decades of grime in the cracks and the tables devoid of linen. He saw a place where he could satisfy the belly, not satisfy the ego; a place to put your elbows on the table and get armpit-deep in dinner.

It wasn't about being perfect, but being itself.

A motley crew was gathered and cutlery went down. Fridges were stocked, food was cooked, people were invited and something grew.

Yves drew on ideals of thrift, interest and intrigue where the irksome elements of fine dining were blissfully extracted from the restaurant's DNA, and food made it onto the menu simply because it tasted good.

It was exactly the environment the words *comme il faut* were invented for.

A flutter was detected at the edges of the culinary zeitgeist. Bistronomy was born.

Yves inspired a culinary revolution, quietly, choosing to make his point on the plate. He became the unofficial godfather of bistronomy, inspiring legions of chefs around the world and a gastronomic army of occupation in Paris.

In the process, he created an irresistible redemption song for French cuisine.

PUFFED RICE, SASHIMI AND SMOKED BUTTER

CHEF: KARL FIRLA

SERVES 4

You will need to begin this recipe two days ahead.

150 g (5½ oz) sushi rice
vegetable oil, for deep-frying
150 g (5½ oz) butter, at room temperature
300 g (10½ oz) sashimi-grade kingfish, sliced

Rinse the rice under cold running water, drain and place in a large saucepan. Cover with 330 ml (11¼ fl oz/1⅓ cups) of water and bring to the boil over high heat. Reduce the heat to low, cover and cook for 12–14 minutes or until the water has been absorbed and the rice is tender. Remove from the heat, strain and allow to cool.

Add 200 g (7 oz) of the cooled rice and 150 ml (5 fl oz) of cold water to a blender. Season and purée the rice until a fine paste consistency is achieved. Line a large baking tray with baking paper and spread the mixture, at a 3 mm (⅛ inch) thickness, across the paper. Dry for at least 48 hours in a warm, dry place. Depending on the weather, this drying process may take longer. When dry, break into bite-size pieces and store in an airtight container.

To make the puffed rice, heat at least 2.5 cm (1 inch) of vegetable oil in a deep-fryer or large, heavy-based saucepan to 180°C (350°F) or until a cube of bread dropped into the oil turns brown in 15 seconds. Flash-fry the rice pieces, individually, until they take on a whitish, translucent appearance. They will expand to around five times their original size. Drain on paper towel and set aside until ready to serve.

To smoke the butter, season it generously and place in a large resealable plastic bag. Using a handheld food smoker with hickory chips, fill the bag with smoke and seal. Set aside for 1 hour then repeat the smoking process. Alternatively, you can smoke the butter in a food smoker. Put the butter in a tray on an upper rack of the smoker. Place a tray of ice on a lower rack as a heat shield and smoke for 2–3 hours. Remove from the smoker. If some separation in the butter has occurred, put the butter in a bowl over ice and whisk until it re-emulsifies. Place the smoked butter in a piping bag and refrigerate until required.

To serve, break the rice crisps into 5 x 15 cm (2 x 6 inch) pieces. Randomly pipe the butter onto the crisps in small quantities and top with pieces of kingfish to serve.

Note: If kingfish is unavailable, use sashimi-grade mackerel.

STEAMED OYSTERS AND AGED APPLE CIDER EMULSION

CHEF: LUKE BURGESS

SERVES 4

1 garlic clove
250 ml (9 fl oz/1 cup) aged apple cider vinegar
100 g (3½ oz) brown sugar
750 ml (26 fl oz/3 cups) grapeseed oil
2 egg yolks
12 Pacific oysters, unopened
bay leaf oil (see *Accompagnement* for recipe), to serve

Place the garlic, cider vinegar and brown sugar in a Thermomix or blender and combine on the highest setting to make a vinegar base. Stream the grapeseed oil into the vinegar at high speed. Add the egg yolks and continue processing on high speed until emulsified. Season with salt and pepper to taste.

Place the oysters in a stovetop steamer and steam on low for 4–5 minutes. Remove from the steamer. To serve, shuck the oysters and place on a serving platter. Drizzle the apple cider emulsion over the oysters and add 5 dots of bay leaf oil to each oyster. Serve immediately.

MARINATED SARDINES, POACHED WHITE ASPARAGUS AND TRUFFLE

CHEF: MICHAEL CABALLO

SERVES 4

4 fresh sardines, approximately 15 cm (6 inches) long, descaled, filleted
fine sea salt
125 ml (4 fl oz/½ cup) white wine vinegar
125 ml (4 fl oz/½ cup) olive oil

POACHED WHITE ASPARAGUS

8 thick white asparagus spears
13 g (½ oz) sea salt
10 g (¼ oz) caster (superfine) sugar
2 teaspoons white wine vinegar
50 ml (1¾ fl oz) olive oil

HAZELNUT VINAIGRETTE

1 French shallot, peeled, finely chopped
1 tablespoon sherry vinegar
50 g (1¾ oz/⅓ cup) hazelnuts, blanched, toasted and coarsely crushed
50 ml (1¾ fl oz) hazelnut oil (see *Accompagnement* for recipe)
15 g (½ oz) chives, finely chopped
12 g (¼ oz) black truffle, finely diced (if not in season, use good quality black truffle paste)
sea salt

CELERY LEAF SALAD

250 g (9 oz) inner leaves of celery heart
15 g (½ oz/½ bunch) chervil
lemon juice
olive oil
sea salt
borage or other edible flowers, to garnish

Lay the sardine fillets on a clean tray and season both sides with sea salt. Cover and leave for 3 hours in the refrigerator to cure. Fill a shallow bowl with a small amount of vinegar – just enough to be able to submerge the fillets. Rinse the fillets in vinegar by dipping them in briefly; do not leave them submerged. Pat dry with paper towel and lay the fillets flat in a single layer on a rimmed plate or in a shallow bowl. Add enough olive oil to cover. Allow to marinate for at least 6 hours.

Remove the bottom fibrous part of the asparagus stems and gently peel the asparagus from just below the tip, reserving all the trimmings. Put the trimmings in a medium saucepan and cover with 750 ml (26 fl oz/3 cups) water. Place over low to medium heat and bring to a gentle simmer. Turn off the heat and let steep for 20 minutes. Strain the poaching liquid into a bowl, add the salt, sugar, vinegar and olive oil and stir to combine.

Place the peeled asparagus in a large frying pan in a single layer and cover with the poaching liquid mixture. Poach over very low heat for approximately 20 minutes: the asparagus should still retain some texture – firm but not crunchy – and yield slightly when pinched. Gently transfer the asparagus to another vessel, lay flat and cover with just enough of the cooking liquid to cover. Allow to cool.

For the hazelnut vinaigrette, toss the shallot with the sherry vinegar in a small bowl and set aside to macerate for 10 minutes. Add the crushed hazelnuts, hazelnut oil, chives and truffle to the bowl and stir gently to combine.

Just before serving, toss together the celery leaves and chervil with a few drops of lemon juice and olive oil. Season with sea salt.

Lay the poached asparagus on a serving plate, drape with a sardine fillet and spoon over the hazelnut vinaigrette. Scatter with the celery leaf salad and garnish with edible flowers.

PRAWN, RED CAPSICUM AND LARDO DI COLONNATA

CHEF: BERTRAND GRÉBAUT

SERVES 10

50 g (1¾ oz/¼ cup) buckwheat
olive oil, for frying
5 red capsicums (peppers)
20 medium raw prawns, peeled, heads and tails intact, deveined
2 lemons, juice
2 tablespoons olive oil, extra
10 generous shavings of Lardo di Colonnata
100 g (3½ oz) red amaranth leaves

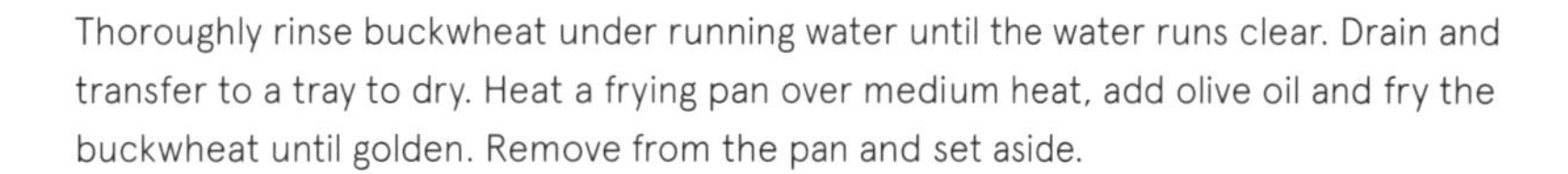

Thoroughly rinse buckwheat under running water until the water runs clear. Drain and transfer to a tray to dry. Heat a frying pan over medium heat, add olive oil and fry the buckwheat until golden. Remove from the pan and set aside.

Cook capsicum over a gas flame, turning occasionally, until skin is blackened and blistered. Transfer to a heatproof bowl, cover with plastic wrap and stand until capsicum cools and softens (20–30 minutes). Peel capsicum and remove seeds, then tear flesh into strips and set aside.

Combine the prawns, lemon juice and olive oil in a bowl. Season and set aside. Heat a barbecue or chargrill on high. Cook prawns, turning once, until just cooked through (2–3 minutes each side).

To serve, layer the Lardo di Colonnata and prawns. Toss the amaranth with the toasted buckwheat and arrange attractively with the capsicum on a serving plate.

Note: If you don't have a gas burner, brush the capsicum with oil and roast at 200°C (400°F/Gas 6) on a baking tray, turning occasionally, for 15–20 minutes or until blackened.

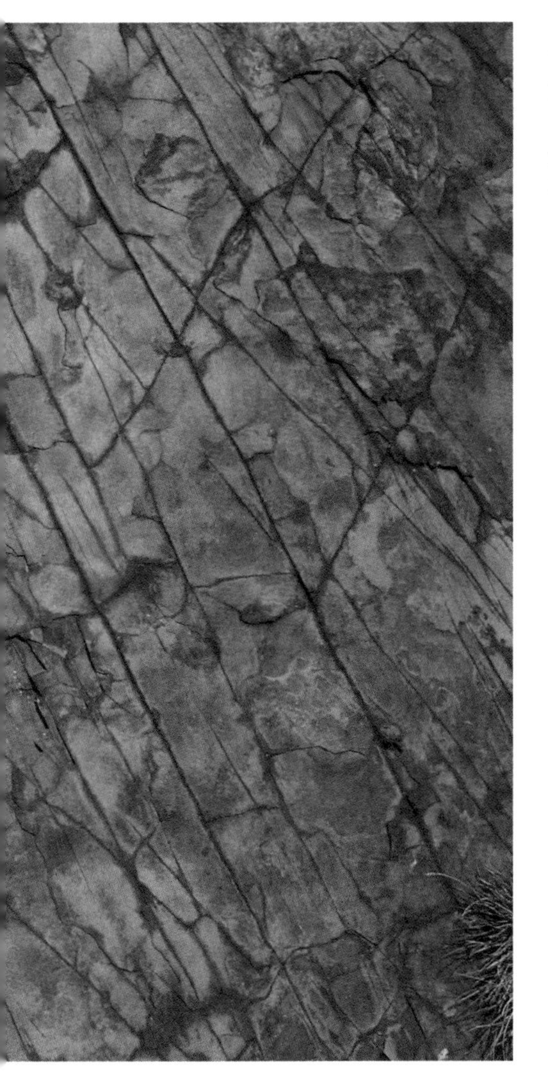

BARBECUED SCALLOPS WITH SEAWEED GREMOLATA

CHEF: ADAM BYATT

SERVES 4

4 extra-large scallops, skirt and roe removed, shells reserved
sea herbs, such as samphire, sea purslane, stonecrop, to serve

FENNEL SAND

75 g (2½ oz) almonds
50 g (1¾ oz/⅓ cup) plain (all-purpose) flour
pinch of Maldon salt
1 garlic clove, crushed
50 g (1¾ oz) butter
18 g (¾ oz) fennel seeds

SEAWEED EMULSION

100 g (3½ oz) seaweed
1 Lebanese (short) cucumber, quartered lengthways, seeds removed
400 ml (14 fl oz) vegetable oil
2 eggs
1 teaspoon dijon mustard

GREMOLATA

1 garlic clove, peeled
1 red chilli, deseeded
25 g (1 oz/1 bunch) chives
150 g (5½ oz/1 bunch) flat-leaf parsley
30 g (1 oz/1 bunch) chervil
1 lemon, zest
200 ml (7 fl oz) olive oil

Preheat the oven to 180°C (350°F/Gas 4). Line a baking tray with baking paper. Combine the ingredients for the fennel sand in a blender and blitz until it resembles coarse breadcrumbs, then spread on the tray and bake for 15 minutes or until lightly golden.

Combine the seaweed, cucumber and vegetable oil for the seaweed emulsion. Blend for 4 minutes at 80°C (175°F) using a Thermomix. Alternatively, leave the seaweed and cucumber in a warm place, then blend the cucumber and seaweed for 10 minutes in a blender. Add vegetable oil and blend for a further 5 minutes. By hand, whisk the seaweed oil in a steady stream slowly into the rest of the ingredients to make a mayonnaise.

To make the gremolata, finely chop the garlic, chilli, chives, parsley, chervil, lemon zest and salt and pepper. Add some of the olive oil to the mixed ingredients, then continue chopping and adding more oil until you form a coarse dressing.

Toss the scallops in the gremolata. Put the scallops back in their shells, wrap with string and cook on a barbecue or chargrill for 7 minutes. Set scallops aside to rest for 2 minutes. Cut the string and remove the top shell.

To serve, spoon a small amount of seaweed emulsion into each shell, top with fennel sand and garnish with sea herbs.

EMOTION + TASTE

Nobody goes to a restaurant just to eat. They go for the experience. And no experience is quite like bistronomy. Haute cuisine *for the people.*

At its most rudimentary, bistronomy is the food without the pomp and circumstance. It is a growing culinary culture that celebrates integrity, simplicity and democracy in dining. Rather than a Chinese whispers version of gastronomy trends and its leaders, it is a food approach based on building a direct relationship between garden, kitchen and diner, with a real sense of place, produce and the wine that might be drunk alongside. It is a combination of bistro (a nod to the traditional dishes that form the starting point for many bistronomy chefs) and gastronomy (a reference to the *haute cuisine* techniques used to update them).

Bistronomy is an elusive style of dining: the sort of laid-back eating experience that offers the gustatory nirvana without the buttock-clenching, wallet-evacuating price tag penance. It marries a no-frills, elbows-on-the-table vibe with phenomenally clever cooking, fuelled by innovative young chefs intent on shaking up the status quo by throwing out the old ceremonies while keeping faith with the main game. The aim is to excel in food, wine and generosity. In this world, the interest is in you, the diner, rather than the angle of the cutlery on the table, and hospitality is more than a catchcry, it is a way of life. It's the kind of effortless culinary cool that takes serious, serious work.

Did this merger of high-end food with pared-back bistro surrounds emerge because our dining tastes have changed? Did it appear because chefs, after years of being hamstrung by the rigours and dictatorship of French kitchens and European styles, throw their tea towels onto the burners and say enough? Did it emerge because the economy spiralled and restaurants had to be smart

'It's not necessarily about a menu or a chef, but a spirit. It's spirit that's important — creating a communal experience, of a neighbourhood, of recognition, of conviviality, of spontaneity and just being able to drop in. It's about a restaurant that can be used at different times of the day.'

STEPHANE JEGO

'We do what tastes good. We take influences from everywhere if they are the right technique for the ingredient and dish. We get inspired by what is available seasonally and what cooking application works with it best. That's it.'

PASI PETANEN

to stay open? It is, no doubt, a combination of all these things. It's a mixture of personalities, economics, timing and a general trend towards a young, original and increasingly democratic dining culture where the purity of what is on the plate trumps the trimmings.

The murmurings of bistronomy began in Paris in 1992 with the opening of La Régalade by chef Yves Camdeborde. While the grand restaurants continued to jump through the hoops of an increasingly out-of-touch, out-of-reach dining system of stars, the corner street bistros persisted with moulding themselves to the trappings of tourism and rather than being the ballast of the Paris restaurant landscape, the bistro became a nostalgic curiosity where you paid a steep price for the privilege of eating 'real' French food. So Yves cast about for new ways to make dining special. He turned to the then down-at-heel 14th arrondissement on the outskirts of Paris to open a restaurant that looked like your grandmother's kitchen with lace curtains, tables devoid of linen and pared back surrounds. His concept was simple. Throw out all formal Michelin-driven dining rules and serve *haute cuisine* in a bistro setting at ridiculously low prices so that everyone could afford to gather around the table. The setting and service were casual, the prices jaw-droppingly small yet the cooking, confusingly, was as phenomenal as any starred establishment. Others followed, and the movement quickly acquired the moniker *bistronomie*, as its popularity continued to spread. Tremors were felt. This was not dining in Paris.

Paris was experiencing a culinary revolution where Michelin was no longer the one pathway to glory. In many ways its stars had morphed to represent a foregone era of fine dining rather than any kind of symbol of France's gastronomic panache. France had long been considered the culinary pacesetter. The rigours of the French kitchen offered the technique and discipline that chefs esteemed and the cuisine we'd dream of eating; an idealised and glamorised lifestyle of truffles and turbot, foie gras and foams. This was the world in which Michelin ruled the scene; but people began to question whether French cuisine had lost its shine. Eating in France had run aground, becoming synonymous with a kind of culinary lethargy. Francophiles would stand by the food and, yes, it was great for those who shopped for cheeses, macarons, breads, or the odd terrine, but dining out had become regimented and stultified. Divorced from reality, top chefs were declaring bankruptcy and, like dominoes, the great began to fall. The white tablecloths were thinning and bistros, brasseries and high-end restaurants were closing at an alarming rate amid the combined mass of culinary and economic woes. And the final nail in the gustatory coffin: Spain had eclipsed France as the culinary leader. The rest of the world had moved into a different era of eating, and this teacher, this leader on our culinary path, was suddenly someone we had outgrown.

While it may have gathered its stronghold in France, the cooking of bistronomy is not a replication of purely French food technique, which is so often based on ritual rather than instinct. The cooking is contemporary and curious, infused with no particular cuisine or style of food; in fact, rarely has a food movement condensed and combined so many world trends. The food is serious, without taking itself too seriously, with a distinct absence of 'clever-clever' food. There is a sense of adventure, a lightness of touch and plenty of humour mixed with the diamond-hard skills of chefs passionate about feeding people. They combine the layered artistry of a composer with the passionate tradition of a grandmother and a teenager's contrarian flair. The bistronomy experience is the sort of food that comes at you from who-knows-where yet never fails to rivet, surprise and satisfy, from chefs concerned about feeding people, not chest-beating ego; chefs who know that precise moment when something fancy must be tempered by the knowledge of when to serve you a really decent pie.

To define bistronomy via a 'restaurant formula', however, would be shortsighted. It's not about defining it, giving a badge of honour to its culinary ambassadors nor frothing at the mouth about who coined the term. Because bistronomy is not designed by committee. It is built on breathtaking, naked passion and all the contradictions, culinary bravado and sense of adventure that comes with it.

Bistronomy is more of a fluid entity, a culinary ethos based on the tenets of freedom, spirit, conviviality and heart. It isn't just the way the bistronomy chef prepares food that sets them apart from the rest of humanity; it is the way they think and talk about food. These restaurants and chefs have been a touchstone for affordable, creative and edgy food long before anyone else talked of natural wines, and it remains, stronger than ever, long after the Spanish foamista chefs passed the baton to their bearded, foraging Nordic successors. The bistronomy experience is simultaneously creative and entirely cerebral. Nothing is scorned as a sin against convention. It isn't rigid. It's natural, an almost instinctual culinary dialect brimming with informed technique and passion. It is a form of gustatory parkour — that wild French trend for running up walls and gutter-pipes and other bits of infrastructure — except, this time, it's inventive chefs, free from the rigours of old-school French kitchens and chronic regionalism, creating perfect havoc with our minds, bellies and senses. And chefs being chefs, there is always wine.

Bistronomy's detractors claim that it is nothing new or special, that it is merely an extension of moving globally towards more relaxed dining environments and cuisine dictated by suffering economies. But with bistronomy, casual and simple does not come at the expense of formidable culinary technique. While it may not be about the triple-star threat of Michelin, there is serious acknowledgement. Fine dining restaurants maintain standards and are the training grounds for many a future generation of chefs. Tradition is at the root of good cooking. Improvisation, flair and creativity are all fundamental, but without a basis

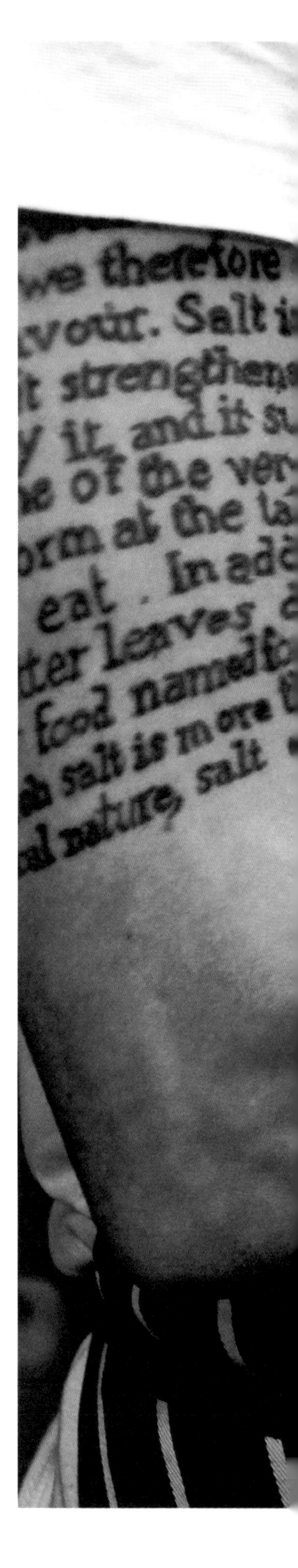

'If you eat the food, sit in the restaurant or meet the chef and you still need to ask what bistronomy is, you're never going to get it.'

DAN PEARSON

of classical technique and an understanding of ingredients and flavours achieved through repetition and study, cooking can never become great. Bistronomy chefs know the rules before they break them. They may not want to run that old type of Michelin-starred establishment but they rely on it to find cooks dedicated enough to prepare food that articulates these techniques even if it is served in a much more casual environment. There is no denying the craft of the cuisinier and this is what truly sets bistronomy apart.

They may be throwing out the rule-book in terms of what, when and how they serve but this is not at the expense of skill; of dishes that involve chefs knowing how to emulsify, to gel, to stuff and to glaze. They have maintained all the essential elements of keeping the craft of cooking alive. It is this, along with their infinite respect for ingredients and raw materials, that is critical. There is a real danger in the continued chorus of the 'simple is best' troupe in flattening the culinary depth of the restaurant industry. To take some examples, the food of Inaki Aizpitarte, Anthony Demetre, Stephane Jego or Pasi Petanen is anything but simple. It is a carefully considered exercise in the juxtaposition of complicated textures and flavours with the utmost respect for the produce. Without question there is an artist at work, one who finely balances simplicity, craftsmanship and flourish. Nowadays, the mouth feel of reductions, emulsions and sauces that have been laboriously refined in the kitchen through diligent skimming and straining is a luxury because of sheer economics. But here, in these spaces, they are on offer at affordable prices where the restaurant's survival is a testament to the chef's skills not only in the kitchen but in balancing the books.

In our efforts to understand bistronomy, we are flocking to define it, to give it rules and shape, while the chefs that live and breathe it are running from any such restrictions; the rules are there are no rules. What we can say with certainty is that bistronomy encapsulates what is good about a movement or culinary style charged by integrity, simplicity and the democratisation of our dining experience. Its ilk, globally, represents a culinary Trojan horse junking tired conventions while respecting others, but more broadly helping to evolve dining from the inside out so that it is the best of the old world and the new. What we can articulate in absolute terms is an unwavering focus on food and the people at the table, by chefs who love to draw on lessons of experience, throw in a dose of the unknown, and stay free enough to follow the mood and the idea of the moment, whatever it may be.

QUI VIENT DU CŒUR
FROM THE HEART

Connecting emotion and perception to take care of people, as cooks and as hosts

SHAVED CALAMARI, OYSTER CREAM AND FERMENTED APPLE JUICE

CHEDDAR FARINETTE, SNAIL BOURGUIGNON, PICKLED LOQUAT

HEIRLOOM PEACH, TOMATO GAZPACHO AND HERBS

BLACK TREVALLY ROE, SEA URCHIN, GREEN ALMOND ESSENCE AND SEABLITE

SOUSED MACKEREL, BURNT APPLE AND DILL

CHICKEN LIVER, ASPARAGUS, GOLDEN RAISINS AND TOAST

MACKEREL, TOMATO WATER AND RASPBERRIES

SMOKED WAGYU, OYSTERS AND GREENS

HALIBUT CONFIT WITH FERMENTED CORN

SMOKED EEL WITH BURNT ONIONS

WHOLE ROASTED PORCINI MUSHROOMS WITH PINE NUT PICADA

Au Passage
N° 043543
5l Fleurette F
2 x 2,5kg Beurre

SHAVED CALAMARI, OYSTER CREAM AND FERMENTED APPLE JUICE

CHEF: DAVE VERHEUL
SERVES 6

You will need to begin the fermented apple juice two weeks ahead and the calamari preparation and dill oil one day ahead.

1 medium calamari tube, cleaned
1 Lebanese (short) cucumber
sea salt
1 granny smith apple, to serve
20 g (¾ oz) dill, to serve

FERMENTED APPLE JUICE
2 granny smith apples
sea salt
30 g (1 oz) biodynamic yoghurt whey

DILL OIL
100 g (3½ oz/4 bunches) dill
60 ml (2¼ fl oz/¼ cup) grapeseed oil

OYSTER CREAM
1 French shallot
1 garlic clove
300 ml (10½ fl oz) milk
2 g (1 teaspoon) agar-agar
2 oysters

To make the fermented apple juice, peel and core the apples, roughly chop and put in a blender. Blend on high speed until thoroughly puréed, quickly pour into a sous-vide bag sitting on a pair of scales. You need to calculate 2% of the weight of the apple purée, then add this weight in sea salt into the mix; for example, 400 g (14 oz) purée = 8 g (¼ oz) salt. Add the whey, quickly mix everything together and seal tightly in the sous-vide bag. Leave for 2 weeks to ferment. You will need to redo the sous-vide process during this time as the fermentation creates gases. Initially you will have to do this daily, but the frequency will decrease as the mixture ages and the amount of gas declines.

Under cold running water, pull away the skin from the calamari tube. Split the tube in half lengthways and place one half on top of the other. Put the halves into a sous-vide bag. Cook at 60°C (140°F) in a water bath for 20 minutes then transfer to an ice bath to chill. When cold, put in the freezer for 6 hours or overnight. Remove from the bag and slice into long fine ribbons using a meat slicer or a mandolin. Let it thaw, then group into 18 small mounds and chill until ready to serve.

To make the dill oil, blend the dill with the grapeseed oil in a blender until thoroughly puréed and slightly warm, then pour into a container and refrigerate overnight. The next day, strain through a fine sieve and chill until ready to serve.

Slice the cucumber lengthways into 2 mm (1/16 inch) thick strips using a mandolin, then cut into 7 mm (¼ inch) ribbons. Roll the ribbons up loosely and set aside in a container. Purée all of the trimmings using a stick blender, then pass the purée through a fine sieve. Weigh the liquid and add 1% salt, stir to combine and pour over the cucumber strips. Put the cucumber into a sous-vide bag and vacuum on high, then chill.

To make the oyster cream, slice the shallot and garlic. Sweat in a small saucepan over low to medium heat without allowing any colour to develop. Add the milk and bring to the boil, then remove from the heat and set aside to infuse for 20 minutes. Strain the liquid into another small saucepan, add the agar-agar, whisk well and bring to the boil. Once it has boiled, pour into a container and chill in the refrigerator until set. When set, put the gel into a blender with the oysters and purée on high speed until smooth. Season with salt and pepper and pass through a fine sieve. Chill until ready to serve.

Strain the fermented apple juice and reserve both juice and pulp separately.

To serve, make a shape in the bottom of each bowl with the cucumber ribbon. Place three small scoops of the fermented apple pulp around the cucumber and dot with the oyster cream. Place three small piles of calamari ribbons on top of the apple pulp. Thinly slice the fresh apple into sticks and arrange with some dill tips sticking out of the oyster cream dots. Make a dressing of two parts fermented apple juice and one part dill oil, stir well and gently pour over.

CHEDDAR FARINETTE, SNAIL BOURGUIGNON, PICKLED LOQUAT

CHEF: ANTHONY DEMETRE

SERVES 6

100 ml (3½ fl oz) olive oil
1 white onion, finely diced
1 medium carrot, finely diced
½ teaspoon garlic purée
50 g (1¾ oz) 'nduja sausage
1 teaspoon dried oregano
1 bay leaf
¼ teaspoon fennel seeds
¼ teaspoon ground cinnamon
50 ml (1¾ fl oz) merlot vinegar, or good quality red wine vinegar
200 ml (7 fl oz) Port (tawny)
250 ml (9 fl oz/1 cup) light red wine
500 ml (17 fl oz/2 cups) beef stock
6 large snails
1 tablespoon butter
parsley, chopped, to finish
capers, to serve
spinach leaves, to serve
pickled loquats (substitute with pickled pear if unavailable)

CHEDDAR FARINETTE

100 g (3½ oz) sourdough bread
milk, to cover
100 g (3½ oz) cheddar cheese, crumbled
1 egg
20 g (¾ oz) plain (all-purpose) flour
nutmeg, to season
butter, for frying

Put the olive oil in a medium frying pan and sweat the onion, carrot and garlic over low to medium heat until translucent. Add the 'nduja sausage, breaking it up to melt easily, then add the oregano, bay leaf, fennel seeds and cinnamon and continue to cook for 10 minutes. Add the vinegar, raise the heat and cook until reduced by two thirds, then add the port and wine and reduce again. Add the beef stock and continue to reduce until the sauce coats the back of a spoon. Just before serving, add the snails to warm through, being careful not to overcook them as they can become dry and rubbery. The sauce doesn't need to be strained, it is much more interesting in its natural form. Monte the sauce with the tablespoon of butter until it looks nice and glossy, then finish with the chopped parsley.

To make the farinette, roughly dice the sourdough bread and cover with warm milk until the bread is soft. Strain any excess milk from the bread and put it in a heatproof bowl with the cheddar cheese. Put the bowl over a bain-marie until the cheese melts slightly. Add the egg and flour, season with salt, pepper and nutmeg and beat until combined. The mixture doesn't have to be completely smooth; it is nice to retain some texture. Warm a non-stick frying pan, add a little butter and fry the mixture until golden brown. Finish in the oven until nicely glazed. Leave to cool until manageable.

Serve with the snail bourguinon, capers, crisp spinach leaves and pickled loquats.

HEIRLOOM PEACH, TOMATO GAZPACHO AND HERBS

CHEF: MATT LAMBERT

SERVES 4

15 French shallots, peeled, thinly sliced
1 garlic clove, crushed
500 ml (17 fl oz/2 cups) extra virgin olive oil
1.5 kg (3 lb 5 oz) heirloom tomatoes, peeled, seeded
400 g (14 oz) heirloom peaches, peeled, stones removed
4 red capsicums (peppers), seeded, roasted and peeled
4 Lebanese (short) cucumbers, peeled
4 tablespoons aged cherry vinegar
garden herbs, to serve

Heat a frying pan over medium heat. Add the shallots and garlic with 2–3 tablespoons of the olive oil and sweat over very low heat until soft and translucent. Remove from the heat and measure 300 g (10½ oz) sweated shallot.

Put the shallot mixture in a blender with the remaining ingredients, except the olive oil, and blend on high speed until well incorporated. Slowly add the olive oil in a thin steady stream until incorporated and emulsified. Strain through a fine sieve and refrigerate. Check seasoning when cold.

To plate, divide the soup evenly among bowls, top with garden herbs and season generously. Serve cold.

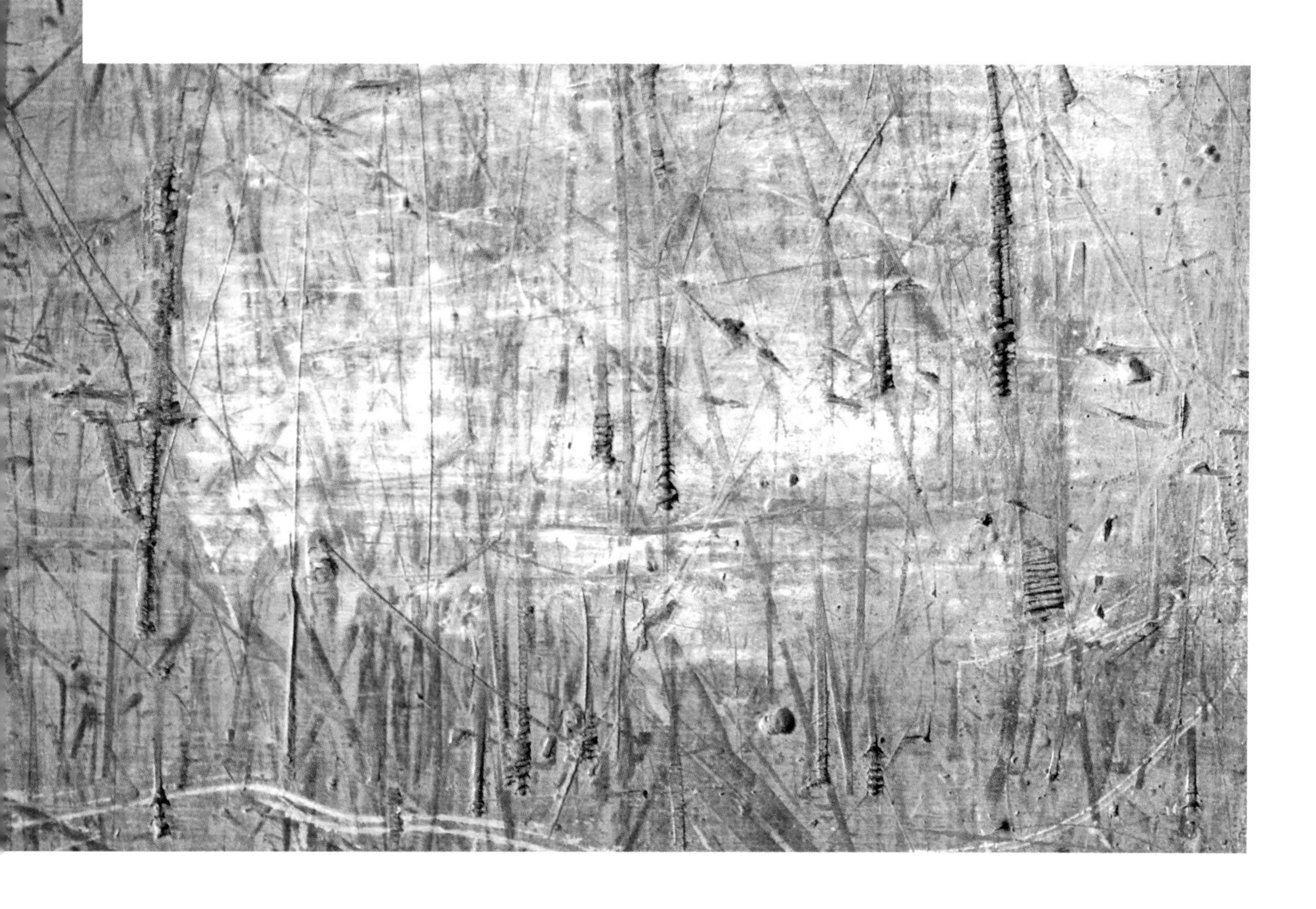

BLACK TREVALLY ROE, SEA URCHIN, GREEN ALMOND ESSENCE AND SEABLITE

CHEF: LUKE BURGESS

SERVES 4

You will need to begin this recipe one day ahead.

- 150 g (5½ oz) fresh black trevally roe
- 9 g (¼ oz) fine sea salt
- 120 g (4¼ oz/2 cups) fresh white breadcrumbs, soaked in milk to soften
- 1 tablespoon Junmai sake
- 1 tablespoon rice vinegar
- 5 g (⅛ oz) horseradish, finely grated
- 1 garlic clove, peeled, finely chopped
- 500 ml (17 fl oz/2 cups) virgin rapeseed oil
- 120 g (4¼ oz) sea urchins
- seablite, to serve
- vinegar, to dress
- green almond essence (see *Accompagnement* for recipe)

Put the trevally roe and sea salt in a small bowl and mix gently and thoroughly. Cover and refrigerate overnight.

Put the salted roe, soaked breadcrumbs, sake, rice vinegar, horseradish and garlic in a blender and process until smooth. Pass through a fine sieve and put into a food processor fitted with the whisk attachment. With the motor running, slowly add the rapeseed oil until the roe mixture is light and thoroughly emulsified. Season to taste and refrigerate until serving. It should have the consistency of a taramasalata.

Shuck the fresh sea urchin roe and reserve in the refrigerator. Pick seablite leaves, wash and reserve in the refrigerator.

To serve, use a palette knife to make a smear of the trevally roe mixture on the plate. Line the smear with 3–4 tongues of sea urchin roe. Lightly dress the seablite in vinegar and scatter across the serving plate. Dot with green almond essence.

SOUSED MACKEREL, BURNT APPLE AND DILL

CHEF: ADAM BYATT

SERVES 4

You will need to begin this recipe two days ahead.

175 ml (5½ fl oz/⅔ cup) cider vinegar
2 large mackerel, cleaned, pin bones removed, skin on
100 g (3½ oz) thick (double) cream
1 granny smith apple, peeled, cored, diced

BURNT APPLE VINEGAR
3 granny smith apples, peeled, cored
2 eggs
3 teaspoons cider vinegar
1 lemon, juice
1 tablespoon dijon mustard
500 ml (17 fl oz/2 cups) vegetable oil

DILL OIL
100 g (3½ oz/4 bunches) dill
600 ml (21 fl oz) vegetable oil

APPLE PICKLE
2 granny smith apples, peeled, cored
1 bunch borage cress, plus extra for garnish
50 ml (1¾ fl oz) rapeseed oil
50 ml (1¾ fl oz) cider vinegar
50 g (1¾ oz) caster (superfine) sugar
50 g (1¾ oz) salt

Combine 100 ml (3½ fl oz) of water with the cider vinegar in a saucepan over medium heat and bring to the boil. Remove from the heat and put in the refrigerator to cool. Once completely cool, steep the mackerel in the liquid for 20 minutes. Remove and set aside for plating.

To make the burnt apple vinegar, burn the apples until blackened on an open flame on a gas stovetop. Cook for 30 minutes, turning every 2 minutes. Char until black as charcoal. Allow the apples to cool before placing in a blender with the eggs, cider vinegar, lemon juice and mustard. Season with salt and pepper and blend well. With the motor running, gradually add the vegetable oil until emulsified. Strain and set the burnt apple vinegar aside.

Prepare the dill oil by putting the dill (including the stalks) in a saucepan of warm, lightly salted water. Blanch for 8 minutes then refresh in iced water. Squeeze the dill dry and put it into a blender. Heat the vegetable oil to 80°C (175°F) and pour it into the blender to just cover the dill. Blend until the dill has made the oil green. Alternatively, put the dill and oil in a Thermomix and blend for 7 minutes until the oil reaches 70°C (150°F). Strain and reserve the oil.

To make the apple pickle, place the apples, 100 ml (3½ fl oz) of water, borage cress, rapeseed oil, cider vinegar, sugar and salt in a blender and blend until smooth. Strain and set aside.

Make a dressing by combining the double cream with 100 ml (3½ fl oz) of the burnt apple vinegar and 200 ml (7 fl oz) of the dill oil in a bowl. Stir to combine.

Char the skin of the mackerel using a blowtorch flame until black and crispy. Alternatively, heat a medium frying pan over high heat. When dry and hot place the fish, skin side down and cook to achieve a dark caramelised colour. Carefully remove the mackerel from the pan. To serve, carefully blowtorch the diced apple flesh until lightly charred.

Spoon some burnt apple vinegar onto the base of each serving plate. Place the mackerel on the plates. Scatter with the diced apple and garnish with the apple pickle. Just before serving, spoon the dressing onto the plate, being careful not to cover the fish.

CHICKEN LIVER, ASPARAGUS, GOLDEN RAISINS AND TOAST

CHEF: OWEN CLARK

SERVES 4

10 chicken livers, rinsed
grapeseed oil, for frying
7 medium French shallots, peeled, thinly sliced
125 ml (4 fl oz/½ cup) brandy
125 ml (4 fl oz/½ cup) mirin (rice wine)
125 ml (4 fl oz/½ cup) rice vinegar
400 g (14 oz) unsalted butter, cubed, at room temperature
freshly ground white peppercorns
6 asparagus spears
celery hearts, microcelery, and wild greens in season, to serve

TOAST TUILES

550 g (1 lb 4 oz/3¾ cups) strong flour
3 tablespoons salt
20 g (¾ oz) baking powder
4 tablespoons sugar
2 tablespoons milk powder
150 ml (5 fl oz) thick (double) cream
250 ml (9 fl oz/1 cup) milk
1 egg, beaten
1 tablespoon active dry yeast

PICKLED GOLDEN RAISINS

50 g (1 ¾ oz/¼ cup) sugar
400 ml (14 fl oz) white verjus
200 g (7 oz) golden raisins (sultanas)

Line a freezer-proof mould with plastic wrap. Blot the chicken livers dry with paper towel. Put a frying pan over high heat and add the grapeseed oil. Once extremely hot (the oil is smoking) sear the livers quickly on all sides for a hard golden crust, being careful not to cook the livers past rare. Remove from the frying pan and set aside.

Reduce the heat to low and gently sweat the shallots in the same pan, until meltingly soft, being careful not to colour them. Add the brandy, mirin, and rice vinegar to the pan and reduce until nearly dry. Put the shallot mixture and seared livers with salt and white pepper in a blender and blend on high until the mixture is fairly smooth. Be careful the mixture doesn't overheat, as this will cause it to become grainy. Reduce the speed to low and slowly incorporate the butter, cube by cube. Season, then pour the mixture into the mould and freeze for 4–6 hours or until solid.

To make the toast tuiles, preheat the oven to 190°C (375°F/Gas 5). Sift the flour, salt and baking powder into a bowl and set aside. Put the sugar, milk powder, cream, milk and egg in a saucepan and whisk lightly to combine. Place over low heat and warm to 37.5°C (99.5°F) or just above body temperature. Remove from the heat, add the yeast and set aside for 10 minutes or until bubbles appear on the surface and the mixture appears frothy. Add the yeast mixture to the dry ingredients and combine into a rough dough. Turn out onto a clean surface and knead for 10 minutes or until smooth in appearance. Put into a large bowl with a damp tea towel (dish towel) over the dough and store in a warm place (the first proving: the dough will double in size). After proving, punch down the dough and roll into a loaf, placing in a loaf (bar) tin, then let it prove once more for about 30 minutes (until it has doubled in size again). Bake in the oven for 35 minutes until golden and cooked through. Allow to cool in the tin before unmoulding. Once cooled, slice very thinly and toast the slices under a grill (broiler) until golden and crisp.

To make the pickled golden raisins, bring the sugar, verjus and a pinch of salt to the boil in a small saucepan over medium heat. Pour the pickling liquid over the raisins and let them sit uncovered in the refrigerator until chilled.

Blanch the asparagus in boiling water and refresh in iced water. Shave 3 asparagus spears into ribbons. Finely chop the remaining asparagus and combine in a bowl. Dress the asparagus with the raisin pickling liquid and gently fold the pickled raisins into the asparagus. Arrange on a plate with the slices of toast. Using a mandolin, shave the frozen liver mousse onto the plate to temper and look like a pile of rags, then garnish with celery hearts, microcelery, and wild greens (such as wood sorrel, alexanders, angelica, nasturtium leaf) before serving.

'Terroir *is about all of the ingredients needing to come together and be eaten together to create a distinctive taste: the dish then being a commitment by everyone involved – the producer, the chef and the diner – if something falls down in this process, the dish is lost and no longer makes sense.*'

STEPHANE JEGO

TERROIR

You don't have to spend much time in a fa-aancy restaurant before someone mentions the T word.

As its basic premise, the elusive French concept of *terroir* (which has no exact translation) is about 'local', 'seasonal' and understanding the characteristics of a specific place — the climate, sunshine, rain, geology, plants and animals — and the impact these elements will have on the taste of a product. Every decade or so the concept and all that comes with it flares up as a food trend. It becomes the marketing speak *de rigueur* in kitchens across the world and the very simple, logical connection between locality, seasons and freshness has become beaten, bloodied and commercialised. Suddenly, to fish, hunt, forage and engage with food — to 'be seasonal' — has morphed into opportunistic fanfare to plaster on a menu or restaurant website. Menu descriptions proclaim an unbridled commitment to the locavore cause, chefs powering their stoves by the wind of their own monologues, throwing around words like 'sustainability' and 'locality' in efforts to bolster their foodie credentials. In clamouring to regurgitate such philosophies they do so without the same grasp, reach, ambition and rigour of the greats. Long before them it was Paul Bocuse, Frédy Girardet, Michel Guérard, Marc Veyrat: these were the kings of *nouvelle cuisine* who were champions of the techniques of classic cooking wedded to rigorously seasonal and local ingredients. Then there is the molecular likes of Ferran Adrià, the purity and seasonality of René Redzepi and the eating-all-the-bits mentality of Fergus Henderson.

But the bistronomy chef just might be *terroir*'s modern day saviour. It would be remiss to say that the quality of ingredients, where they come from and the way the chefs handle them are not of the utmost importance — they most certainly are — but it is the intersection of these elements in a functional, idealistic and economic way that places the bistronomy concept of *terroir* on a different plane. Bistronomy is a phenomenal exercise in picking and choosing: an approach that balances the purity of ingredients with economic sensibility and kitchen practicality. It is cost control with efficient service developed by chefs who reveal a rare talent as both cooks and restaurateurs.

Gone are the romantic notions of the horny-handed peasantry tilling the ancient land, pulling figs from the trees for sustenance, or the ideals of petty nationalism,

'We are driven by the moment, by singular, perfect ingredients that define our terroir, by things from the forest and the sea: still so wild and ancient, pure and elegant.'

MICHAEL CABALLO

the idea that my apple is better than yours. That obnoxious concept of microsourcing — *'A farmer found this rare sorrel variety on the south-facing slope of his neighbour's vineyard and we got the first leaf!'* — and obsession with offering food that you can't precisely get anywhere else or at any other moment has also been eradicated. *Terroir* is not a way for a bistronomy chef to demonstrate that he or she is 'a la minute', it is exactly what it is. A really basic, fundamental key to good cooking.

Bistronomy chefs are undeniably tuned into their environment. They know they are only as good as their ingredients and are committed to sourcing produce from the best farms, fishermen and foragers with precise and inventive cooking that allows the quality of the raw materials to reveal itself. They feel a responsibility to the Earth and its bounty and the ideals of *terroir* feed a natural curiosity for life beyond the kitchen. They're just not slaves to it. *Terroir* happens everywhere and nowhere. There is no need for mystique: it is simply fresh product grown locally. That's it. It is important. Dramatically so, but the chefs are consciously aware that the sanctimony attached to it is often too much and the dining public only care so much about a cook who is turning himself into a boy scout trying to put the insides of an unspoiled rainforest on the plate.

The cooking of the bistronomy chef manages what so few others achieve. It is an expression of a sense of place. The proposition is pretty straightforward: the best ingredients fished, foraged and farmed from as close to the restaurant as possible, in as sustainable a manner as possible, combined with a recession-busting push towards cheaper ingredients, translating the food into something deeper, more sensual and much more robust. At the heart of this food lie flavours that recognise location, and their influences are plainly decipherable: the herbs and vegetables grown on the roof (sorrel and mint, broad beans and radishes), or honey from their own beehives.

There is an emphasis on seasonality and the cult of the ingredient. The dishes that emerge from the bistronomy kitchen are simply a vivid reflection of the season: roots and squashes roasted into toffee-like lusciousness; brassicas with cream for comfort; the earthy perfume of mushrooms; and sorbets of quince, or rosehip and crabapple; or pears in mulled wine with cinnamon cream. Every dish is beautifully presented and allows each ingredient to stand out individually, with all of the individual flavours coming together to form a magnificent whole. There is minimum buggering around, with no heavy sauces to hide behind. The flavours are clean. Precise. And produce is king.

In the world of the bistronomy chef, *terroir* is the ideal that a perfect sardine is better than a mediocre lobster. One ingredient does not have more value than another; a producer or farmer hasn't put any less love into farming a potato than collecting caviar. In their approach is an inherent understanding that creativity is at the service of technical ability, which is itself at the service of quality ingredients. They get the best ingredients they can simply because they know that is where great cooking begins.

Bistronomy also brings the concept of *terroir* back to utility. Ultimately, it comes down to cost. Chances are good, you've eaten something that someone found; and that they didn't pay for it. It is why offcuts, offal and gizzards are celebrated on the bistronomy menu. The approach may be consistent with the bistronomy style of utilising everything but it is also a nod to the thriftiness necessary for small-run restaurants to remain open and profitable. When produce is dictatorial, the menu often changes daily and, unlike at other restaurants, prices change in reflection of the ingredients used. This can reduce costs, helping the chefs to match their creative integrity with customers' needs: one of the most important and challenging balancing acts faced by any cook.

Some of the chefs call it *reverse terroir*: everything has to fit a business model to stay afloat. It is a way of saying, these are the items available in the kitchen or garden or farmer's honesty box, so let's make a tasty dish out of them; it's working backwards in a far more pragmatic way. If a chef controls the growing and sourcing process there is easier access, better control over produce and waste, and naturally improved economic control. It's the realisation (outside of taste) that if there is no business there is no craft and therefore no art. It keeps the local community stable, it's better for the farmer, and the produce hasn't travelled as far, so it's going to taste better.

Terroir is also about connection. The philosophy has always been to bring farmers into the community and cut out the middleman; an almost sociological way of looking at food and showing how food and community are entirely entwined. These restaurants are run by people (mostly the chefs) with skin in the game. They're about intimacy, connection and relationships; in particular, relationships with suppliers of great produce, which they can translate on the plate to connect with the customer. This understanding of *terroir* is encapsulated by their innate sense of where the pleasure in food comes from — the thrill and fire of the food — the very thing we come for.

'Of course I forage. I'd forage a cow if I wasn't going to get arrested for it. It's about necessity as much as freshness: if I'm picking it, I'm not paying for it. And that helps me keep the doors open. I just don't pick it if there's shit on it.'

DAN PEARSON

MACKEREL, TOMATO WATER AND RASPBERRIES

CHEF: BERTRAND GRÉBAUT
SERVES 10

2 kg (4 lb 8 oz) mixed variety of organic tomatoes, very ripe, halved
20 g (¾ oz/1 bunch) thyme
600 g (1 lb 5 oz) mackerel fillets, skin on
200 ml (7 fl oz) olive oil
2 lemons, juice
fleur de sel
100 g (3½ oz) raspberries (use redcurrants if raspberries not in season)
3 large shiso (perilla) leaves
olive oil, to serve

Put the tomatoes in a large, deep-sided frying pan over low heat. Simmer slowly for about 15 minutes. Strain through a fine sieve to achieve a clear consommé. Add the thyme while still hot and set aside for at least 30 minutes for the flavours to infuse. Strain again through a fine sieve and set aside to cool.

Just before serving, cut the mackerel into 5 cm (2 inch) cubes. Season with the olive oil, lemon juice and fleur de sel. Place 4–5 pieces of mackerel skin side up on a serving plate, using a mix of the silver belly and spotted side. Roughly chop the raspberries and nestle in a serving bowl with shiso leaves, tearing any large pieces. Gently spoon a small ladle of tomato water into the bowl and finish by drizzling with a few drops of olive oil. Serve cold.

SMOKED WAGYU, OYSTERS AND GREENS

CHEF: BERTRAND GRÉBAUT

SERVES 10

500 g (1 lb 2 oz) sawdust
800 g (1 lb 12 oz) wagyu beef, fat and sinew removed, cut into 8 x 15 cm (3¼ x 6 inch) pieces
10 oysters, cut into bite-size pieces
2 lemons, juice, to serve
fleur de sel, to serve
samphire and in-season wild greens, to serve

PICKLED CUCUMBER

300 g (10½ oz) Lebanese (short) cucumber, thinly sliced
2 litres (70 fl oz/8 cups) rice vinegar
1 kg (2 lb 4 oz) sugar

BREADCRUMBS

200 g (7 oz) artisanal bread, frozen
80 g (2¾ oz) salted butter, plus extra (if needed)

SAUCE VERTE

500 ml (17 fl oz/2 cups) thin (pouring) cream
70 g (2½ oz/1 bunch) sorrel
150 g (5½ oz/1 bunch) parsley
30 g (1 oz/1 bunch) tarragon
olive oil, to emulsify

Preheat a coal-bedded kettle barbecue to low heat and set up for indirect grilling, using the top rack. Add one-quarter of the sawdust around the coals and cook until smoke appears. Place the beef on the top rack and smoke, adding extra sawdust as required, for approximately 4 minutes each side. Remove from the heat, roll the beef in plastic wrap and freeze for up to 3 hours or until firm enough to slice. Slice thinly and reserve for plating at room temperature.

To make the pickled cucumber, put the sliced cucumber in a large bowl. Put the rice vinegar, sugar and 3 litres (105 fl oz/12 cups) of water in a large saucepan and bring to the boil. Remove from the heat and allow to cool, then pour the pickling liquid over the cucumbers. Cover with plastic wrap and set aside until ready to serve.

For the breadcrumbs, blend the frozen bread in a food processor to achieve a medium crumb that retains some texture (not too fine). Heat the butter in a non-stick frying pan over medium heat until it is foaming, then add the breadcrumbs and cook slowly over a low heat, continuously stirring for even colour. Add more butter if the mix becomes dry. Remove the breadcrumbs when toasted and crisp. Allow to cool.

To make the sauce verte, boil the cream until reduced by half and set aside. Blanch the sorrel, parsley and tarragon in boiling water and refresh in iced water. Squeeze dry. Put the herbs in a blender and purée, adding the cream slowly to loosen the mix and follow with the olive oil, adding it gradually to create an emulsion. Pass through a sieve. Season with salt and pepper.

Using a teaspoon, place three small quenelles of sauce verte on each plate. Lightly season the beef slices with a squeeze of lemon and some fleur de sel and place three slices of beef on each plate. Place a morsel of oyster near each piece of meat. Follow with some pickled cucumber. Place 3 half-teaspoons of breadcrumbs on the dish, concentrating the clusters near the edge of the sauce verte. Finish with samphire and other in-season wild greens.

HALIBUT CONFIT WITH FERMENTED CORN

CHEF: ARI TAYMOR

SERVES 4

You will need to start this recipe at least one day ahead.

450 ml (16 fl oz) olive oil
450 g (1 lb) halibut fillets or firm white fish, such as black pomfret, cod or snapper
1 lemon, peel zested
generous pinch dried chilli flakes
½ bunch coriander
1 lemongrass stem, bruised
purslane leaves, to serve

FERMENTED CORN

4 ears of corn, shucked, kernels cut from cob
1 jalapeño, seeded, finely diced
1 onion, peeled, finely diced
3 capsicums (peppers), finely diced
5 cm (2 inch) piece young ginger, peeled, grated
2 peaches, stones removed, puréed with skin
2 lemons, juice
1 tablespoon sea salt

DRIED TOMATOES

12 cherry tomatoes
1–2 handfuls hickory wood chips

MARINATED CAPSICUM

2 capsicums (peppers)
100 ml (3½ fl oz) sherry vinegar
100 ml (3½ fl oz) olive oil
sea salt

YOUNG CORN AND GINGER SAUCE

3 ears of corn, shucked, kernels cut from cob
5 cm (2 inch) piece young ginger, peeled, grated
sea salt

Prepare the fermented corn by combining all ingredients in a bowl. Stir, then put into a plastic or glass container, cover with muslin (cheesecloth) and leave at room temperature for 24–48 hours. It will taste slightly sour. Reserve in the refrigerator until using.

To make the dried tomatoes, preheat the oven to 135°C (275°F/Gas 1). Lay the hickory wood chips across the base of a baking tray and place the cherry tomatoes on top. Bake for 3–4 hours or until the skins are puckered and slightly dry.

Reduce the oven to 100°C (200°F/Gas ½). Heat the olive oil to 80°C (175°F) in a saucepan over high heat. Arrange the fish fillets, lemon zest, chilli flakes, coriander and lemongrass in a baking dish to fit the fish very snugly then add the olive oil to cover. Bake until just cooked (15 minutes). Set aside in oil until ready to serve.

To make the marinated capsicum, roast the capsicums over an open flame until charred on all sides. Put in a bowl, cover with plastic wrap and set aside for 30 minutes to allow the skins to sweat. Remove the skins, seed and slice the capsicum into wide strips. Marinate in the sherry vinegar, olive oil and salt.

To make the young corn and ginger sauce, juice the corn kernels in a vegetable juicer. Pour into a medium saucepan over low heat, stirring constantly. After 2 minutes, add the ginger, continuing to stir as the sauce begins to thicken with the natural starches. Once thickened to the texture of custard, remove from the heat, add a pinch of salt and strain through a fine sieve.

To plate, remove the fish from the oil, break into small pieces and add to a bowl with salt, olive oil and lemon juice to taste. Place two spoonfuls of fermented corn on a serving plate. Place the fish around it. Refresh the capsicum strips with the sherry vinegar, and curl on the plate. Place 4 tomatoes per person around the other components. Make 4 large dots of corn sauce on each plate. Garnish with purslane.

SMOKED EEL WITH BURNT ONIONS

CHEF: GIOVANNI PASSERINI

SERVES 4

4 sweet onions
½ garlic clove, peeled
1 tablespoon red wine vinegar
4 lemons
4 oranges
1 carrot, sliced
2 tablespoons yuzu juice
50 g (1¾ oz) butter, chopped
1 whole smoked eel, filleted, skinned, cut into 4 portions (approximately 200 g/7 oz each)
lemon juice, extra
1 tablespoon olive oil
500 g (1 lb 2 oz) English spinach
2 teaspoons sesame oil

Preheat the oven to 180°C (350°F/Gas 4).

Put the onions on a chargrill and carefully char them until completely black (about 20 minutes), turning regularly with tongs. Line a baking tray with baking paper, place the charred onions on the tray and bake in the oven for 25 minutes. Remove from the oven and add to a blender with the garlic and red wine vinegar. Season generously with salt and pepper and process until completely smooth. Strain the mixture through a fine sieve and set aside to keep warm.

Peel the lemons and oranges, reserving the flesh. Put the peel in a saucepan, cover with water and bring to the boil. Strain and repeat the process three times, using fresh water each time. Juice the flesh of the lemons and oranges. Pour the juice into a saucepan, adding the peel and carrot. Simmer gently over very low heat until the juice has significantly reduced and the peel is confit. Put the mixture in a blender and purée on high. With the motor running, add the yuzu juice and the chopped butter and purée until smooth and emulsified. Strain and keep cold until ready to serve.

Turn the oven down to 80°C (175°F/Gas ¼). Put the eel portions in an ovenproof dish, cover with foil and cook for 5 minutes. Remove and season with lemon juice.

Place a large frying pan over medium heat, add the olive oil and quickly fry the spinach. Drain on paper towel and season generously with salt, pepper and sesame oil.

To serve, place a spoonful of the burnt onion purée in the middle of each plate, place a piece of eel on top, cover with the spinach and finish with the citrus purée.

WHOLE ROASTED PORCINI MUSHROOMS WITH PINE NUT PICADA

CHEF: MICHAEL CABALLO
SERVES 4

30 g (1 oz) butter
4 fresh whole porcini mushrooms, approximately 50 g (1¾ oz) each, cleaned with damp towel
1 thyme sprig
sea salt
3 teaspoons dry Madeira
15 g (½ oz) chives, finely chopped
¼ lemon, rind finely grated

PINE NUT PICADA
100 ml (3½ fl oz) olive oil
2 garlic cloves, peeled
100 g (3½ oz/⅔ cup) pine nuts
20 g (¾ oz) diced white country-style bread or baguette (not sourdough), crusts removed
250 g (9 oz/1½ large bunches) flat-leaf (Italian) parsley leaves, picked
sea salt

To make the pine nut picada, heat the olive oil in a saucepan over medium–high heat. Add the garlic and fry until soft and lightly golden. Remove with a slotted spoon, season with salt and set aside. Repeat the process with the pine nuts, and then the bread, reserving the olive oil.

Set aside the olive oil to cool. Put the garlic, pine nuts and bread into a mortar and, using a pestle, crush to a coarse paste. Add the parsley and mix well before stirring through the cooled olive oil. Adjust seasoning if required.

Preheat the oven to 150°C (300°F/Gas 2). Melt the butter in a shallow ovenproof sauté pan until foaming. Add the whole mushrooms and thyme. Toast all sides of the mushrooms, basting constantly until lightly golden. Season with salt and add the Madeira and 3 teaspoons of water. Cover and roast in the oven for 10 minutes or until a skewer penetrates the mushrooms easily. Remove the mushrooms, discarding the thyme. Add the chives and lemon rind to the juices in the pan and stir.

To serve, spoon the picada into the base of a serving plate, top with porcini mushrooms and spoon the juices over. Serve immediately.

SUR LE PASS

ON THE PASS

These are the chefs with skin in the game

DUTCH CREAMS, BONE MARROW, AIR-DRIED TUNA AND COFFEE

STEAMED MUD CRAB, SILKY MACADAMIA AND CHAMOMILE

VENISON TARTARE

QUAIL, BREAD SAUCE AND CHERRIES

OCTOPUS IN COCONUT MILK, RED ONION CEVICHE, PLANTAIN CHIPS

KING SALMON CONFIT, LEEKS AND EGGS

HALIBUT WITH OYSTER MUSHROOMS AND LEEKS

VEAL TONGUE WITH PEA ICE

GLOBE ARTICHOKE SOUP, SCALLOPS AND TRUFFLE

SMOKED EEL, CARROT AND CHAMOMILE

CUTTLEFISH, CLAMS AND FIGS

PORK SHOULDER TERRINE, KIMCHI PURÉE, CUCUMBER PICKLE AND LOBSTER CRACKER

SMOKED BONITO, SALTED GRILLED PLUMS AND ONION

DUTCH CREAMS, BONE MARROW, AIR-DRIED TUNA AND COFFEE

CHEF: MATT GERMANCHIS

SERVES 2–4

You will need to begin this recipe one day ahead.

4 dutch cream (waxy) potatoes, scrubbed clean
50 g (1¾ oz) butter
60 g (2¼ oz) bone marrow, cut into 1 cm (3/8 inch) dice
10 g (¼ oz) finely ground coffee

AIR-DRIED TUNA

200 g (7 oz) sashimi-grade tuna belly, sinew removed
50 g (1¾ oz) salt
50 g (1¾ oz) sugar
1 lemon, zest finely grated
150 g (5½ oz) hickory wood chips, soaked in cold water and drained

POTATO ESPUMA

500 g (1 lb 2 oz) dutch cream (waxy) potatoes, extra
250 ml (9 fl oz/1 cup) thin (pouring) cream
60 g (2¼ oz) butter
1.5 g xanthan gum
2.5 g iota carrageenan
375 ml (13 fl oz/1½ cups) chicken stock
10 g (¼ oz) salt

Make a cure for the tuna by combining the salt, sugar and lemon zest in a small bowl. Rub the mixture vigorously into the fish and set aside to cure for 45 minutes. Wipe the cure from the tuna.

To smoke the tuna, line the base of a large, heavy-based saucepan with the hickory wood chips. Ignite them until you see them start to smoke then place the lid on top to capture the smoke. Working quickly, place a greased wire rack over the top of the wood chips, add the tuna and close the lid again. Set aside for 10 minutes for the smoke flavours to infuse the fish. Remove from the saucepan and put the tuna in a dehydrator overnight, or dry in a 50°C (120°F) oven. The aim is to dry the tuna to a jerky consistency that is firm enough to grate.

Put the 4 scrubbed potatoes in a large saucepan, cover generously with water and bring to the boil over high heat. Reduce the heat to medium and simmer for 20 minutes or until the potatoes are cooked through. Drain and set aside.

Make a beurre noisette by heating a frying pan over medium heat until hot, add the butter and cook, swirling constantly, until it turns a nut-brown colour. Set aside.

To make the potato espuma, boil the extra potatoes with the skin on for 20 minutes or until cooked through. Strain and set aside. When cool enough to handle, peel the potatoes. Heat the cream and butter in a saucepan over medium heat until the butter has melted. Add the xanthan gum and iota carrageenan to the heated cream, stirring to combine. Place the potato, cream mixture, chicken stock and salt in a blender and blend until smooth. Pass through a sieve into a pouring jug and keep warm until ready to serve.

To serve, warm the 4 whole potatoes then break them into bite-size chunks. Add the beurre noisette, season generously with salt and pepper and toss gently to combine. Boil the bone marrow for 1 minute in a saucepan of boiling water placed over medium heat. Strain and add the marrow to the buttered potatoes before scooping into serving bowls. Pour the puréed potato mixture into an espuma gun loaded with two chargers until it is three-quarters full, being careful not to overfill the gun. Shake the espuma gun and trigger potato foam over the top of the potato and marrow mix. Sift ground coffee over the top of the foam and grate about 10 g (¼ oz) of air-dried tuna over the top of each individual serve.

STEAMED MUD CRAB, SILKY MACADAMIA AND CHAMOMILE

CHEFS: DAN PUSKAS, JAMES PARRY

SERVES 6

You will need to begin this recipe one day ahead.

1.2 kg (2 lb 10 oz) mud crab

SILKY MACADAMIA MILK

500 g (1 lb 2 oz) macadamia nuts
500 ml (17 fl oz/2 cups) filtered water

TO SERVE

olive oil
macadamia nut oil
macadamia nuts, shaved
12 fresh chamomile flowers, or chamomile essential oil

To make the silky macadamia milk, preheat the oven to 160°C (315°F/Gas 2–3). Roast 50 g (1¾ oz) of the nuts on a baking tray for about 6–10 minutes, then combine them with the remaining unroasted nuts. Process the nuts with the filtered water for 1½ minutes in a blender on high speed, until a white paste forms.

Put the nut paste in a container and let it stand overnight so the nuts release their oils and become more flavourful. The next day, squeeze out the milk by placing small amounts in a flexible sieve or oil filter and squeezing out as much liquid as possible. Alternatively, strain using a fine sieve lined with multiple layers of muslin (cheesecloth). Keep the liquid in the refrigerator for about 2 hours before use to allow it to thicken slightly.

Put the crab in the freezer for 1 hour before cooking. Wrap the crab in baking paper before sealing in a large sous-vide bag. This prevents the claws punching holes in the bag. Steam the crab in a combi-oven set on 90°C (195°F) until the shell turns red. For a 1.2 kg crab this will take approximately 50 minutes. Alternatively, place the crab in a heatproof shallow dish in a bamboo steamer over a wok filled three-quarters full of water. Bring to the boil, then steam until just cooked, adding boiling water to the wok if necessary.

Once cooked, let the crab stand at room temperature for 10 minutes, then douse in cold water for 10 minutes, then in iced water for 10 minutes. Once cold, pick the crabmeat and divide into 25 g (1 oz) portions.

To serve, place a portion of crabmeat on each plate, loosen the crabmeat in a circle and cover with approximately 1 tablespoon of macadamia milk (enough to just cover, being careful the milk doesn't run). Dress with a few drops of olive oil and a few drops of macadamia nut oil. Arrange shaved macadamia nuts over the top to cover then place chamomile flowers, two per serve, on top. If fresh flowers are not available, put a few drops of chamomile essential oil on some paper towel and wipe across the serving plate to add aroma.

VENISON TARTARE

CHEF: MATT AITA
SERVES 4

280 g (10 oz) venison short loin, cut into 3 mm (1/8 inch) dice
1 small French shallot, minced
24 g (1 oz) wholegrain mustard
20 g (¾ oz) camelina oil, or substitute linseed (flaxseed) oil
immature juniper berries, to serve
microgreens, to serve
walnuts, toasted and crushed, to serve

TARRAGON PURÉE
7 g (1/8 oz) agar-agar
5 g (1/8 oz) sea salt
70 g (2½ oz) tarragon leaves

LEMON PURÉE
115 g (4 oz) lemon peel
140 ml (4½ fl oz) lemon juice, strained
40 g (1½ oz) sugar
4 g (1/8 oz) salt

For the tarragon purée, bring 500 ml (17 fl oz/2 cups) of water, the agar-agar and sea salt to a boil in a saucepan over medium heat. Boil for 1 minute, stirring constantly. Pour into a container, cover and place in the refrigerator to set for 20 minutes. Blanch the tarragon in boiling water until bright green and tender. Refresh in iced water, squeeze to remove excess water then add to a food processor with the cooled agar-agar base and process until smooth. Set aside.

For the lemon purée, place the peel in a saucepan of water and bring to the boil over medium heat. Drain and repeat the process twice more. Place the cooked peel and remaining purée ingredients in a medium saucepan and simmer until the lemon peel is tender. Purée in a blender, adding water as needed to thin to a creamy consistency.

To prepare the venison, suspend a stainless steel bowl over a bowl of ice, ensuring the top bowl is touching the ice so it stays cool. Put the venison in the chilled bowl, along with the shallot, mustard and camelina oil. Season and beat vigorously with a wooden spoon for 3 minutes.

Arrange the venison on a serving plate and scatter with juniper berries, microgreens and walnuts. Dot the lemon purée and tarragon purée around the plate. Serve immediately.

QUAIL, BREAD SAUCE AND CHERRIES

CHEF: MATT LAMBERT

SERVES 4

You will need to begin this recipe one day ahead.

2 quail, deboned, bones reserved
1 tablespoon butter
1 thyme sprig
1 garlic clove, bruised
oil, for deep-frying
red ribbon sorrel and rocket (arugula) flowers, to serve

PICKLED CHERRIES

100 g (3½ oz) cherries, halved, pitted
200 g (7 oz) cherries, quartered, pitted
500 ml (17 fl oz/2 cups) cider vinegar
75 g (2¾ oz) caster sugar
5 cloves
2 cinnamon sticks
1 star anise
2 g (1/16 oz) salt

MASTER STOCK

250 ml (9 fl oz/1 cup) soy sauce
10 star anise
3 oranges, juice
150 ml (5½ fl oz) black vinegar
40 g (1½ oz) ginger, peeled, sliced
2 teaspoons coriander seeds
3 dried bird's eye chillies
3 cinnamon sticks
750 ml (26 fl oz/3 cups) brown chicken stock

BREAD SAUCE

350 ml (12 fl oz) cream
200 ml (7 fl oz) milk
1 rosemary sprig
1 bay leaf
1 large onion, chopped
oil, for frying
115 g (4 oz/2 cups) fresh sourdough breadcrumbs

QUAIL JUS

1 litre (35 fl oz/4 cups) brown chicken stock
1 tablespoon butter

To make the pickled cherries, reserve 100 g (3½ oz) of the quartered cherries, and put the remaining ingredients into a medium saucepan with 250 ml (9 fl oz/1 cup) of water. Bring to the boil over medium heat and boil for 2 minutes. Remove from the heat, pour into a container and refrigerate to chill. Cover the reserved cherries with the cold pickling liquid and allow to macerate overnight. Strain the cherries and reserve the liquid for the quail jus.

Put all of the master stock ingredients into a saucepan over medium heat and bring to 70°C (150°F) for 10 minutes. Remove from the heat and allow to steep for 30 minutes. Strain into a clean saucepan. Return to low heat, add the quail legs and poach at 50–60°C (120–140°F) for 30 minutes. Remove the quail legs from the master stock and chill them in the refrigerator until ready to serve.

To make the bread sauce, put the cream, milk, rosemary and bay leaf in a saucepan over low to medium heat and simmer for approximately 6 minutes. Remove from the heat and set aside to steep for 1 hour before removing the herbs. Put the onion in a frying pan with a dash of oil and caramelise over high heat. Stir the breadcrumbs and onions into the milk and cream. Allow about 15 minutes for the crumbs to absorb some of the liquid, then blend on high in a blender while the mixture is still warm, until silky smooth and shiny. Season with salt, then pour the bread sauce into a small squeeze bottle and keep warm.

Prepare the quail jus by putting the brown chicken stock, reserved quail bones and 2 tablespoons of the reserved cherry pickling liquor in a saucepan and reduce by two-thirds over medium heat. Put the butter in a separate saucepan and emulsify over medium heat. Season with salt and reserved pickling liquid, to taste: you want the taste to be rich, a little sweet and a little tart.

Place the quail breast skin side down in a frying pan and cook over medium heat, pressing down in the centre of the breast to crisp the skin, for 3–5 minutes until just cooked through. Halfway through cooking, add 12 pickled cherry halves and cook to achieve a light pan roast on the edges. Add the butter, thyme and garlic to the pan and baste the raw side of the quail breast. While the breast is cooking, preheat oil in a deep-fryer to 175°C (345°F) or until a cube of bread dropped into the oil turns brown in 15–20 seconds. Add the poached quail legs and cook for 1–2 minutes or until golden.

On a tray lined with a cold tea towel (dish towel), place the quail breast skin side up, with the cherries and quail legs.

To serve, take the warm bread sauce and place 3 dots, about the size of a teaspoon on each plate. Add 3 roasted cherry halves, 3 of the pickled halved cherries and 3 of the pickled quartered cherries to each plate. Place a crisp fried leg and a breast on each plate. Drizzle with jus and garnish with red ribbon sorrel and rocket flowers.

OCTOPUS IN COCONUT MILK, RED ONION CEVICHE, PLANTAIN CHIPS

CHEF: JOSÉ CARLES

SERVES 8

4 celery stalks, thinly sliced
2 leeks, white part only, thinly sliced
1 garlic bulb, cloves crushed
1 large brown onion, peeled, thinly sliced
1.8 kg (4 lb) octopus, frozen

COCONUT MILK SAUCE
450 g (1 lb) fresh coconut flesh
75 g (2¾ oz) onion, finely chopped
30 g (1 oz) green capsicum (pepper), finely chopped
30 g (1 oz) garlic, finely chopped
30 g (1 oz) aji dulce (cachucha pepper)
10 g (¼ oz) annatto seed (achiote) paste
1 tablespoon tomato paste (concentrated purée)
8 coriander stems, washed
1–2 tablespoons butter
lemon juice, to season

SPICED MUSTARD
200 g (7 oz) English mustard
150 g (5½ oz) smoked vegetable hot sauce (mild) (see *Accompagnement* for recipe)

RED ONION CEVICHE
1 red onion
100 ml (3½ fl oz) lime juice
1 tablespoon brown sugar
½ teaspoon grated garlic
½ teaspoon grated ginger
½ teaspoon curry powder
½ teaspoon ground cumin
2 tablespoons finely chopped coriander (cilantro)

PLANTAIN CHIPS
1 green plantain
2 tablespoons butter
100 g (3½ oz) garlic, finely chopped
25 g (1 oz) aji dulce (cachucha pepper), finely chopped
40 g (1½ oz) tomato concasse
3–4 parsley sprigs, finely chopped
vegetable oil, for deep frying

Put 5 litres (175 fl oz/20 cups) of water, the celery, leek, garlic and onion in a large stockpot and bring to the boil. Plunge the octopus into the boiling water three times for 20 seconds each time. After the third repetition, wait until the liquid returns to the boil, add the octopus and cook for approximately 1 hour. Remove octopus and transfer to an ice bath. Allow to cool, cut off the legs and refrigerate.

To make the coconut milk sauce, put the coconut flesh and 1.5 litres (52 fl oz/6 cups) of water in a large saucepan. Bring to the boil, then remove from the heat. Blend in a food processor and strain through a fine sieve, pushing out as much coconut milk as possible. Set aside.

Put the onion, capsicum, garlic, aji dulce, annatto seed paste, tomato paste and coriander in a frying pan with the butter. Cook over low heat for about 10 minutes until soft. Add the coconut milk and reduce until you have about 200 ml (7 fl oz) and the liquid is the consistency of a sauce. Strain into a bowl, adding half of the solids. Season generously with salt, pepper and lemon juice. Allow to cool completely before adding the octopus legs. Cover and refrigerate until ready to serve.

To make the spiced mustard, combine the English mustard and smoked vegetable hot sauce in a bowl and stir until well combined. Set aside until ready to serve.

To prepare the red onion ceviche, peel the onion and slice it 3 mm (⅛ inch) thick on a mandolin. Put all the ingredients into a bowl, stir gently to combine, cover and set aside until ready to serve.

To make the plantain chips, slice the plantain 2 mm (1/16 inch) thick on a mandolin. Put the butter in a frying pan over low heat. Add the garlic and aji dulce and sweat until soft, with no colour. Remove from the heat, add the tomato concasse and parsley. Season with salt and pepper and reserve. Heat vegetable oil in a deep-fryer or large, heavy-based saucepan and heat to 180°C (350°F) or until a cube of bread dropped into the oil turns brown in 15 seconds. Add the plantain slices and cook for 3 minutes. Remove, drain on paper towel and then combine with the tomato mixture.

Put the marinated octopus legs in a sous-vide bag and cook in a water bath for 10 minutes at 85°C (185°F). Gently remove from the bag: the octopus should look glazed. To serve, place the octopus in the centre of the plate. Stack about 8 plantain chips next to the octopus. Serve with several drops of spiced mustard and a generous spoonful of the red onion ceviche.

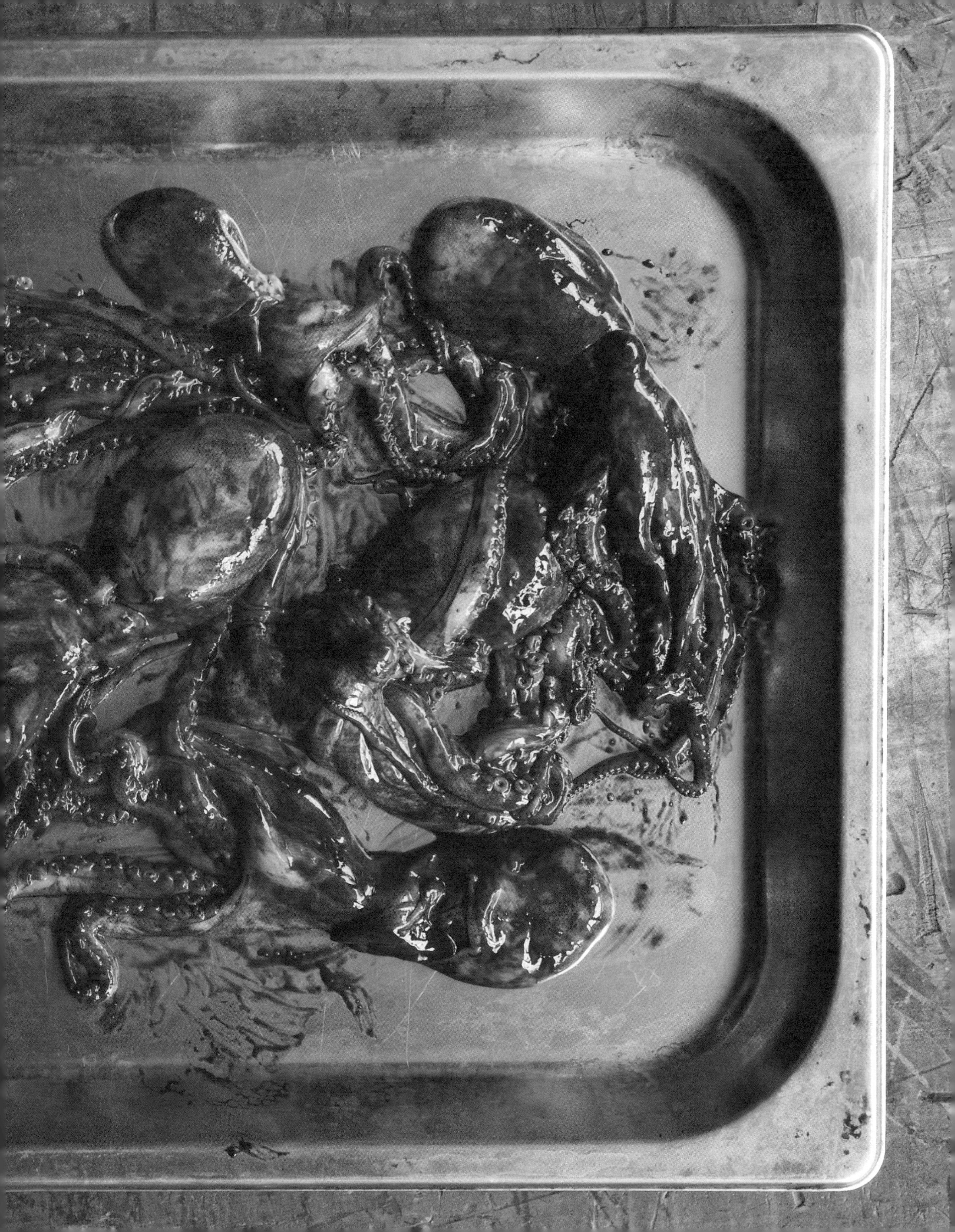

THE MENU

The bistronomy menu is usually set. Like it or lump it.

There are a few cheffy indulgences but its composition is genuinely directional without being a pretentious display of a chef's ego. Ranging from anywhere between three and ten courses, the bistronomy menu is not a laboured sales pitch but an executive summary of the season and an introduction to the chef and the journey they want to take you on. It's a dalliance, the culinary equivalent of a discreet flash of thigh or the sense of intrigue that runs down the nape of an exposed neck. It is a younger, more free-form invention with no rules and few limits.

The kind of tasting menu offered by bistronomy is short, sharp and enticing. It is far more likely to leave the diner happily sated than uncomfortably full and, while it still follows the traditional structure of a tasting menu graduating from light dishes to a climax of heavier, protein-rich plates, it moves away from the idea of holding the diner hostage as they labour through course after course, numerous table interruptions, palate fatigue and, inevitably, some sameness on the plate. We are not referring here to Japanese *kaiseki* or *omakase* menus either. Both are old dining traditions with underlying structures that chefs and diners comprehend. Rather, the bistronomy menu is engineered to shock, delight and surprise. Its conciseness is exciting to eat through and there is a structural freedom where refined and robust happily coexist: a world where salads can be comfortably 'composed' or 'tossed'.

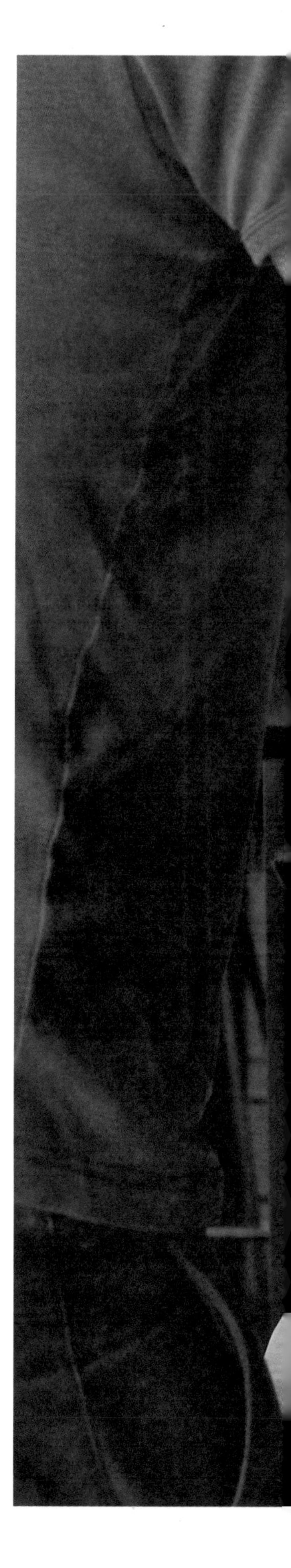

'Guidelines only restrict our vision. The food can be a vast collection of many cultures and awesome ingredients. We cook and drink what we like.'

BEAU VINCENT

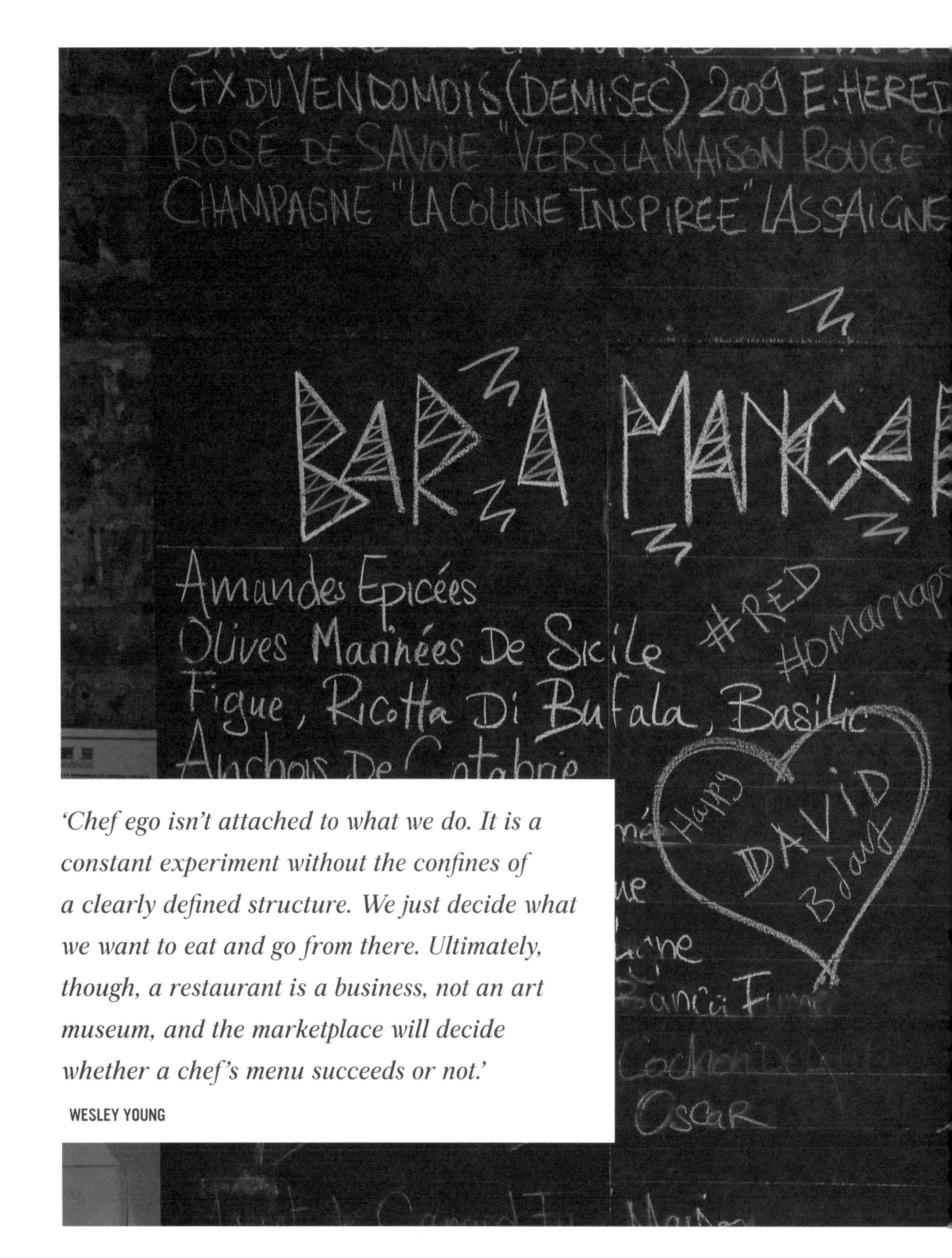

'Chef ego isn't attached to what we do. It is a constant experiment without the confines of a clearly defined structure. We just decide what we want to eat and go from there. Ultimately, though, a restaurant is a business, not an art museum, and the marketplace will decide whether a chef's menu succeeds or not.'

WESLEY YOUNG

This menu structure is not for everyone, and is a culinary challenge that no chef dives into casually. A restaurant whose sole product is a take-it-or-leave-it meal sets a dauntingly big challenge for itself. It's not simply about serving a lot of courses, it's about balance. A tasting menu is a showcase for indulgent, multicourse journey-type meals, and only really talented, pioneering cooks can get away with this format. In the hands of the true bistronomy chef who grasps the challenges and possibilities of the form, the tasting menu yields a series of delights that a shorter meal can never contain. It is more like a succession of small thrills, eyebrow-raising surprises and experiments in sensual gratification, which, when done well, create rhythm and momentum as the menu maps a chef's influences. It enables them to experiment with new techniques and offer something that isn't at risk of being dumbed down or sanitised by trend or tradition.

Unlike other menus that often compensate for lousy food by adding as many adjectives and verbs to the menu as possible, the bistronomy menu is written with an economic sensibility — much like the *nouvelle vague* philosophy of bistronomy itself — with a sense of humour and touch of nostalgia. Perhaps it is that sense of capturing the ephemeral that has liberated the bistronomy chef from the constraints of a menu that is too serious. The description of food is whimsical, yet serious, often funny, fun, challenging and new. It is short and to the point, written with minimal explanation that at times verges on the obtuse. But that is part of the fun. It's like witnessing classically trained musicians behind the decks at a basement club. There's a certain style, without doubt, but their joy comes from being able to let loose. The elusiveness and cryptic wording is intended to be a series of provocations, not mechanical pleasures and, like many things culinary and *avant-garde*, it provokes an enquiring belly and mind: that's something every food scene — be it fine dining, a food truck or a relaxed bistro — needs.

KING SALMON CONFIT, LEEKS AND EGGS

CHEF: SCOTT PICKETT

SERVES 4

2 leeks, white part only, finely chopped, ½ leek reserved
1 onion, peeled, finely chopped
50 g (1¾ oz) butter
2½ tablespoons grapeseed oil
250 ml (9 fl oz/1 cup) milk
250 ml (9 fl oz/1 cup) cream
½ a sebago (all-purpose) potato, peeled, sliced
250 g (9 oz) salmon belly, skin and sinew removed
50 g (1¾ oz) grey salt
50 g (1¾ oz) sugar
1 litre (35 fl oz/4 cups) olive oil
4 quail eggs, soft-boiled
4 teaspoons salmon caviar
4 teaspoons beluga caviar

Preheat the oven to 260°C (500°F/Gas 9). Lay the reserved half leek on a foil-lined baking tray. Roast for 10–20 minutes or until blackened, dry, and crisp. Allow to cool. Break into fine shards. Leek ash will keep for up to 3 days in an airtight container at room temperature.

Put the chopped leek, onion, butter and grapeseed oil into a frying pan over low heat, and sweat until soft and translucent. Season with salt and pepper and reserve 8 tablespoons of the leek mixture for serving. Add the milk, cream and potato to the pan and cook for 15–20 minutes until the potato is soft. Purée the mixture in a blender until smooth, season with salt and pepper, then pass through a fine sieve. Put the mixture in an espuma gun with a double charge and set aside until ready to serve. Be careful not to fill the gun past three-quarters full.

Lightly cure the salmon in the grey salt and sugar for 30 minutes. Rinse gently and pat dry with paper towel, leaving it uncovered until ready to cook. Poach the salmon in the olive oil at 52°C (126°F) for 8–10 minutes. Remove from the oil and drain on paper towel.

To serve, put some sweated leeks in the bottom of each bowl, place some salmon belly pieces on top, garnish with a quail egg, salmon caviar and beluga caviar. Use the espuma gun to create potato foam, spoon it over the salmon, then sprinkle with leek ash and serve warm.

HALIBUT WITH OYSTER MUSHROOMS AND LEEKS

CHEF: WESLEY YOUNG

SERVES 2–4

285 g (10 oz) halibut (black pomfret) fillet, no more than 3.75 cm (1½ inches) thick
10% brine: 100 g (3½ oz) salt dissolved in 1 litre (35 fl oz/4 cups) water
1 sheet kombu, rehydrated
grapeseed oil, for frying
85 g (3 oz) oyster mushrooms
55 g (2 oz) leeks, white part only, julienned
pea shoots, to garnish

DASHI EGG WASH

½ egg yolk
1 tablespoon dashi stock (see *Accompagnement* for recipe)
½ teaspoon dehydrated mushroom powder

Soak the halibut fillet in the brine for 2 hours.

Make the dashi egg wash by combining all ingredients in a small bowl and whisking to combine. Set aside.

Preheat the oven to 60°C (140°F). Pat dry the halibut fillet and gently wrap it in the rehydrated kombu. Place on a baking tray lined with baking paper and bake for 25 minutes or until the fish looks opaque.

Heat a frying pan over medium-low heat and put the grapeseed oil and salt in the pan. Add the oyster mushrooms evenly and cook for 3–4 minutes or until the mushrooms develop a deep caramelisation. Do not shake the pan during this time. Add the leek evenly on top of the mushroom and toss gently to incorporate. The liquid released from the leek will deglaze the caramelisation of the pan. When the leek is just cooked (about 30 seconds), remove everything from the pan, ready for plating.

To plate, cut the seaweed along the edges of the halibut, leaving one side uncut. Roll the seaweed back like the lid of a sardine can to expose the top of the fillet. Glaze the fish with the dashi egg wash and put it under the grill (broiler) for 20 seconds. Place the mushroom and leek mixture on top of the fish. Garnish with pea shoots and serve immediately.

VEAL TONGUE WITH PEA ICE

CHEF: SHAUN KELLY

SERVES 4-6

You will need to begin this recipe one week ahead.

1 veal tongue, approximately 500 g (1 lb 2 oz)
1 tablespoon dijon mustard
fresh salad leaves, such as mustard greens, watercress, pea shoots, to serve

BRINE

125 g (4½ oz) salt
70 g (2½ oz/⅓ cup) dark brown sugar
20 g (¾ oz) sodium nitrate (optional)
4 sage sprigs
12 juniper berries, crushed
2 garlic cloves
1 teaspoon white peppercorns, crushed

PEA ICE

500 g (1 lb 2 oz) frozen peas
olive oil

Make the brine by combining all of the ingredients with 2 litres (70 fl oz/8 cups) of water in a large saucepan over high heat and cook for 1–2 minutes or until the salt and sugar have dissolved. Refrigerate until completely cooled. Once cooled, add the tongue, placing a weight on top to ensure it stays completely submerged in the liquid. Cover and refrigerate for 7 days.

Remove the tongue from the brine, reserving 500 ml (17 fl oz/2 cups) of the liquid, and place in a large saucepan. Cover with water and bring to the boil over high heat. Strain and immediately return to the saucepan, cover with fresh water and reserved brining liquid. Simmer for 3 hours over low to medium heat. To test, pierce the tongue using a skewer at the thickest part and the tip: both should be tender.

Remove the tongue from the saucepan, reserving the cooking liquor, and, while warm, remove the thick leather membrane. Start at the back or throat end of the tongue and use a small knife to lift up the first piece of skin. Then, using your fingers, peel the skin off as though you were removing a glove. Be careful when you reach the tip of the tongue that you don't tear it off. Discard the skin.

Make the pea ice by blanching and refreshing the peas. Put the peas in a blender with 1–2 tablespoons of the tongue's cooking liquor and a drizzle of olive oil. Purée until smooth and season generously with salt and pepper. Put the mixture in an ice-cream machine and churn until a fine ice is achieved. Alternatively, you can serve it as a chilled purée.

Thin the mustard with 1–2 tablespoons of the tongue's cooking liquor. When ready to serve, thinly slice the tongue. Place a piece of tongue on each plate with a little of the mustard, top with a spoonful of pea ice and scatter with the fresh salad leaves.

GLOBE ARTICHOKE SOUP, SCALLOPS AND TRUFFLE

CHEF: JOSH MURPHY

SERVES 6

1 celery stalk
1 leek, white part only
½ onion, peeled
¼ fennel bulb
4 garlic cloves
2 thyme sprigs
1 tablespoon olive oil
600 ml (21 fl oz) light chicken stock
1.5 kg (3 lb 5 oz) globe artichoke hearts, cleaned
200 g (9 oz) all-purpose potatoes, such as desiree, peeled, sliced
1 bay leaf
pinch of dried chilli flakes
½ teaspoon fennel seeds
½ teaspoon coriander seeds
125 g (4½ oz) thick (double) cream
white pepper
18 scallops
2 globe artichokes, extra, for frying
sunflower oil, for frying
lemon juice
sherry vinegar, to season
fresh black truffle, shaved

In a large, heavy-based saucepan gently sweat the celery, leek, onion, fennel, garlic and thyme with the olive oil, taking care to avoid any colouring. When soft and aromatic, add the stock, followed by the artichoke, potato, bay leaf, chilli flakes, fennel seeds and coriander seeds. Simmer gently until the potatoes are cooked. Purée in a blender until smooth, then pass through a sieve and return to the heat. Add the cream and bring to a simmer. Remove the soup from the heat and set aside to cool. Season with white pepper and salt.

To prepare the scallops, make a brine by whisking 100 g (3½ oz) table salt into 1 litre (35 fl oz/4 cups) of water. Shuck the scallops from the shells, clean and drop them into the brine for 10 minutes. Set aside on a dry tea towel (dish towel). Carefully remove any small pieces of shell from the scallops.

Thinly slice the extra artichokes using a mandolin. Fry in sunflower oil at 135°C (275°F) for 3 minutes or until golden. Drain on paper towel and season lightly with salt.

Season the top of the scallops with salt. Heat a heavy-based frying pan over medium-high heat, brush the pan with oil and place the scallops evenly in the pan, top side down. Sear in the hot pan on one side until golden then turn them over with a spoon. Add the lemon juice to the scallops in the pan and remove them immediately to a tray. It is best to do this in batches.

Arrange the scallops in a bowl and garnish with a few artichoke chips. Season with a little sherry vinegar and top with shaved fresh black truffle. Meanwhile, heat the soup, season with salt and pepper and finish with a little lemon juice. Pour the soup, about 120 ml (4 fl oz) per serve, beside the scallops and serve.

SMOKED EEL, CARROT AND CHAMOMILE

CHEF: SCOTT PICKETT

SERVES 9

You will need to begin this recipe one day ahead.

- 40 g (1½ oz) dried chamomile flowers (looseleaf tea)
- 1 litre (35 fl oz/4 cups) milk
- 10 g (¼ oz) agar-agar
- 5 g (⅛ oz) salt
- 4 large celery stalks, rinsed, lightly peeled, sliced 1 cm (½ inch) thick
- 500 ml (17 fl oz/2 cups) apple juice
- 4 large carrots, juiced
- 150 g (5½ oz) brioche, roughly torn
- 1½ tablespoons olive oil
- 2 smoked eels, 700 g (1 lb 9 oz) each, skinned, backbone discarded
- black lava salt
- chickpea cress leaves, to serve

Put the chamomile and milk in a saucepan over medium heat. Bring to a soft boil then remove from the heat. Cover and allow the flavours to infuse overnight in the refrigerator. Strain the milk into a clean saucepan, add the agar-agar and salt and place over low heat. Bring the milk to 90°C (195°F), whisking constantly until the ingredients are incorporated. Pour the mixture into a tray and allow to cool in the refrigerator for 1 hour. When set, transfer to a blender and blend until the mixture resembles thick cream, then set aside.

Place the celery pieces in a tight-fitting container. Cover with the apple juice and set aside.

Strain the carrot juice into a saucepan and simmer over low heat until the juice is reduced by half and a silky texture is achieved. Stir regularly to ensure the mixture doesn't catch. Set aside.

To make the brioche crumbs, preheat the oven to 180°C (350°F/Gas 4). Place the torn brioche on a baking tray and bake until lightly toasted (4–5 minutes). Reduce the heat to 90°C (195°F/Gas ½) and bake for a further 10 minutes or until the bread has dried out. Set aside to cool then process in a food processor until fine crumbs form. Put the crumbs in a frying pan with the olive oil and fry over medium heat until golden. Set aside.

To serve, drizzle the carrot reduction over a plate, add dollops of chamomile cream and pieces of celery. Warm the eel in the oven, cut it into bite-size pieces and place them on the plate. Season with black lava salt then add a light sprinkling of brioche crumbs and some chickpea cress.

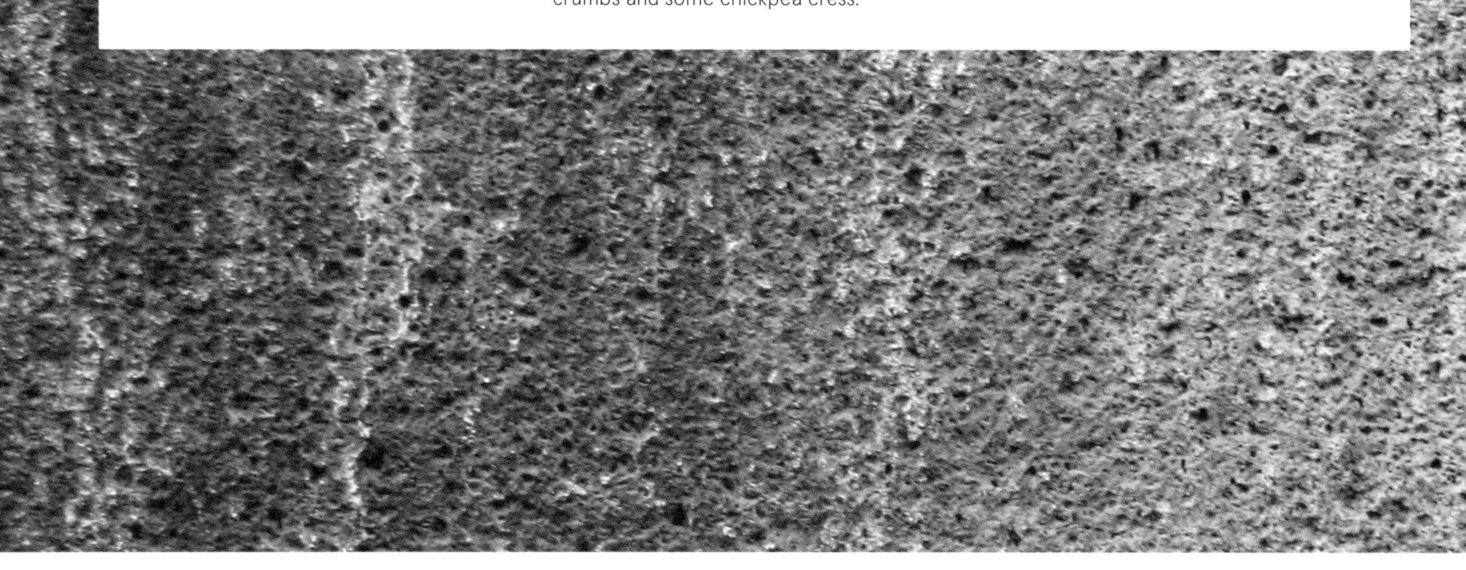

CUTTLEFISH, CLAMS AND FIGS

CHEF: INAKI AIZPITARTE
SERVES 4

20 g (¾ oz) capers
1 cuttlefish, approximately 500 g (1 lb 2 oz)
20 clams (vongole)
1 teaspoon fino sherry vinegar
1 teaspoon Jerez vinegar
4 figs
bronze fennel seeds, to serve

FIG OIL
500 ml (17 fl oz/2 cups) grapeseed oil
1 bunch fig leaves

Preheat the oven to 80°C (175°F/Gas ¼). Put the capers on a baking tray lined with baking paper and dehydrate for 6 hours.

Make the fig oil by heating the grapeseed oil to 60°C (140°F). Add the fig leaves, remove from the heat and set aside to steep for a minimum of 1 hour. Strain and set aside, discarding the leaves.

Clean the cuttlefish, cut it into small bite-size pieces and set aside. Cook the clams in a large saucepan of boiling water without salt until they open. Let them stand for 15 seconds, then cool them down with ice. Drain the clams, reserving the liquid; then add the combined vinegars to the clam liquid.

To serve, season the cuttlefish with salt, pepper and fig oil. Arrange the cuttlefish on the centre of each plate. Pour the liquid from the clams over the cuttlefish, then arrange five clams on each serving and top with a sprinkling of dried capers.

Cut each fig into 5 sections and arrange around the cuttlefish. Add a few drops of fig oil and sprinkle with bronze fennel seeds. Serve immediately.

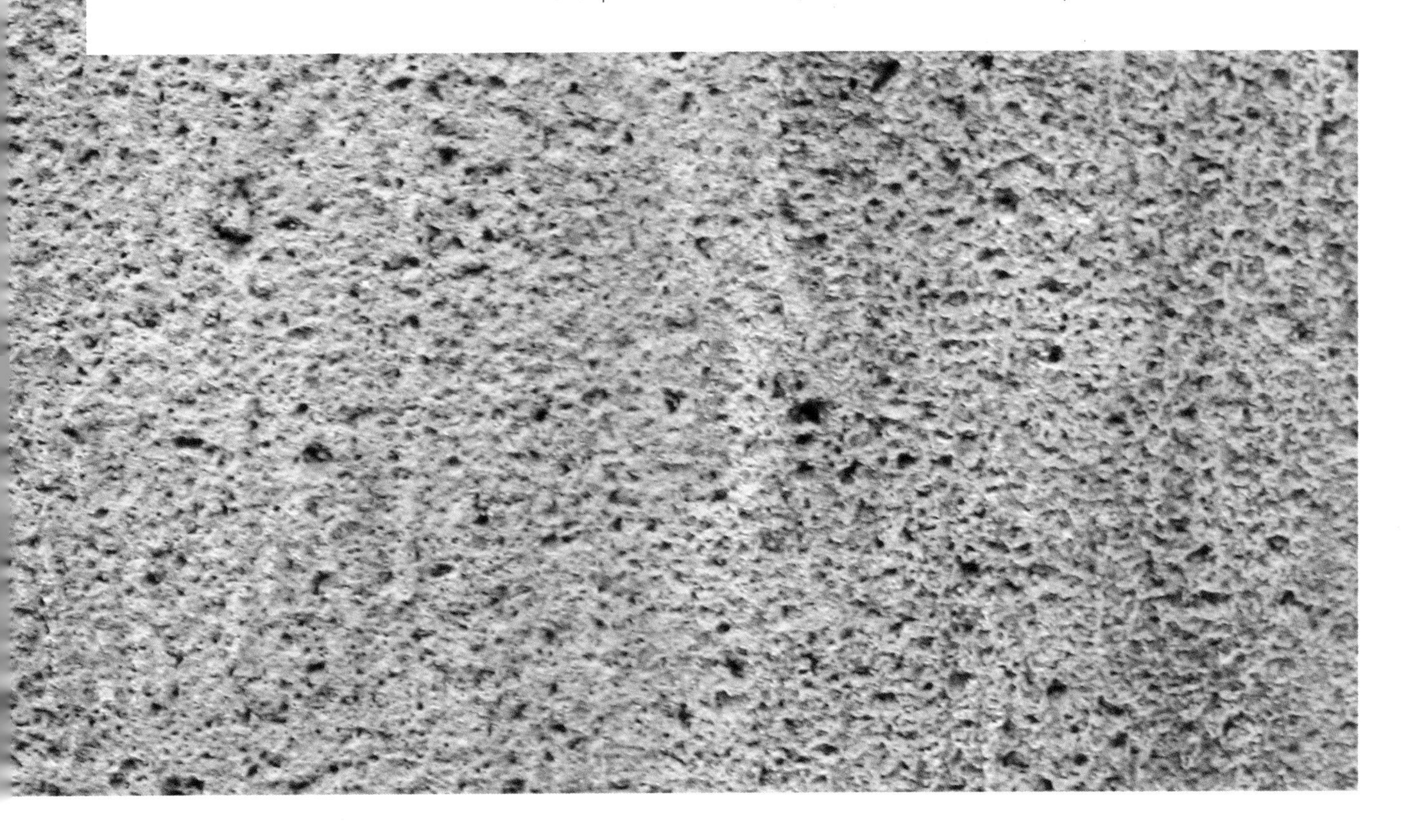

SUNFLOWER SEEDS
CAYENNE PEPPER
TUMERIC
NUTMEG
CUMIN SEEDS
SWEET PAPRIKA
SeSame

PORK SHOULDER TERRINE, KIMCHI PUREE, CUCUMBER PICKLE AND LOBSTER CRACKER

CHEF: BEAU VINCENT

SERVES 6–8

You will need to begin this recipe two days ahead.

2.5 kg (5 lb 8 oz) pork shoulder, bone in
4 bay leaves
10 g (¼ oz/½ bunch) thyme
8 sage leaves
2 small garlic bulbs, cut crossways
2 litres (70 fl oz/8 cups) chicken stock
150 g (5½ oz/1 cup) plain (all-purpose) flour
3 eggs, beaten
60 g (2¼ oz/1 cup) panko breadcrumbs
vegetable oil, for deep-frying

LOBSTER CRACKER

100 g (3½ oz) tapioca pearls
250 g (9 oz) raw lobster meat, finely chopped
shichimi togarashi
vegetable oil, for deep-frying

CUCUMBER PICKLE

250 ml (9 fl oz/1 cup) white wine vinegar
110 g (3¾ oz/½ cup) caster (superfine) sugar
375 ml (13 fl oz/1½ cups) apple juice
2 telegraph (long) cucumbers, approximately 350 g (12 oz)

KIMCHI PURÉE

½ Chinese cabbage (wong bok), heart only, approximately 500 g (1 lb 2 oz)
½ green apple, peeled
15 g (½ oz) ginger, peeled
½ white onion, peeled
1 red chilli
6 garlic cloves
shichimi togarashi
100 ml (3½ fl oz) soy sauce
35 ml (1¼ fl oz) sesame oil
15 g (½ oz) bonito flakes
fish sauce, to taste

Preheat the oven to 100°C (200°F/Gas ½). Put the pork shoulder in a large, deep-sided tray with the bay leaves, thyme, sage leaves, garlic and chicken stock. Cover the tray with foil, place in the oven and cook for 20 hours. After cooking, carefully remove the shoulder from the stock and place on a tray. The pork should be very tender and falling off the bone, and all the fat should have come away from the skin. Discard the skin and any bones so that only the fat and meat are remaining. Mix the meat and fat together using some of the reserved cooking liquid to moisten. Season well, then use plastic wrap to tightly roll the pork into uniform long cylinders, approximately 2–3 cm (¾–1¼ inches) in diameter. Place in the refrigerator until set, at least 2 hours. When cold and firm, cut crossways to desired length, about 5–10 cm (2–4 inches) long. Remove the plastic wrap and crumb in panko breadcrumbs, first using the flour, then the beaten eggs, then the panko breadcrumbs. Return to the refrigerator until ready to cook.

To make the lobster cracker, place the tapioca and 1 litre (35 fl oz/4 cups) of water in a large saucepan over low heat, stirring occasionally, for approximately 45 minutes or until the tapioca becomes translucent. Let cool. Mix the lobster meat and 600 g (1 lb 5 oz) of the cooked tapioca in a blender until smooth. Season with salt and shichimi togarashi to taste. Line two baking trays with baking paper and spread the mixture in a very thin layer across the trays. Keep in a warm area (such as above an oven) until the mixture has dried. Depending on weather and humidity the time for this process varies between 1 and 2 days. (The same result can be achieved by spreading over greaseproof paper and placing in a dehydrator for 4–6 hours.) Heat vegetable oil in a deep-fryer or large, heavy-based saucepan to 180–200°C (350–400°F), or when a cube of bread dropped into the oil turns brown in 5–15 seconds, and fry pieces of lobster cracker until crisp and puffed. Set aside until ready to plate.

To make the kimchi purée, trim the cabbage and place in cold salty water for 24 hours. Wash the cabbage and dry with a tea towel (dish towel) before putting the cabbage and remaining ingredients in a blender and blending to a smooth paste consistency. Set aside until ready to plate.

To make the cucumber pickle, put the vinegar, sugar and apple juice in a saucepan and bring to the boil. Remove from heat and allow to cool to room temperature. Peel the cucumbers, put them in a sous-vide bag and add the pickling liquid. Seal the bag in a vacuum sealer, removing the air and compressing the pickling liquid into the cucumber. Set aside to infuse. Just before serving, remove from the bag and slice on angles down the cucumber.

To finish, heat the vegetable oil in a deep-fryer to 190°C (375°F). Add the pork croquettes, being careful not to overcrowd the fryer, and cook for approximately 3–4 minutes or until the pork is brown and crisp and thoroughly heated through. Remove croquettes from the fryer and season with salt and pepper. Warm the kimchi purée, then spoon it onto a plate, place pork onto the purée and scatter lobster crackers and cucumber pickles along the side.

SMOKED BONITO, SALTED GRILLED PLUMS AND ONION

CHEF: JAMES HENRY

SERVES 8

20 sweet onions, peeled,
2 litres (70 fl oz/8 cups) chicken stock
4 fresh bonito fillets, skin removed
30 g (1 oz) salt
50 g (1¾ oz) brown sugar
8 mirabelle plums
Banyuls wine vinegar, to season
apple wood chips, for smoking

Heat a large chargrill or barbecue on medium-high heat. Add the onions and grill until charred, about 5 minutes. Set one onion aside for later use. Combine the chicken stock with the remaining charred onions in a bowl and steam over a double boiler for 4 hours. Pass the mixture through a fine sieve and put it in a clean saucepan over medium heat. Reduce the liquid by two-thirds.

Meanwhile, put the bonito fillets in a non-reactive container. Sprinkle with the salt and sugar and stand for 3 hours in the refrigerator. Wipe the fillets clean.

Cold smoke the fillets by preheating a coal-bedded kettle barbecue to low heat and set it up for indirect grilling using the top rack. Add half of the wood chips around the coals and cook for 3-4 minutes until smoke appears. Place the fillets on the oiled top rack, cover with lid and smoke at medium-high smoke, being careful not to cook the fish at all. You can add a tray of ice to help keep it cool. Alternatively set a piece of wood over a fire, snuff it out and put it in a tray. Place the bonito in a perforated tray that fits snugly over the other tray and cover with foil.

To assemble, cut the mirabelle plums in half, remove the stone and lightly salt the flesh. Sear the plums, cut side down, in a frying pan over medium heat.

Separate layers of the reserved onion and drizzle with Banyuls wine vinegar. With the sharpest knife possible slice two pieces of fish per person. Place two slices of fish on each plate. Add two seared plum halves and pieces of reserved onion. Lightly dress with the onion sauce and serve.

CUISINIERS REBELLES
REBEL COOKS
Young, freethinking arch-progressives

PRAWN CEVICHE, PONZU AND FOIE GRAS PARFAIT

MONKFISH BOUILLABAISSE

SOLE MEUNIÈRE

SNAIL AND GARBANZO

GRILLED LANGOUSTINE WITH POTATO AND BEEF PURÉE, CORN AND SOFRITO

RABBIT, BEER GRAINS, WHITE CARROT AND SAMPHIRE

SHIO KOJI BARBECUED DUCK HEARTS WITH HORSERADISH

STEAMED HAPUKU, WILD NETTLE AND TOASTED RYE BUTTER

STINGRAY, SPICED CRAB SOUP AND GIROLLES

LAMB LEG TARTARE WITH SMOKED CAPSICUM AND SHICHIMI TOGARASHI

SKEWERED LAMB SWEETBREADS, SUN-DRIED TOMATOES, EGGS AND BUTTON MUSHROOMS

BEETROOT RISOTTO

PRAWN CEVICHE, PONZU AND FOIE GRAS PARFAIT

CHEF: BEAU VINCENT

SERVES 10

50 g (1¾ oz) ginger, julienne, to deep-fry
plain (all-purpose) flour, for coating
vegetable oil, for deep-frying ginger
20 raw prawns, peeled, deveined
baby shiso (perilla), to serve
3 radishes, thinly sliced, to serve
2 green apples, thinly sliced, to serve

PONZU

5 g (1/8 oz) sugar
50 ml (1¾ fl oz) mirin (rice wine)
25 ml (1 fl oz) yuzu juice
3 teaspoons soy sauce
5 g (1/8 oz) bonito flakes
90 ml (3 fl oz) grapeseed oil

RYE CRUMB

2–3 slices rye bread, one or two days old
50 g (1¾ oz) clarified butter

FOIE GRAS PARFAIT

(all ingredients at room temperature)
300 ml (10½ fl oz) Port (tawny)
100 ml (3½ fl oz) brandy
5 g (1/8 oz/¼ bunch) thyme
2 rosemary stalks
½ garlic clove, unpeeled, chopped
250 g (9 oz) chicken livers, cleaned
½ teaspoon salt
¼ teaspoon white pepper
2 eggs
100 g (3½ oz) clarified butter

To make the ponzu, dissolve the sugar with 3 teaspoons of water in a saucepan over medium heat. Remove from the heat and add the mirin, yuzu juice, soy sauce and bonito flakes and stir until combined. Slowly whisk in the grapeseed oil until emulsified. Set aside until ready to serve.

Blitz the rye bread in a food processor until you achieve a crumb consistency. Melt the clarified butter in a frying pan over medium heat, toast the rye breadcrumbs until they are deep golden then season with salt and place on paper towel to drain. Set aside until ready to serve.

To make the foie gras parfait, bring the port and brandy to the boil in a large saucepan, then set the mixture alight to burn off the alcohol. Once the flame subsides, add the thyme, rosemary and garlic, and simmer over medium heat to reduce until syrupy. Strain the liquid through a fine sieve and allow to cool to room temperature. In a Thermomix, blend the chicken livers on high speed, adding the salt and white pepper and the reduced syrup until puréed. Set Thermomix to 40°C (105°F), add the eggs one at a time and then clarified butter to allow emulsification. Once thoroughly emulsified, increase the heat to 80°C (175°F) and blend on high speed again until the temperature has been reached and the mixture has thickened. Alternatively, blend the chicken livers with the salt and pepper and reduced syrup in a food processor, then add the eggs and butter to create an emulsion. Place the purée in an ovenproof dish and place the dish in a water bath in an oven preheated to 100°C (200°F/Gas ½). Cook until the parfait has reached 80°C (175°F) in the centre. Strain through a fine sieve, into a container, then cover and refrigerate at once.

Coat the sliced ginger julienne in flour and deep-fry in vegetable oil in a heavy-based saucepan, then drain on paper towel.

Put the foie gras parfait in a piping (icing) bag and place 5 hazelnut-sized dots in a 10 cm (4 inch) circle on each plate. Blanch the prawns for 15 seconds in boiling water, then slice in half lengthways so you have two pieces the same size and shape. Place the prawns on the foie gras parfait, dress liberally with ponzu, and then add shiso, deep-fried ginger and rye breadcrumbs. Finish with green apple and radish slices, arranged in a circular pattern.

MONKFISH BOUILLABAISSE

CHEF: MATT AITA

SERVES 4

grapeseed oil, for frying
500 g (1 lb 2 oz) monkfish tail
8 prawns (shrimp), peeled and deveined, tails intact
12–16 cockles
8 baby fennel bulbs, blanched
16 baby potatoes, halved and cooked
24 samphire stalks
24 torn croutons (deep-fried and tossed with salt and Espelette pepper)
black garlic purée (see Accompagnement for recipe)
Espelette pepper, for dusting

SACHET

1 bay leaf
20 g (¾ oz) basil
10 g (¼ oz) thyme
20 g (¾ oz) tarragon
5 g (⅛ oz) star anise
8 g (¼ oz) black peppercorns
12 g (½ oz) fennel seeds

BROTH

2.3 kg (5 lb) fish bodies, bones and scraps
10 lobster heads
220 g (7¾ oz) prawn (shrimp) shells
grapeseed oil, extra
800 ml (28 fl oz) white wine
200 ml (7 fl oz) olive oil
500 g (1 lb 2 oz) onions, roughly chopped
375 g (13 oz) fennel, roughly chopped
100 g (3½ oz) celery, roughly chopped
40 g (1½ oz) fresh red cayenne pepper, roughly chopped
200 g (7 oz) red capsicum (pepper), roughly chopped
100 g (3½ oz) garlic
75 g (2¼ oz) leek, white part only, roughly chopped
small pinch of saffron threads
125 g (4½ oz/½ cup) tomato paste (concentrated purée)
15 g (½ oz) salt

Place the ingredients for the sachet in a small square of muslin (cheesecloth), draw up the edges and tie tightly with kitchen string.

To make the broth, rinse and clean the fish bodies and roughly chop; clean and scrape the lobster heads and chop into 5 cm (2 inch) pieces. Cook the fish bodies, prawn shells and lobster heads with grapeseed oil in a roasting pan over medium heat until the flesh on the bodies is translucent and the juices are reduced. Add the wine and reduce by half.

Put the olive oil, onion, fennel, celery, cayenne, capsicum, garlic, leek and saffron in a large saucepan and cook over low to medium heat until the vegetables are breaking down and starting to stick. Add the tomato paste and cook for an additional 3 minutes. Add the fish bodies mixture and 3 litres (105 fl oz/12 cups) of water plus the sachet. Bring to the boil, then reduce the heat and simmer for 45 minutes. Strain, reserving bones and broth.

Put 400 g (14 oz) of the reserved bones and 1.25 litres (44 fl oz/5 cups) of the broth in a blender. Pulse a few times to break up the bones. Pass the liquid through a fine sieve and season with the salt.

Preheat the oven to 230°C (450°F/Gas 8). Heat a large ovenproof frying pan over medium heat and add grapeseed oil to coat the surface. Season the monkfish tail with salt and pepper. Sear the monkfish on one side then roast it in the oven until cooked and firm.

Meanwhile, put 70 ml (2¼ fl oz) the broth with the prawns, cockles, fennel and potato in a large saucepan and gently heat until the cockles open and the prawns are just cooked. Add the samphire at the last minute before you plate.

Put the contents of the saucepan in serving bowls. Slice the monkfish, place on top then garnish with the croutons, 5 drops of black garlic purée per serve and Espelette pepper.

Note: If monkfish is not available, use rocklobster or any firm white-fleshed fish.

SOLE MEUNIERE

CHEF: INAKI AIZPITARTE

SERVES 4

2 tablespoons grapeseed oil
4 whole sole (flounder) fillets, 300 g (10½ oz) each, skin removed
plain (all-purpose) flour, for dusting
100 g (3½ oz) butter
½ lemon, juice
2 lemons, extra, to serve

Put the grapeseed oil in a heavy-based frying pan over medium heat. Generously dust both sides of the sole fillets with flour on a clean surface or large plate.

Place the skinned side of the fillets first in the frying pan, cooking for about 3 minutes. Turn and cook the other side for the same amount of time. Keeping the fillets warm, glaze with fresh butter and the juice of half a lemon, scraping the juices from the base of the pan and scooping them over the fillet.

Serve immediately, topped with leftover lemon butter from the pan. Cut two lemons in *dents de loup* (wolf tooth) fashion and serve one half with each sole.

SNAIL AND GARBANZO

CHEF: MATT AITA
SERVES 10–12

1.2 kg (2 lb 12 oz) dried garbanzo beans (chickpeas)
pinch of saffron threads
130 g (4½ oz) garlic, crushed
20 g (¾ oz) aniseed, toasted
1 kg (2 lb 4 oz) snails
15 g (½ oz) butter
black garlic purée (see *Accompagnement* for recipe)
basil leaves, coarsely torn, to serve

BOUQUET GARNI
2 rosemary stalks
3 thyme stalks
1 bay leaf

CRISP GARBANZO
100 g (3½ oz) garbanzo beans (chickpeas), soaked overnight
grapeseed oil, for frying
sea salt
Aleppo pepper

Put the garbanzo beans, saffron, garlic and aniseed in a large saucepan. Cover generously with about 2.5 litres (87 fl oz/10 cups) water, place over medium heat and simmer for 40 minutes or until the garbanzo beans are tender.

Make the bouquet garni by enclosing the herbs in a piece of muslin (cheesecloth) and knotting it at the top. Remove the garbanzo bean mixture from the heat, add the bouquet garni and allow to steep for 6 minutes before removing. Season generously with salt, return to the heat and add the snails. Simmer for 1 minute. Remove from the heat and allow to cool.

For the crisp garbanzo, put the soaked garbanzo beans in a medium saucepan of simmering water and cook for 30–40 minutes until tender. Drain and spread out in a single layer to cool. Heat grapeseed oil in a frying pan over high heat until shimmering, add the garbanzo beans and shallow-fry for 5–10 minutes until golden and crisp. Remove the garbanzo beans with a slotted spoon and drain on paper towel. Toss with sea salt and Aleppo pepper to taste and set aside.

To serve, fry the snail and garbanzo bean mixture with the butter in a large frying pan over medium heat until glazed. Place about 200 g (7 oz) per person in shallow serving bowls, dot with small dollops of black garlic purée and scatter with basil leaves and crisp garbanzo.

GRILLED LANGOUSTINE, WITH POTATO AND BEEF PUREE, CORN AND SOFRITO

CHEF: JOSÉ CARLES

SERVES 6

You will need to begin this recipe two days ahead.

6 large fresh langoustines, cleaned, heads and shells reserved
200 ml (7 fl oz) grapeseed oil
10 g (¼ oz) annatto seed (achiote) paste
8 coriander (cilantro) stalks
2 limes, zest
40 g (1½ oz) garlic
pinch of ground cumin
pinch of curry powder
dill, to garnish

POTATO AND BEEF PURÉE

200 g (7 oz) any first-class cut of beef, such as rib eye
200 ml (7 fl oz) olive oil
20 g (½ oz) annatto seed (achiote) paste
20 g (½ oz) garlic
8 coriander (cilantro) sprigs
5 g (¼ oz) salt
5 g (¼ oz) black pepper
wood chips, for smoking
600 g (1 lb 5 oz) waxy potatoes
200 ml (7 fl oz) milk
150 g (5½ oz) butter

CORN REDUCTION

1 tablespoon grapeseed oil
350 g (12 oz/1¾ cups) fresh corn kernels
70 g (2½ oz) butter
1 white onion, peeled, thinly sliced
50 g (1¾ oz) celery stalks, thinly sliced
50 g (1¾ oz) leek, white part only, thinly sliced
10 g (¼ oz) annatto seed (achiote) paste
10 g (¼ oz) tomato paste (concentrated purée)
1 teaspoon lemon juice, to season
15 g (½ oz) butter, to season

SOFRITO

2 g annatto seed (achiote) paste
25 g (1 oz) butter
1 small onion, finely diced
20 g (½ oz) green capsicum (pepper), finely diced
½ garlic clove, finely chopped
10 g (¼ oz) aji dulce (cachucha pepper), finely chopped
50 g (1¾ oz) tomato concasse
2 coriander (cilantro) sprigs, leaves finely chopped
1 parsley sprig, finely chopped

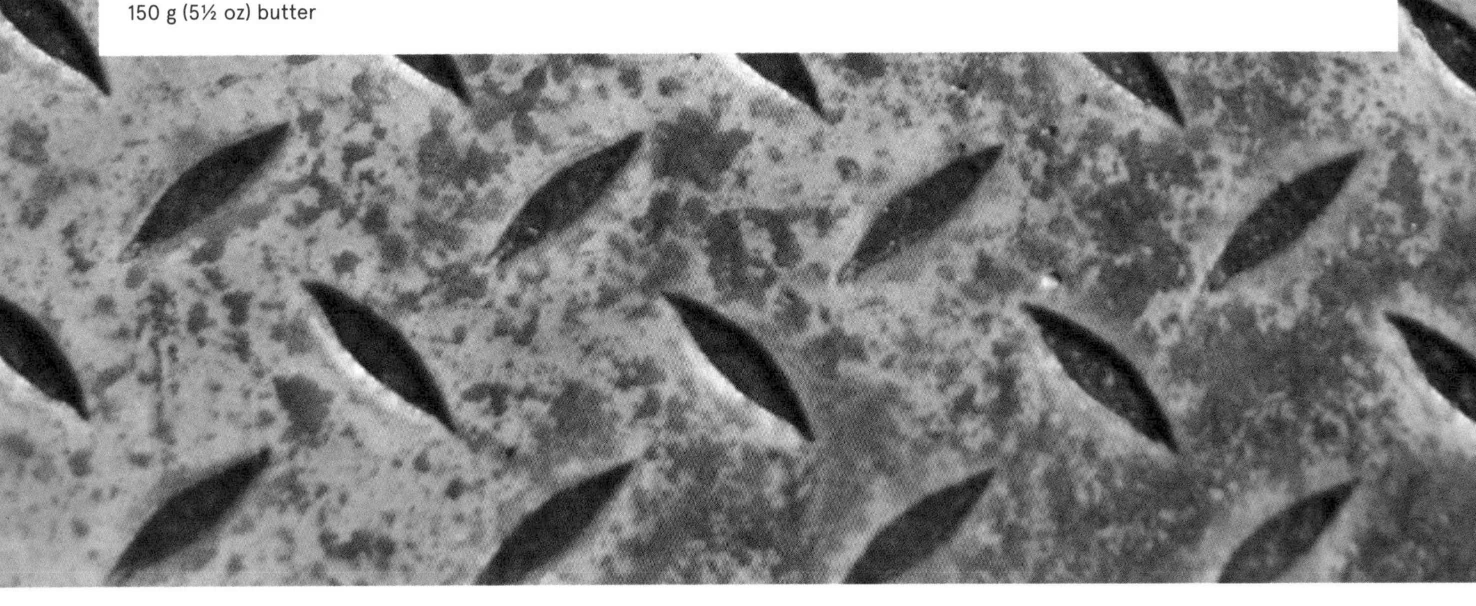

For the potato and beef purée, clean the beef and slice into 2.5 cm (1 inch) pieces. Make a marinade for the beef with the olive oil, annatto seed paste, garlic, coriander, salt and pepper and vacuum seal or place in a bowl, cover with plastic wrap and set aside in the refrigerator for at least 2 days.

Preheat a coal-bedded kettle barbecue to low heat and set up for indirect grilling. Add one-quarter of the wood chips around the coals and cook until smoke appears. Place the beef on a rack, cover and smoke, adding extra wood chips as required, until cooked through (30–40 minutes) or the meat reaches 60°C (140°F) internal temperature. Remove from heat and set aside to cool to room temperature. Finely chop 200 g (7 oz) of the beef and set aside for the purée.

Put the potatoes in a large saucepan of boiling water and cook until soft. Pass through a mouli grater, then put in a bowl with the milk, butter and finely chopped beef and stir to combine. Cover and refrigerate until serving.

Meanwhile, combine the langoustines in a bowl with the grapeseed oil, annatto seed paste, coriander stalks, lime zest, garlic, cumin, curry powder and salt and toss to coat. Cover and refrigerate overnight to marinate.

To make the corn reduction, heat the grapeseed oil in a pressure cooker. When it is starting to smoke, add the reserved langoustine heads and shells and roast, crushing the shells as they cook. Remove the shells, reduce the heat slightly and add the corn kernels. Caramelise the kernels without burning them then add the butter and remaining ingredients except the seasonings. Add 2 litres (70 fl oz/8 cups) of water and close the pressure cooker, cooking on high heat for 25 minutes.

Let cool at room temperature without opening. After an hour or so all the fat will set on the top of the liquid. Carefully scoop off as much fat as possible, transfer the stock to a large saucepan and reduce to a glaze-like consistency. Finish by seasoning with lemon juice and butter.

For the sofrito, slowly cook the annatto seed paste in the butter in a small saucepan over medium heat. Add the onion, capsicum, garlic and aji dulce. Cook until soft and fragrant. Add the tomato concasse, season with salt and pepper and finish with the herbs.

To assemble, grill the marinated langoustines on a barbecue or chargrill. On the centre of each serving plate, place a small amount of the potato and beef purée. Drizzle the corn reduction around it. Place a langoustine on the centre of the purée and top with the sofrito. Finish with a few sprigs of dill.

RABBIT, BEER GRAINS, WHITE CARROT AND SAMPHIRE

CHEF: KARL FIRLA

SERVES 8

You will need to begin this recipe two days ahead.

100 g (3½ oz) cracked wheat
1.5 kg (3 lb 5 oz) rabbit, deboned, bones reserved
750 g (1 lb 10 oz) butter
2 bay leaves
3 thyme stalks
2.5 litres (87 fl oz/10 cups) chicken stock
200 g (7 oz) white carrots, thinly sliced
pinch bicarbonate of soda (baking soda)
grapeseed oil, to fry beer grains
100 g (3½ oz) samphire
50 g (1¾ oz) young almonds, peeled, blanched

MIREPOIX

225 g (8 oz) white onion, chopped
100 g (3½ oz) carrot, chopped
100 g (3½ oz) celery, chopped
4 garlic cloves
1 bay leaf
3 thyme sprigs

BUTTER EMULSION

100 ml (3½ fl oz) white wine
pinch of salt
250 g (9 oz) butter, softened

To make beer grains, put the cracked wheat and 200 ml (7 fl oz) of hot water in a saucepan over low heat. Cook, maintaining a temperature of 70°C (150°F) for 1 hour, agitating the grains every 5 minutes. Use a sugar thermometer to monitor the temperature. Strain and dry the grains on baking paper for 48 hours.

Preheat the oven to 85°C (185°F/Gas ¼–½). Place the whole back legs and belly of the rabbit in a roasting dish with the butter, bay leaves and thyme. Cover with foil and roast for 3 hours. When cooked, remove the meat from the leg bone, layer the leg meat over the belly meat and cover with a tray weighted with tins. Put it in the refrigerator for 24 hours: you want to compress the leg and belly meat together. Reserve the loin meat.

Meanwhile, preheat the oven to 160°C (315°F/Gas 2–3). Roast the rabbit bones in the oven for 15 minutes until golden. In a large saucepan over medium heat, put the chicken stock, roasted bones and the mirepoix ingredients. Simmer for 3 hours, then strain into a clean saucepan and bring to the boil, simmering for 15 minutes until reduced to a sauce consistency.

In a small frying pan, sauté the white carrot with the bicarbonate of soda until soft. Season and purée using a food processor.

Reduce the oven to 65°C (145°F). In a medium frying pan, sear the pressed rabbit meat then cook in the oven for 3 minutes.

Poach the reserved rabbit loin in the combined butter emulsion ingredients for 10 minutes.

Toast the beer grains in a little grapeseed oil in a frying pan for 1 minute until golden. Stir constantly. Strain off excess oil and reserve for plating.

To serve, place a tablespoon of the carrot purée on each plate. Arrange the rabbit loin to one side and the compressed belly to the other. Spoon toasted beer grains over the centre. Place samphire on top and scatter with almonds.

SHIO KOJI BARBECUED DUCK HEARTS WITH HORSERADISH

CHEF: JAMES HENRY

SERVES 4

You will need to begin this recipe one day ahead

4 duck hearts
1 tablespoon shio koji (fermented rice)
fleur de sel
3 cm (1¼ inch) piece horseradish

Trim the duck hearts of any fat and sinew. Put them in a sous-vide bag or resealable plastic bag with the shio koji and leave to marinate overnight.

Heat a barbecue or chargrill to high. When it is very hot, grill the duck hearts for 1 minute on each side. Remove from the heat and rest for 2 minutes. Cut each heart evenly in half, season lightly with fleur de sel then, using a microplane, grate a healthy sprinkling of horseradish over the hearts and serve immediately.

THE BISTRONOMY CHEF

For the bistronomy chef, professional cooking is not about accruing 'stars' or signature dishes.

It is not a name-up-in-lights reckoning of celebrity chefdom either. It is about craftsmanship and engaging with farmers, providores and diners in new and meaningful ways. There is an ever-present, gung-ho enterprising determination found in bistronomy from a group of chefs for whom cooking in their restaurant kitchens on a daily basis is their prime source of succour ... and survival.

The restaurant industry has always been mercurial, but the bistronomy chef is the battle-weary survivor. It is an approach brazenly driven by the market (in all senses of the word) and a tenacity for survival by cooking. For the majority, the chef wears many hats: having to play chef, investor and restaurateur, all the while outlasting slowing economies, ever-present industrial relations issues and competition. In this economic environment — and as the cultural trend for formal dining continues to be an endangered species — the bistronomy chef has had to cast about for new ways to make dining special, and in doing so has created restaurants that deliver real heart and passion.

It is a journey of appetite, courage and varying resources. Chefs are restless souls and the bistronomy CV and style are indicative of their food tendencies: they don't tend to hang around anywhere very long. They travel. They pick up skills. They learn recipes. They move on again, trading what they've already obtained for what else they can get. It is out of this jumble of short-lived stints that this eclectic, individual style is formed and their food speaks several languages fluently, slang included. These chefs are the kid not overthinking it at the top of the waterslide; the drunk in the midnight choir. They are exactly the kind of cook you want in charge of your dinner, not because of their mastery of technique — though they certainly have that in spades — but because of their intensely creative, to the point,

'A chef's life is one of the last few bastions of true apprenticeship.'

JOE BASTIANICH

'Every chef has their own vision. Like an artist who paints, they have their own way of connecting with locality, culture and people through their food — their canvas. We are spiritual brothers with similar beliefs in our approach but we all do our own food. It is a continual process of discovery, like making love to a woman then discovering she is even more beautiful than when you seduced her.'

STEPHANE JEGO

left of field, contrarian approach and insanely good taste. They have an innate understanding of the good things in life and have created a setting that enables us to align our wallets and our ethics with hedonism. It's genius, and it means we can support their unique and, at times, discordant culinary voices.

The bistronomy chef has moved on from previous fixations with *avant-garde* Euro mentors to develop more personal, less derivative and looser styles. They are the freethinkers and foragers who transform unloved, wild and premium produce into dishes that reflect their admiration for other cooking styles. They don't seek to merely copy; technical game-playing for its own sake is no longer the choice *de rigueur*; instead, they are young, freethinking archprogressives who happen to be as talented as they are blissfully out of step with the dominant dining paradigm. They display the virtuosity not of cooks, but of culinary artists by unapologetically pursuing a path that redefines the modern chef. They don't cook because they think it leads to fame or fortune. They cook to nourish people. So a wood oven and a wood-burning grill are as important as any immersion circulator or blast chiller in the kitchen where doing things from scratch is more the rule than the exception.

They do not entertain subtle. If they give you an ingredient, you taste the ingredient. It's striking and it perpetuates one of the great virtues of the kitchen: taking something ostensibly inedible and, by application of human cunning, transforming it into a delicacy. It becomes a showcase of produce, of ingenuity and finesse, and often, a mixture of all three. It takes guts for pushing the bounds, plucking up the courage, and daring to dare.

Bistronomy is a movement within which the chefs feel safe enough to fail and play with their dishes. An environment where they can take on a more rudimentary process of building and tinkering rather than refining and promoting; they can get things gloriously wrong, stupendously so, by trying dishes and experimenting with foods and techniques they may or may not have encountered before, free from the judgment and circle jerk of cheffy one-upmanship. It is the idea that a dish can never really be finished. These are the chefs with lifeblood. They cook for family. For friends. For love. For food itself. They embrace and honour their freedom to constantly be perfecting and honing and refining and fine-tuning every single thing they do on the plate.

They may change the menu as whim and produce dictates, but their key concession to us, the willing eater, is that they will go a long way out of their way to make sure what's on the plate tastes as good as it can taste. They revisit and recreate their menus to always be pushing ahead, tasting more, doing more, and making it better for you and me whenever we get to eat there.

STEAMED HAPUKU, WILD NETTLE AND TOASTED RYE BUTTER

CHEFS: DAN PUSKAS, JAMES PARRY

SERVES 5

400 g (14 oz) hapuku, skin and bones removed, cut into five equal portions
12 nettle leaves, to garnish
1 tablespoon grapeseed oil, for frying

NETTLE PURÉE

250 ml (9 fl oz/1 cup) chicken stock
500 g (1 lb 2 oz) nettle leaves or sweet potato leaves
3 sheets titanium-strength gelatine, bloomed
2 teaspoons butter
pink salt

TOASTED RYE BUTTER

100 g (3½ oz) malted rye
500 g (1 lb 2 oz/2 cups) thick (double) cream

To make the nettle purée, put the chicken stock and nettle leaves in a large saucepan over medium heat. Boil the leaves for 2–3 minutes until soft. Drain, reserving the stock, then put the leaves in a blender and blend to a purée. To achieve purée consistency, you may need to loosen with some of the reserved stock. Weigh out 250 g (9 oz) of purée, reserving any leftover for future use.

While the purée is still warm, add the softened gelatine and blend again, ensuring the gelatine has melted and is fully incorporated. Add the butter and season with salt. Pass the purée through a fine sieve to remove any grit then spread very thinly – about 2 mm (1/16 inch) – over a sheet of acetate. Carefully transfer the sheet to a baking tray and place the tray in the freezer until the spread is solid, a minimum of 1–2 hours. Once frozen, gently peel from the sheet of acetate and cut into 5–6 squares, roughly 8 cm (3¼ inch) square. Return to the freezer until ready to serve.

To make the toasted rye butter, infuse the malted rye into the cream by first bringing the cream to the boil in a saucepan over medium heat. Once boiled, remove from the heat, add the rye and set aside to cool. Strain the mixture into a food processor fitted with a paddle attachment and beat until stiffly whipped. Continue until the whipped cream collapses and separates into butterfat globules. The buttermilk will separate from the butter and slosh around the bowl. Line a clean sieve with muslin (cheesecloth), add the butter and place over a bowl for the buttermilk to drain. Turn out the butter into a medium frying pan and cook over medium heat, swirling constantly until the butter is a nut-brown colour. Drain, reserving the solids until ready to serve.

Preheat the oven to 180°C (350°F/Gas 4). Place a large, ovenproof frying pan over medium heat. Add the fish and caramelise very lightly on both sides. Remove from heat, top each piece of fish with 1 square of the frozen nettle purée then place in the oven to finish cooking for 4–6 minutes or until the fish has just cooked through and the nettle purée square has melted, giving the fish a nice even coating. As you pull the fish from the oven, top with some rye butter solids.

Shallow-fry the 12 nettle leaves in the grapeseed oil in a medium frying pan over high heat until crisp. Season generously with salt. To finish, place a piece of fish on each plate. Garnish with the fried nettle leaves and serve.

Note: If hapuku is not available, substitute blue-eye trevalla or any fish with firm white flesh.

STINGRAY, SPICED CRAB SOUP AND GIROLLES

CHEF: JAMES HENRY
SERVES 4

2 kg (4 lb 8 oz) étrille crabs (blue swimmer crabs)
grapeseed oil, for frying
1 onion, finely diced
2 garlic cloves, finely diced
1 carrot, finely diced
1 piece fennel, finely diced
2 dried chillies
3 teaspoons ras el hanout
2 large heirloom tomatoes
125 ml (4 fl oz/½ cup) white wine
8 heirloom cherry tomatoes
1 kg (2 lb 4 oz) stingray, trimmed and cut into 4 pieces
6 tablespoons butter
500 g (1 lb 2 oz) girolles (chanterelles)
purple basil leaves, to garnish
olive oil, to drizzle

Sedate the crabs by putting them in the freezer for 1 hour before cooking. Cut the crabs in half down the centre and sweat them in grapeseed oil in a large frying pan over medium heat until caramelised. Add the onion, garlic, carrot and fennel to the crabs in the pan and sweat until caramelised, taking care not to colour the vegetables. Add the chillies, ras el hanout and tomatoes and continue to cook until almost all of the liquid has evaporated. Add the wine and cook for a further 5 minutes.

Cover with water and cook for 1 hour over medium heat. Pass the stock through a fine sieve, then return the liquid to a clean saucepan and reduce over medium heat, to taste. Keep warm.

Stab the cherry tomatoes with the point of a sharp knife, plunge them into boiling water and then into iced water and peel.

Preheat the oven to 200°C (400°F/Gas 6). In a large, ovenproof frying pan over medium heat, start cooking the stingray in grapeseed oil. Once it is starting to colour, add 4 tablespoons of butter and put it in the oven for 4 minutes. Remove the stingray from the oven and baste it with the pan juices. The middle cartilage should pull out cleanly.

Add the peeled cherry tomatoes to the crab soup to warm through.

Pan fry the girolles in the remaining butter and season with salt and pepper.

To serve, put a piece of stingray in a bowl. Add some soup, tomatoes and girolles and finish with a garnish of purple basil leaves and a drizzle of olive oil.

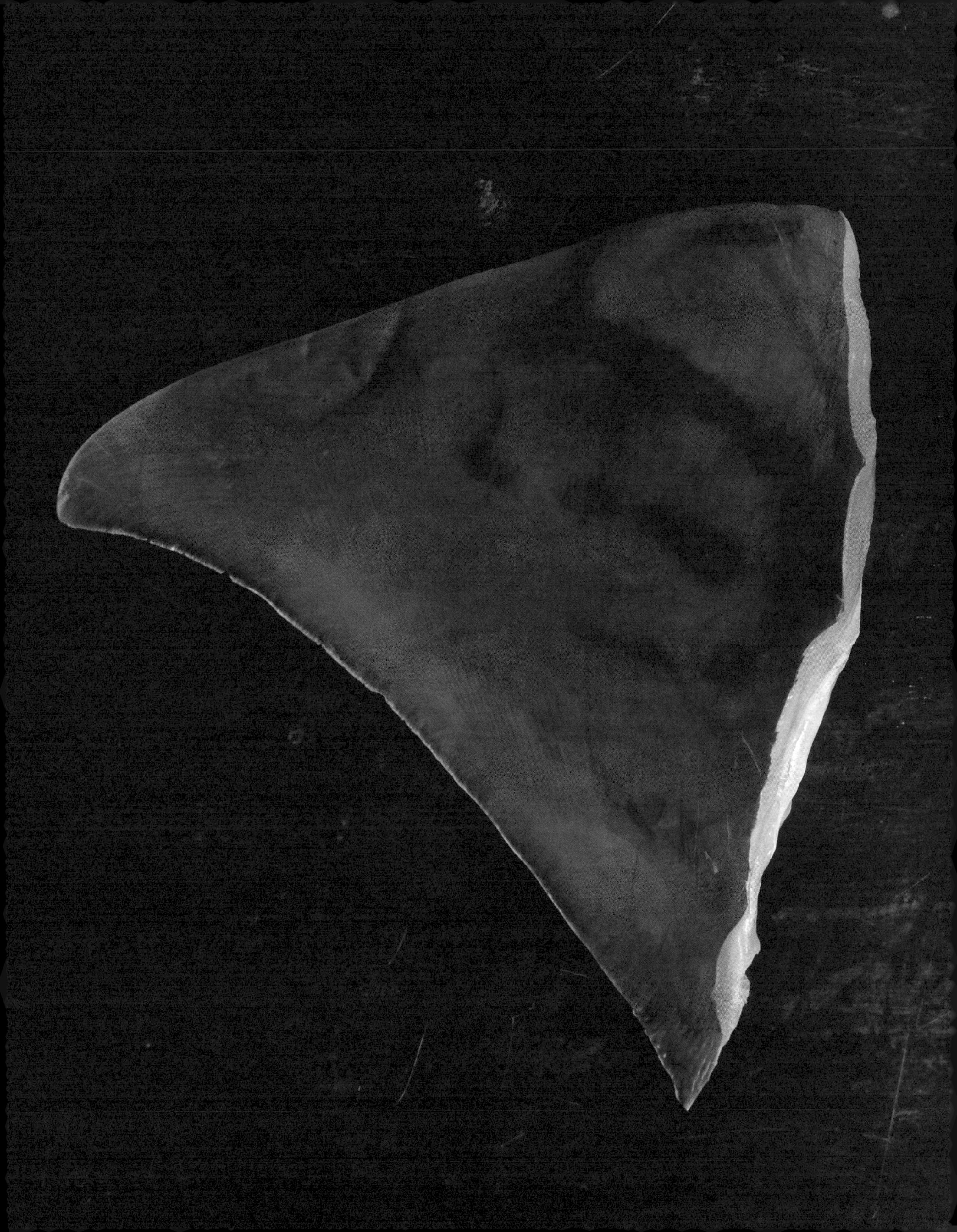

LAMB LEG TARTARE WITH SMOKED CAPSICUM AND SHICHIMI TOGARASHI

CHEF: PASI PETANEN

SERVES 12–14

You will need to begin this recipe one day ahead.

1 Suffolk lamb leg, approximately 3 kg (6 lb 12 oz), fat and sinew removed

SHICHIMI TOGARASHI

200 g (7 oz) red capsicum (pepper), sliced
100 g (3½ oz/½ cup) jasmine rice
400 ml (14 fl oz) vegetable oil, for deep-frying
40 g (1½ oz) red rice
40 g (1½ oz/¼ cup) white sesame seeds, toasted
20 g (¾ oz) black sesame seeds, toasted
20 g (¾ oz) onion powder
10 g (¼ oz) dry orange zest, blanched 3 times, finely chopped
40 g (1½ oz) dry wakame, finely chopped
2 g (1/16 oz) cayenne pepper
2 g (1/16 oz) sweet paprika

CAPSICUM PURÉE

200 ml (7 fl oz) olive oil
500 g (1 lb 2 oz) brown onions, sliced
4 garlic cloves, sliced
1 kg (2 lb 4 oz) red capsicum (pepper), sliced
1 teaspoon freshly ground black pepper
1 teaspoon ground cumin
2 teaspoons sea salt

SMOKED CAPSICUM

200 g (7 oz) red capsicum (pepper)
hickory wood chips, for smoking

Make the shichimi togarashi by putting the sliced capsicum, jasmine rice and 400 ml (14 fl oz) of water in a saucepan over medium heat. Bring to a simmer, cover and cook for 40 minutes until the liquid has evaporated and the mixture has cooked through. Put the mixture in a blender and blend until it is a smooth purée. Line two baking trays with baking paper and spread the purée on the trays to dry in the oven overnight at 50°C (120°F). Alternatively, use a dehydrator at 55°C (130°F) for 4–6 hours or until completely dry.

Break the dried paste into pieces. Heat the vegetable oil in a large, heavy-based saucepan or deep-fryer to 180°C (350°F) or until a cube of bread dropped into the oil turns brown in 15 seconds. Briefly fry the red rice. It will puff and burn quickly. Remove from the oil, draining any excess, and allow the rice to dry slightly before crushing to a powder using a mortar and pestle. Combine with the remaining ingredients and store in an airtight container until ready to serve.

To prepare the lamb, fill a large bowl or your kitchen sink with ice. Put the lamb leg in another bowl over the ice. Remove the muscle (alternatively you could ask your butcher to do this) from the leg, keeping the meat over the ice at all times. Clean all the muscle of any sinew. Finely dice the cleaned meat for a smooth tartare consistency. Cover and refrigerate until ready to serve.

To make the capsicum purée, heat a little of the olive oil in a large frying pan over medium heat. Add the sliced onions, garlic and capsicum and sauté for 5 minutes until soft. Add the spices and remaining olive oil and cook over low heat for 1 hour or until all the liquid has been absorbed and you are left with a rich red oil and capsicum paste. Pour into an airtight container with any excess oil on top.

To make the smoked capsicum, roast the capsicums over an open flame until charred on all sides. Place in a bowl, cover with plastic wrap and set aside for 30 minutes to allow the skins to sweat. Peel off the skins, cut the capsicums in half and remove all the seeds. Preheat a coal-bedded kettle barbecue to low heat and set up for indirect grilling using the top rack. Add half of the hickory wood chips around the coals and cook until smoke appears (3–4 minutes). It is very important for cold smoking to have your coal base well established and glowing before adding the wood chips. Once smoking turn off the heat. Layer the capsicum halves on smoking trays and cold smoke for 10 minutes. Cut the smoked capsicum into small dice and reserve until serving.

To plate, remove the lamb from the refrigerator 20 minutes before serving. For every 50 g (1¾ oz) of meat, mix through 1 teaspoon of capsicum purée and 1 teaspoon of smoked capsicum. Season generously with salt and pepper. Place on a plate, sprinkle generously with shichimi togarashi and serve.

SKEWERED LAMB SWEETBREADS, SUN-DRIED TOMATOES, EGGS AND BUTTON MUSHROOMS

CHEF: STEPHANE JEGO

SERVES 4

You will need to begin this recipe one day ahead.

4 lamb sweetbreads, sinew trimmed
300 g (10½ oz/2 bunches) flat-leat (Italian) parsley
extra virgin olive oil, to emulsify
16 sun-dried tomatoes
100 g (3½ oz) butter, coarsely chopped
red wine vinegar, to taste
120 g (4¼ oz/1 bunch) basil, finely chopped
4 large button mushrooms with white, firm flesh, thinly sliced
lemon juice, to serve
3 hard-boiled eggs, coarsely chopped
olive oil, extra, to serve

Refrigerate the sweetbreads in cold water for 12 hours, changing the water at least twice. Drain the sweetbreads then blanch in a saucepan of boiling salted water for 30 seconds. Remove the sweetbreads with a slotted spoon and drain on paper towel. Set aside to cool to room temperature.

Bring a medium saucepan of water to a rapid boil. Add the parsley. After 20 minutes, shock the parsley by removing it and plunging it into iced water to retain its bright green colour. Pat dry. Reserve the parsley liquid.

Finely chop the sweetbreads and process in a food processor with the parsley for 1–2 minutes until smooth. Season with salt and pepper. Add extra virgin olive oil in a thin steady stream, continuing to process until the mixture is emulsified. Roll the mixture between your hands into bite-size pieces.

Prepare 4 skewers, alternating the sweetbread pieces with the sun-dried tomatoes. If using wooden skewers, soak them in water for 30 minutes prior to using.

Heat the butter in a frying pan over medium–high heat, put in the sweetbread skewers and cook, turning and spooning the butter over the sweetbreads occasionally, for 3–4 minutes until golden. Add a few drops of red wine vinegar just before they are done. Set aside and keep warm.

To serve, arrange some of the reserved parsley liquid on each plate, add the basil and mushrooms with a little lemon juice, then top with a sweetbread skewer and some chopped egg. Drizzle with olive oil and season with salt and pepper to taste.

Tip: Create a little hot-cold sensation by using the iced parsley liquid and hot skewers.

BEETROOT RISOTTO

CHEF: YVES CAMDEBORDE

SERVES 4

1 white beetroot
1 yellow beetroot
1 Chioggia beetroot
1 French shallot, peeled, finely chopped
1 tablespoon olive oil
200 g (7 oz/scant cup) arborio rice
200 ml (7 fl oz) dry white wine
5 red beetroot, juiced
chicken stock (optional)
50 g (1¾ oz) butter, cubed, cold
200 ml (7 fl oz) milk
20 g (¾ oz) horseradish
4–8 slices excellent quality jambon
butter, to serve
lime juice, to serve
Espelette pepper

Cook the white, yellow and Chioggia beetroot in lightly salted water. Once cooked, allow to cool then peel. Cut thin slices of the white beetroot, yellow beetroot and Chioggia, then use a small 5–8 cm (2–3¼ inch) cookie cutter to cut rounds out of the beetroot slices.

Put the shallot and olive oil in a large, heavy-based saucepan over medium heat and sweat, then add the rice, turning to coat with oil until it appears slightly translucent. Deglaze the pan with the wine and cook, progressively adding beetroot juice until the rice is *al dente*. If there is not enough beetroot juice, chicken stock can be used to supplement it. Bind the risotto with the cold butter. Season generously with salt and pepper.

While the rice is cooking, put the milk and horseradish in a saucepan and bring to the boil. Pass the liquid through a fine sieve and allow to cool.

To plate, put the risotto into shallow dishes. Arrange the beetroot on top, alternating the colours, and finish with slices of jambon. Emulsify the horseradish milk and make a foam using a stick blender. Place dollops of foam on the plate. Add butter and lime juice to taste, season with salt and Espelette pepper.

LE BORD

THE EDGE

From the abstract to the concrete, the practical to the fanciful, this is the food shaping the cuisine of tomorrow

ROAST CABBAGE, MUSSEL BUTTER, POMELO AND BONE MARROW

LAMB BREAST, PEAS, CARROTS AND MINT SAUCE

BUTTERNUT SOUP, BRAISED PORK BELLY AND TOASTED BUCKWHEAT

SHORT RIB OF BEEF, CHILLED NORMANDY APPLES,
COUNTRY STYLE APPLE CIDER JELLY

FLAT IRON STEAK, ANCHOVY, CRACKLING AND PEPPER SAUCE

BABY LAMB LEG COOKED ON STRING, CHAR LEEKS AND CRISP SALTBUSH

DUCK, GOLDEN BEETS, DANDELION AND SPROUTED WHEAT

POACHED CHICKEN, SHAVED ARTICHOKE, RICOTTA AND AVRUGA

PARSNIP RISOTTO, WALNUT, APPLE AND HORSERADISH

PIGEON, YEAST SOUBISE AND BLUEBERRY WHEY COMPOTE

ROAST CABBAGE, MUSSEL BUTTER, POMELO AND BONE MARROW

CHEF: PASI PETANEN

SERVES 16

You will need to begin this recipe one day ahead.

100 g (3½ oz) bone marrow
1 savoy cabbage, outer leaves removed, cut into 16 wedges
100 g (3½ oz) unsalted butter
olive oil, for frying
1 pomelo, peeled, segmented

CABBAGE POWDER

300 g (10½ oz) cavolo nero leaves

MUSSEL BUTTER

300 g (10½ oz) unsalted butter, at room temperature, plus 1 tablespoon extra
3 French shallots, peeled, finely chopped
1 garlic clove, finely chopped
6 g (⅛ oz/½ cup) parsley
1 kg (2 lb 4 oz) mussels, scrubbed, beards removed
100 ml (3½ fl oz) dry white wine
½ lemon, juice

LEMON PURÉE

10 Meyer lemons
100 g (3½ oz) caster (superfine) sugar
50 g (1¾ oz) unsalted butter, diced
100 g (3½ oz) beurre noisette (browned butter)

Soak the bone marrow in iced water, leaving overnight to remove any blood. Slice into 10 g (¼ oz) slices and set aside.

To make the cabbage powder, blanch the cavolo nero in boiling water for 30 seconds. Refresh in iced water then dry on a tea towel (dish towel). Place the leaves on a baking tray lined with baking paper and dry overnight in an oven at 55°C (130°F) or use a dehydrator. Crumble the dried leaves to a fine powder in a food processor and set aside until ready to serve.

To make the mussel butter, heat a frying pan over medium–high heat and sauté the shallot, garlic and parsley in the extra tablespoon of butter. Add the mussels and white wine and continue to cook until the mussels open. Remove from the heat and remove the mussels from the shells. Reserve 16 mussels for later use, cover and store in the refrigerator. Strain the cooking liquid through a sieve lined with muslin (cheesecloth) into a clean saucepan. Place over low heat and reduce by half or until a thick syrup-like consistency is achieved. Reserve 300 ml (10½ fl oz). From the remaining mussels, remove the stomachs and chop the meat very finely. Combine with the room temperature butter, lemon juice and remaining strained mussel juice in a bowl and season with black pepper. Turn out the mixture onto a flat surface lined with plastic wrap and roll the butter mixture into a log. Wrap in the plastic wrap, seal at the ends and store in the refrigerator until ready to serve.

To make the lemon purée, put a saucepan of water over medium heat, immediately add the lemons and blanch from a cold water start. Repeat the process twice more. Cut the lemons in half and remove the seeds. Cover the base of a large saucepan with the sugar and diced butter. Put the lemon halves over the sugar mixture and cook over medium-low heat until slightly golden in colour. While still warm, blend in a high-speed blender, adding the beurre noisette and warm water as needed. Reserve the purée until ready to plate.

Heat the reserved mussel juice in a saucepan over medium heat. Add the 100 g (3½ oz) butter, cook until melted and use a stick blender on high speed to make a mussel emulsion.

To serve, heat a frying pan over medium heat. Add a dash of olive oil and fry the cabbage wedges on one side slowly until golden brown. Be careful not to overcrowd the pan. Turn over and add 2 tablespoons mussel butter, basting the cabbage as you would a piece of steak. The idea is to have the thin end of the cabbage nice and soft while the thicker end retains some crunch. Heat the reserved mussels, bone marrow and pomelo in the mussel emulsion. Plate a wedge of cabbage. Place a mussel, bone marrow slice and pomelo segment on top and dust with the cabbage powder. Serve with a dollop of lemon purée on the side.

LAMB BREAST, PEAS, CARROTS AND MINT SAUCE

CHEF: JAMES KNAPPETT

SERVES 6

You will need to begin this recipe one day ahead.

2 boneless lamb breasts,approximately 1.7 kg (3 lb 12 oz)
rapeseed oil, for frying
1 bunch each red heirloom carrots and golfball carrots, trimmed, scrubbed
1½ tablespoons butter, for frying carrots and peas
250 g (9 oz) fresh peas, podded, reserved in ice bath
200 g (7 oz/¾ cup) natural yoghurt
pea shoots, to serve

MINT SAUCE

150 ml (5 fl oz) white wine vinegar
150 g (5½ oz/⅔ cup) caster (superfine) sugar
100 g (3½ oz/1 large bunch) mint, leaves picked, stalks reserved

Season the lamb with salt and pepper, place in a sous-vide bag and seal. Cook the lamb in a water bath at 63°C (145°F) for 24 hours. Remove from the water bath and place in the refrigerator to chill before removing it from the bag.

To pickle the mint for the mint sauce, bring the white wine vinegar and sugar to the boil in a medium saucepan until sugar has dissolved. Remove from the heat, add the mint stalks and leave to infuse for 1 hour. Strain the mixture, discarding the stalks, and put the liquid in the refrigerator to chill.

Heat a little rapeseed oil in a frying pan over medium heat. Put the lamb in the frying pan and cook on both sides until golden brown and crisp. Remove the lamb breasts from the frying pan and allow the meat to rest.

Separate the carrots by colour, season and seal in separate sous-vide bags. Place the bags in a large saucepan of simmering water. Cook carrots for 1–2 minutes or until just cooked. Remove carrots from the bags. In a frying pan, heat the carrots in a little butter and water, keeping the colours separate.

In a frying pan over low heat, gently heat the peas in a little butter.

Season the yoghurt with salt and set aside until the yoghurt reaches room temperature.

Put the mint leaves into a blender and blend with enough of the mint pickle to bring to a sauce consistency. Season the mint sauce with salt. It is important to make the mint sauce at the last minute so that it is as fresh-flavoured and colourful as possible.

To serve, spread the yoghurt on the plates. Carve the lamb breast and place a portion off-centre. Scatter carrots and peas over the yoghurt. Next, lightly drizzle mint sauce around the plate and garnish with pea shoots.

BUTTERNUT SOUP, BRAISED PORK BELLY AND TOASTED BUCKWHEAT

CHEF: DAN PEARSON

SERVES 4–6

You will need to begin this recipe two days ahead.

3 tablespoons maple syrup
1 tablespoon cumin seeds, toasted, roughly ground
1 tablespoon sea salt flakes
1 kg (2 lb 4 oz) pork belly, deboned, trimmed, sinew removed
500 ml (17 fl oz/2 cups) apple cider
2 litres (70 fl oz/8 cups) chicken stock
4 tablespoons olive oil
2 butternut pumpkins (squash), peeled, seeded and roughly chopped
1 garlic bulb, peeled, smashed
3 rosemary stalks
3 thyme stalks
30 ml (1 fl oz) grapeseed oil
200 g (7 oz/1 cup) buckwheat
200 g (7 oz) butter
75 g (2½ oz/½ cup) plain (all-purpose) flour, seasoned with salt and pepper
1 turnip, peeled, thinly sliced, to serve
watercress, to serve

MAPLE SYRUP DRESSING

50 ml (1¾ fl oz) maple syrup
150 ml (5 fl oz) olive oil
white balsamic vinegar

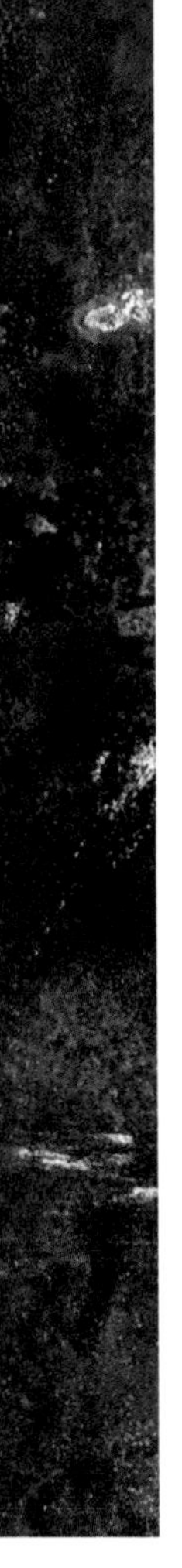

Combine the maple syrup, cumin and sea salt in a small bowl. Rub into the pork, cover and refrigerate overnight.

Preheat the oven to 90°C (195°F/Gas ½). Lightly wash the pork and pat dry with paper towel. Roll and tie with a strong butcher's string and sear in a large frying pan over medium heat, caramelising all sides. Transfer to a large braising pan and deglaze the frying pan with the apple cider. Pour the pan juices and chicken stock into the braising pan, cover with foil and cook in the oven for 18 hours.

Once cooked, cool at room temperature in the stock. When the pork is cool enough to handle, remove it from the stock, wrap it in plastic wrap and store in the refrigerator until ready for serving. Strain the braising liquid and reserve it for the soup, covered, in the refrigerator.

Preheat the oven to 200°C (400°F/Gas 6). Heat a deep baking tray in the oven with the olive oil until the oil is almost smoking. Add the prepared butternut, smashed garlic, rosemary and thyme and roast until caramelised, tender and dark golden (1–1½ hours). Put the cooked butternut in a blender with 1 litre (35 fl oz/4 cups) of the pork braising liquid and blend until smooth. Strain and season generously with salt and pepper.

Wash the buckwheat under cold running water until the water runs clear. Transfer to a saucepan of boiling water and cook for 5 minutes or until soft. Strain and rinse under cold running water until cool. Drain and pat dry between tea towels (dish towels).

Gently heat some of the grapeseed oil in a frying pan over medium heat and add enough buckwheat to cover the base of the pan. (Don't overcrowd the pan as the buckwheat won't caramelise properly and will stick together.) When the buckwheat starts to colour add the butter and a little salt and pepper. Keep the pan moving or stir constantly to prevent the buckwheat from burning. It will cook quickly and have an aroma reminiscent of popcorn. Remove and season with salt while still hot.

Make the maple syrup dressing by putting all the ingredients in a bowl and whisking vigorously until emulsified.

To serve, preheat the oven to 200°C (400°F/Gas 6). Cut the pork belly into medallions and roll in the seasoned flour, shaking off any excess. Caramelise all sides in a non-stick ovenproof frying pan over medium-high heat then place pan in the oven to warm through.

Bring the butternut soup to serving temperature and pour into soup bowls. Place a medallion of pork belly in the centre then add the sliced turnip around it. Sprinkle with a generous amount of toasted buckwheat, then a small swirl of maple syrup dressing. Finish with a couple of sprigs of watercress.

SHORT RIB OF BEEF, CHILLED NORMANDY APPLES, COUNTRY STYLE APPLE CIDER JELLY

CHEF: STEPHANE JEGO

SERVES 6

You will need to begin this recipe one day ahead.

50 g (1¾ oz) butter
600 g (1 lb 5 oz) short rib of beef
400 g (14 oz) mirepoix
50 g (1¾ oz) good quality bacon lardoons
2 garlic cloves, peeled and sliced
3 French shallots
250 ml (9 oz/1 cup) beef stock
6 normandy apples (or best in season)
1 lemon, juice
½ lemongrass stalk, white part only, finely chopped
200 g (7 oz) baby spinach leaves
olive oil
croutons, to serve

CIDER JELLY

500 ml (17 fl oz/2 cups) sparkling apple cider
½ lemon, juice
4 sheets gold-strength gelatine, bloomed
50 g (1¾ oz) caster (superfine) sugar
apple cider vinegar, to taste

Heat the butter in a large cast-iron casserole dish over medium heat and brown the beef for 8–10 minutes. Transfer to a plate using a slotted spoon. Add mirepoix, bacon lardoons, garlic and French shallots to the casserole dish and sauté for 5–7 minutes until softened. Return the beef to the casserole dish, add the beef stock and bring to the boil. Simmer over low heat, occasionally skimming off any fat that rises to the surface, for 2–2½ hours or until the meat is tender. Remove the meats and vegetables, reserving the broth. Cover everything with plastic wrap and refrigerate overnight.

Prepare the cider jelly by combining 250 ml (9 fl oz/1 cup) of water, half the cider, and the lemon juice in a bowl. Pour 250 ml (9 fl oz/1 cup) of the liquid into a saucepan and heat to just below boiling temperature. Add the gelatine leaves and stir well until completely dissolved. Add the remaining cider and the caster sugar. Season to taste with the apple cider vinegar, stirring to incorporate before pouring into attractive dessert cups. Place the cups in the coldest part of the refrigerator to set.

Remove the meat from the refrigerator and bring it to room temperature. Heat a barbecue or chargrill to medium–high. Grill the meat slowly, turning often until golden brown and crisp when done.

Gently fry the bacon lardoons and set aside until ready to serve.

Slice off the tops of the apples and hollow them out without bruising. Brush with half the lemon juice to keep them from turning brown. Finely chop the scooped-out apple and combine with the remaining lemon juice, the lemongrass and the spinach. Coat with olive oil and set aside. Combine at the last minute to keep the salad from wilting.

To serve, cut the meat into thin slices. Use breakfast bowls (the larger the better). Place the hollowed-out apples in the centre of each bowl and fill to overflowing with the apple and spinach salad and the slices of meat prepared in advance. Add the lardoons and two or three croutons on top. Serve with the cups of jelly on the side. If you can't fit all the filling into the apples, plate the rest separately. Don't forget to season well.

FLAT IRON STEAK, ANCHOVY, CRACKLING AND PEPPER SAUCE

CHEF: JOSH MURPHY

SERVES 6

You will need to begin this recipe one day ahead.

2 flat iron (oyster blade) steaks, 425 g (15 oz) each, cartilage reserved (ask your butcher to do this for you)
sunflower oil, for frying
12 anchovies

KOHLRABI LEAF

4 kohlrabi leaves
½ teaspoon olive oil, for frying

PEPPER SAUCE

3 tablespoons olive oil
1 tablespoon butter
60 g (2¼ oz) garlic
130 g (4¾ oz) French shallots
40 g (1½ oz) sugar
3 tablespoons brandy
100 ml (3½ fl oz) light soy sauce
2 tablespoons white balsamic vinegar
15 g (½ oz) black peppercorns, ground
15 g (½ oz) white peppercorns, ground
5 g (¼ oz) sichuan peppercorns, ground
1 tablespoon fish sauce
250 ml (9 fl oz/1 cup) brown chicken stock
1 teaspoon xanthan gum

PEPPER CRUST

3 tablespoons white peppercorns
3 tablespoons black peppercorns
3 tablespoons Kampot pepper

WHIPPED POTATO

200 g (7 oz) potatoes, peeled and diced
250 ml (9 fl oz/1 cup) milk
1 garlic clove
400 ml (14 fl oz) blended olive oil
white pepper, to season
lemon juice, to season

PICKLED SHALLOT

2 French shallots
50 ml (1¾ fl oz) white wine vinegar
50 g (1¾ oz) sugar

Put the thick piece of cartilage from the centre of the oyster blade in a saucepan with enough water to cover and boil it for 5–6 hours until soft. Scrape any remaining meat off, slice thinly and dehydrate overnight in a dehydrator.

Remove any sinew and cut the steak into 140 g (5 oz) portions. Set aside.

Bring a medium saucepan of salted water to the boil. Cook the kohlrabi leaves in the boiling water for 1 minute, then refresh in iced water. Drain and set aside.

To make the pepper sauce, heat the olive oil and butter in a saucepan over low to medium heat, then gently cook the garlic and shallot until golden. Add the sugar and brandy and simmer until completely reduced. Add the soy sauce, balsamic vinegar, combined ground peppercorns, fish sauce and chicken stock. Bring to a simmer and cook for 5 minutes. While the stock is still hot, transfer it to a blender and purée. With the machine running, add the xanthan gum and purée for 1 minute. Pour into a bowl and set aside.

Prepare the pepper crust. Grind the white, black and Kampot peppercorns. Discard the fine powder, leaving only the crust. Repeat three times. This removes most of the heat from the peppercorn, allowing for a thick crust that is not too overpowering. Set aside.

Boil the potato in a large saucepan of salted water until soft. Pass through a mouli grater into a large bowl. Warm the milk with the garlic clove in a small saucepan. Gradually whisk the oil into the potato until it splits from the potato. Gradually mix the milk into the potato mixture until it is emulsified, smooth and creamy. Pass through a fine sieve and season with salt, white pepper and lemon juice. The acid of the juice will thicken the potato mixture a little so use some more of the warm milk to adjust the consistency if necessary.

To make the pickled shallot, peel the shallots and slice into thin rings. Warm the vinegar and sugar with 2 tablespoons of water in a saucepan over low to medium heat, until the sugar has dissolved. Cool and pour over the shallot. Stand until ready to serve.

Preheat the oven to 180°C (350°F/Gas 4). Coat the steak portions in the pepper crust. Sear the steak in a hot ovenproof frying pan for 2 minutes on each side. Finish the beef in the oven, cooking for 3–5 minutes depending on the thickness, until the steak is done to medium. Once the steak is cooked, rest in a warm place for at least 8 minutes.

Meanwhile, heat a small saucepan of sunflower oil to 200°C (400°F) or until a cube of bread dropped into the oil turns brown in 5 seconds. Fry the cartilage slices in the oil until they puff completely. Drain on paper towel and season with a little salt. Heat a heavy-based frying pan and add ½ teaspoon of olive oil. Fry the kohlrabi leaves one at a time, until they start to blacken on one side.

Once the beef has rested, reheat gently. Carve into 5 mm (¼ inch) slices and season with salt. Lay 1–2 kohlrabi leaves and 4 slices of pickled shallot on each plate and place a spoonful of whipped potato on top. Put the beef portions beside the potato and add 2 pieces of fried cartilage, and 2 anchovies. Finish with 1 teaspoon of pepper sauce.

THE RESTAURANT

Unlike high-end restaurants that are meant to keep the world at bay, the bistronomy restaurant is where the real world blusters in intrusively, and is welcomed in all its glorious and random untidiness.

A bit bare, sometimes a bit hit-and-miss, these are personal spaces that are simple in concept and infinitely various in practice. The restaurants do not look set-designed; rather, they are simple spaces that ring true to the idealistic sensibility of the French café. That urbane everyday kind of eating place, a place that feels truly lived in; the living rooms, the kitchen tables, the dining rooms and the schools of greater human life.

On paper the locations of the restaurants are not just random but unlikely. Most are tucked into the armpit of neighbourhood obscurity. Their locations in down-at-heel areas in the throes of gentrification guarantee they balance the uppity and financial necessity of cultural and culinary renaissance with pockets of seediness, anonymity and that obligatory touch of filth to keep things interesting. It helps. It makes them feel like the sort of place you can holler down the table to pass the salt, as well as give a sense of occasion should the moment require it. They are destination restaurants that feel like your favourite neighbourhood local, where the stripped back affair is simply somewhere to sit down, eat in and entertain family and friends. These are the restaurants that survive not only on clever food, but their dynamic and unexpected charisma and the attraction of the local, visceral and authentic.

Heavy on the charm rather than the thickness of the table linens, the bistronomy restaurant is stripped of many of the trimmings. They aren't much to look at, generally just a single-fronted shop space tarted up for food. Inside, you can feel the makeshift roots: with the bare walls, exposed beams and a sparse aesthetic.

'We meet the demand for quirk and the unexpected. The surrounding buzz, the edgy feel and being a bit rough around the edges gets us a following of diners who love the sense of discovery in unknown or unexpected parts of town.'

LUKE BURGESS

'There's enough adventure to satisfy the foodies, but not so much to deter the drop-ins who call the places their "great little local"'.

WESLEY YOUNG

They are relatively small spaces, seating between 10 and 40 people. The menus are set and delivered to unadorned tables on basic flatware by a skeleton staff with a welcome absence of white gloves. There is no artifice; no distraction. The desire to keep adding elements to make the customer experience more comfortable and the kitchen more exciting for the chef is simply not a plausible financial position. Putting all the modern services a kitchen and restaurant demand today into old, often characterful or transitory spaces is incredibly tricky but these restaurants are living proof of how much can be achieved out of so little. The bare-bones approach, while developed from economic necessity, is also an art within itself; to execute such controlled restraint and feel it in motion is both a rarity and a breath of fresh air.

The bistronomy kitchens vary from matchbox-sized afterthoughts to not so much open as explosively cleaved down the middle; the chef's inner workings being splayed open and offered to the few tightly located tables that grace its space. Unlike many open kitchens and chef's tables, this is not so much a monument to ego, it is simply an easier way for the chef to speak more easily with diners. Chefs are no longer operating in isolation, cut off from their customers to be preoccupied with the perfection of the finished dish, here they are an active part of the dining experience. At l'Ami Jean in Paris, Stephane Jego is likely to yell to you across the restaurant to check you are enjoying your meal, while at Kitchen Table, London chef James Knappett merely leans across the bar to talk you through a dish, an ingredient or to explain the wine pairing. At Esq, Brisbane, it might be the regular sitting cheek-by-jowl beside you who informs you your ordering has been impeccable right up until dessert at which point they hand over their plate and encourage you to stick your spoon into theirs so you 'know for next time'. It creates an ambience of such raw energy and warmth you are unsure whether you want to eat, drink or just inhale.

There will always be reactionary types who'll hate the bistronomy experience, its tablecloth-free lack of schmooze, the unadorned space of almost Presbyterian plainness and the tyranny of a limited or no-choice *a la carte* menu. Yes, there are hiccups, for sure with this kind of dining environment, but they are forgivable and certainly don't cramp the pleasures of something that is altogether more liberated, unstarchy, affordable and fun. Besides, these are the restaurants that have manners not rules, a relaxed elegance without formality that tries to be nothing other than unpretentious and honest with a balanced mix of the fancy (on the plate at least) and the familiar.

BABY LAMB LEG COOKED ON STRING, CHAR LEEKS AND CRISP SALTBUSH

CHEF: MATT GERMANCHIS

SERVES 6

12 garlic cloves
250 ml (9 fl oz/1 cup) vegetable oil
1.5 kg (3 lb 5 oz) baby lamb leg, thighbone removed
4 tarragon stalks
4 summer savory stalks (you can use mint if unavailable)
extra virgin olive oil, for frying, plus extra, to serve
100 g (3½ oz) of saltbush, picked, to serve
1 lemon, juice, to serve

CHAR LEEKS

4 finger-size leeks
250 ml (9 fl oz/1 cup) olive brining liquid (use the liquid from a jar of olives)
250 ml (9 fl oz/1 cup) chicken stock

To confit the garlic, combine the vegetable oil and garlic in a small saucepan, adding extra oil if necessary to cover the garlic. Cook over low heat for 25–30 minutes until very tender. Drain and set aside to cool, reserving the oil for another use.

Bring the lamb leg to room temperature. Rub with 2 cloves of the confit garlic, and place the tarragon and summer savory in the bone cavity of the leg. Season generously.

Preheat a barbecue with a rotisserie attachment. Tie the lamb leg with butcher's string or use a hook and hang above the grill up to 40 cm (16 inches) from the flame if possible. Cook for approximately 1¼ hours, continuing to rotate until the inner temperature of the meat reaches 55°C (130°F) or it is cooked to your liking. Remove from the heat and rest, covered, for 15 minutes.

Meanwhile, preheat the oven to 100°C (200°F/Gas ½). Trim the leeks and place in a tight-fitting ovenproof dish. Pour over the olive brine and chicken stock. Cover with foil and steam in the oven for 15–20 minutes until cooked. Alternatively, place the leeks in a sous-vide bag with the olive brine and chicken stock. Seal the bag and cook in a water bath at 80°C (175°F) for 15 minutes.

When ready to serve, put the leeks and remaining liquor in a saucepan and simmer over low heat for 5 minutes. Strain the leeks, place in a frying pan over medium heat and char lightly on all sides.

Heat olive oil in a frying pan and flash-fry the saltbush until crisp (about 20 seconds).

To serve, slice the charred leek lengthways and place on a plate. Slice the rested lamb across the grain, and plate approximately 160 g (5¾ oz) per serve. Drizzle with some extra virgin olive oil and a squeeze of lemon juice. Scatter with a generous amount of crisp saltbush and serve.

DUCK, GOLDEN BEETS, DANDELION AND SPROUTED WHEAT

CHEF: OWEN CLARK

SERVES 5

You will need to begin this recipe two days ahead.

5 duck breasts, skin on
80 g (2¾ oz/1 bunch) dandelion greens
1 tablespoon butter
1 garlic clove
1 thyme stalk
dandelion leaves, extra, to serve

SPROUTED WHEAT

220 g (7¾ oz/2 cups) milling wheat grains (hard red wheat berries)
2 French shallots
15 g (½ oz) chives
75 g (2½ oz/½ bunch) flat-leaf (Italian) parsley
1 lemon, zest and juice

BRINE

3 large white onions, peeled, chopped
3 large carrots, peeled, chopped
½ head of celery, chopped
3 garlic bulbs, split, peeled, chopped
10 allspice berries
10 cloves
1 tablespoon coriander seeds
1 tablespoon whole black peppercorns
1 tablespoon fennel seeds
20 g (¾ oz/1 bunch) thyme
10 bay leaves
45 g (1½ oz/½ cup) Turkish coffee beans
630 g (1 lb 6 oz/2 cups) salt
220 g (7¾ oz/1 cup) sugar

ROASTED BEETROOT

10 baby beetroot, washed, tops removed
3 large golden beetroot, washed
2 tablespoons olive oil
3–4 thyme stalks

POTATO PURÉE

4 russet potatoes, peeled, skins reserved
4 thyme stalks
1 garlic bulb, peeled, split
good quality fruity olive oil (less peppery)

VEGETABLE DRESSING

1 egg yolk
25 g (1 oz) salted anchovies
125 ml (4 fl oz/½ cup) balsamic vinegar
1 tablespoon worcestershire sauce
1 tablespoon soy sauce
375 ml (13 fl oz/1½ cups) grapeseed oil

Put the wheat berries in a bowl, cover with water and soak overnight. Drain and lay out the berries in a thin layer on a large baking tray lined with a damp tea towel (dish towel). Cover with another damp tea towel and set aside for 24 hours for the berries to sprout.

Prepare the brine for the duck by sweating the vegetables in a large saucepan or stockpot over medium heat until tender. Toast the spices in a small frying pan, add them to the vegetables and cook until fragrant. Add 5.5 litres (190 fl oz/22 cups) of water and bring to the boil. Reduce heat to low and simmer gently for 45 minutes or until the flavours infuse. Add the herbs, coffee beans, salt and sugar, steep for 15 minutes then allow to cool completely. When cold, pour over the trimmed duck breasts, cover and leave in the refrigerator for at least 8 hours, preferably overnight.

Put the sprouted berries in a large saucepan with 1 litre (35 fl oz/4 cups) of water. Simmer over medium heat until tender. Cool in the cooking liquid, strain and season with salt. Finely chop the shallots, chives, parsley and lemon zest. Combine with the berries in a bowl and season with lemon juice, salt and pepper. Set aside until ready to serve.

Preheat the oven to 190°C (375°F/Gas 5). Place the baby beetroot and golden beetroot in two separate roasting tins and drizzle with oil. Season with salt and pepper and scatter with the thyme sprigs. Cover each roasting tin with foil and roast the baby beetroot for 30 minutes and the golden beetroot for 1¼ hours or until just tender. Peel the beetroot by rubbing off the skins while still warm. Using a mandolin, slice the golden beetroot and set aside.

To make the potato purée, put the potatoes and skins in a large saucepan. Cover with water and add the thyme, garlic and a few generous pinches of salt to season. Cook over medium heat for 15 minutes or until tender and thoroughly cooked but not falling apart. Drain and press potatoes through a potato ricer or mash in a bowl. Fold through enough olive oil to make the potato shiny with a slight fruity olive flavour. Season generously with salt and pepper and keep warm.

To make the vegetable dressing, blend the egg yolk, anchovies, vinegar, worcestershire sauce and soy sauce in a blender until smooth. With the motor running, slowly add the grapeseed oil and emulsify until a creamy dressing is achieved. Set aside.

Blanch the dandelion greens in a saucepan of boiling water then shock in iced water to halt the cooking process. Purée in a blender and season with salt and pepper. Cover and reserve in the refrigerator until serving.

Lightly season the duck breast with salt and pepper. Score the fat. Heat a frying pan over low heat and add the duck, skin side down. Cook, rendering the fat on the breast for 5–6 minutes until it is golden brown and crisp. Drain off the fat as it renders. Turn the heat to high and sear the flesh side of the breast, then return to medium heat. Add the butter, garlic and thyme and baste the flesh until golden in colour. Cook 3–4 minutes for medium rare. Transfer to a warm plate, cover loosely with foil and rest for 5 minutes.

To serve, warm the potato purée, add a spoonful of the dandelion purée and mix gently until smooth. Spoon onto the plate and add the beetroot slices and seasoned baby beetroots. In a separate frying pan, warm the sprouted wheat and herb mixture and season to taste, spooning over the beetroot and dandelion purée. Lightly coat the beetroot slices and dandelion greens in the vegetable dressing. Slice the duck breasts into three pieces and arrange on top, laying the extra dandelion greens on top.

POACHED CHICKEN, SHAVED ARTICHOKE, RICOTTA AND AVRUGA

CHEF: DAVE VERHEUL

SERVES 6

You will need to begin this recipe one day ahead.

3 x 250 g (9 oz) free-range chicken breasts
5 tablespoons thyme leaves
2 garlic cloves
half a lemon, zest
1 bay leaf
30 ml (1 fl oz) olive oil
sea salt
chicken jus (see *Accompagnement* for recipe)
3 baby violet artichokes, peeled, trimmed
lemon juice, to serve
olive oil, to serve
4 black garlic cloves, thinly sliced, to serve
salad burnet leaves, to serve
chicken skin crisps (optional), to serve

RICOTTA GNUDI

200 g (7 oz) ricotta cheese
8 g (¼ oz) parmesan cheese
4 g (⅛ oz) plain (all-purpose) flour
1 egg yolk
sea salt
200 g (7 oz) fine semolina

ROASTED GARLIC

4 garlic cloves

AVRUGA CRÈME FRAÎCHE

50 g (1¾ oz) crème fraîche
30 g (1 oz) Avruga
sea salt

To make the ricotta gnudi, gently mix the ricotta, parmesan, flour and egg yolk together in a bowl. Season well with salt and pepper and roll into thumbnail-size balls. Sprinkle a layer of semolina in the base of a flat container, place the ricotta balls at even spacings taking care that they don't touch each other, then completely cover with the remaining semolina. Refrigerate overnight. The next day, bring a saucepan of water to a gentle simmer, remove the gnudi from the semolina – shaking off any excess – and drop the gnudi in the water. When they rise to the top, scoop out and chill.

Trim the chicken breasts of any sinew and remove the small fillet. Put the breasts into a sous-vide bag with the thyme, garlic, lemon zest, bay leaf and olive oil and season with salt. Seal the bag and cook in a water bath at 65°C (145°F) for 1 hour, remove and keep warm.

To roast the garlic, put the cloves in a 140°C (275°F/Gas 1) oven until tender and caramelised. Peel and pass through a sieve.

To make the Avruga crème fraîche, gently mix the crème fraîche and Avruga together, and season well with salt and pepper.

Warm the chicken jus in a large saucepan over low to medium heat and season to taste with the roast garlic purée and sea salt. Add the gnudi to warm through. Shave the artichokes very thinly on a truffle slicer, and season with lemon juice, olive oil and sea salt. Place 3 slices of black garlic on each plate, followed by 4 gnudi and some Avruga crème fraîche. Slice each chicken breast lengthways, and place 3 slices on each plate. Put a spoonful of chicken jus beside the chicken. Scatter the artichoke over the gnudi, and place the salad burnet and chicken skin crisps, if using, on top.

PARSNIP RISOTTO, WALNUT, APPLE AND HORSERADISH

CHEF: DAN PEARSON

SERVES 6–8

1.5 litres (52 fl oz/6 cups) vegetable stock
100 ml (3½ fl oz) olive oil
1 white onion, peeled, finely diced
2 garlic cloves
600 g (1 lb 5 oz/2¾ cups) carnaroli rice
4 large parsnips
200 g (7 oz) butter
500 ml (17 fl oz/2 cups) cream
250 g (9 oz) mascarpone
50 g (1¾ oz) parmesan cheese, finely grated
walnuts, toasted, to serve
2 apples, thinly sliced on a mandolin, to serve
chervil leaves, to serve
horseradish, finely grated, to serve

In a large saucepan, bring the vegetable stock to the boil over high heat, then reduce the heat and keep the stock at a simmer to be used for the risotto. Line a large baking tray with baking paper. Heat the olive oil in a large saucepan and sauté the onion and garlic for 1–2 minutes or until translucent, without browning. Add the rice and cook, stirring constantly, for 1–2 minutes; do not allow to brown. Add the boiling stock to the rice mixture, one-third at a time, each time stirring until the rice has absorbed the liquid. Each addition should take about 6 minutes to be absorbed. Season to taste with salt and pepper. Remove from the pan, press flat in the prepared tray and cover with baking paper to prevent a skin forming. Chill in the refrigerator for 1 hour until completely cooled.

To make parsnip stock, cut off the tops, peel the parsnips and slice them in half lengthways. Remove the core of each parsnip with a teaspoon, put the tops and trimmings in a medium saucepan and just cover with water. Place over medium heat and bring to the boil, remove from the heat and put the saucepan to one side to cool. Strain into a clean container, discarding the pulp. Chop the parsnip into cubes. Put the butter in a medium frying pan over low to medium heat and cook until foaming. Add the parsnip and cook until caramelised, about 5 minutes. Add the cream to cover and cook for an additional 5–10 minutes or until the parsnip is soft. Transfer to a blender and mix until smooth. Strain into a clean bowl and season to taste with salt and pepper.

Spoon 4 tablespoons of risotto per person into a large frying pan. Add a generous ladleful of parsnip stock and cook until warm. When you toss the pan, the risotto should have a wavelike consistency off the back of the pan. If not, add a little more parsnip stock. Add parsnip purée to taste, 6 tablespoons of mascarpone and the grated parmesan. Season with salt and pepper to taste.

To serve, spoon the risotto into the centre of each plate. Top with toasted walnuts, sliced apples and chervil leaves. To finish, generously grate fresh horseradish over the dish with a microplane. Serve warm.

PIGEON, YEAST SOUBISE AND BLUEBERRY WHEY COMPOTE

CHEF: ARI TAYMOR
SERVES 4

4 pigeons, cleaned; necks, hearts and livers reserved
2 eggwhites
6 cups grey salt

PIGEON JUS
1 onion, charred
red wine, for deglazing
chicken stock, to cover
butter, to season
Banyuls wine vinegar, to season

YEAST SOUBISE
4 white onions, peeled, chopped
butter or oil, for frying
2 tablespoons fresh yeast
60 ml (2 fl oz/¼ cup) milk

ROASTED SPRING ONION
1 teaspoon grapeseed oil
16 spring onions (scallions), peeled and trimmed
1 tablespoon butter

BLUEBERRY WHEY COMPOTE
390 g (13¾ oz/2½ cups) blueberries
250 ml (9 fl oz/1 cup) whey
1 teaspoon caster (superfine) sugar

Preheat the oven to 230°C (450°F/Gas 8). To make pigeon jus, roast the pigeon necks, hearts and livers until caramelised. Add the charred onion and a little red wine to deglaze the pan. Cover the mixture with chicken stock and simmer for 4 hours, skimming constantly. Pass through a fine sieve and season to taste with butter, salt and Banyuls wine vinegar.

To make the yeast soubise, sweat the onions in a little butter or oil in a saucepan over low heat until translucent. Add yeast, milk and 60 ml (2 fl oz/¼ cup) of water. Bring to a gentle simmer, then purée and season to taste. Pass through a fine sieve and set aside until ready to serve.

Prepare the pigeons for roasting. Mix the eggwhite and salt to form a wet, sandlike paste, adding more salt or eggwhite if necessary. Press the paste over the pigeon breasts, place in a roasting tin and cook in the preheated oven for 9 minutes. Rest for 2 minutes, then crack the crust and debone the bird. Sear in a frying pan over high heat, skin side down.

To make the roasted spring onion, heat a frying pan over medium heat, add the grapeseed oil and spring onion. Cook until tender. Finish with the butter and season with salt. Set aside until ready to serve.

To make the blueberry whey compote, mix the blueberries, whey and sugar in a saucepan over low to medium heat for 3–5 minutes until the blueberries soften and the mixture thickens. Set aside until ready to serve.

To serve, warm the soubise, spring onions, blueberry whey compote and jus all separately. Decorate four plates with the soubise, pigeon and spring onions. Finish with the blueberry whey compote and drizzle with pigeon jus.

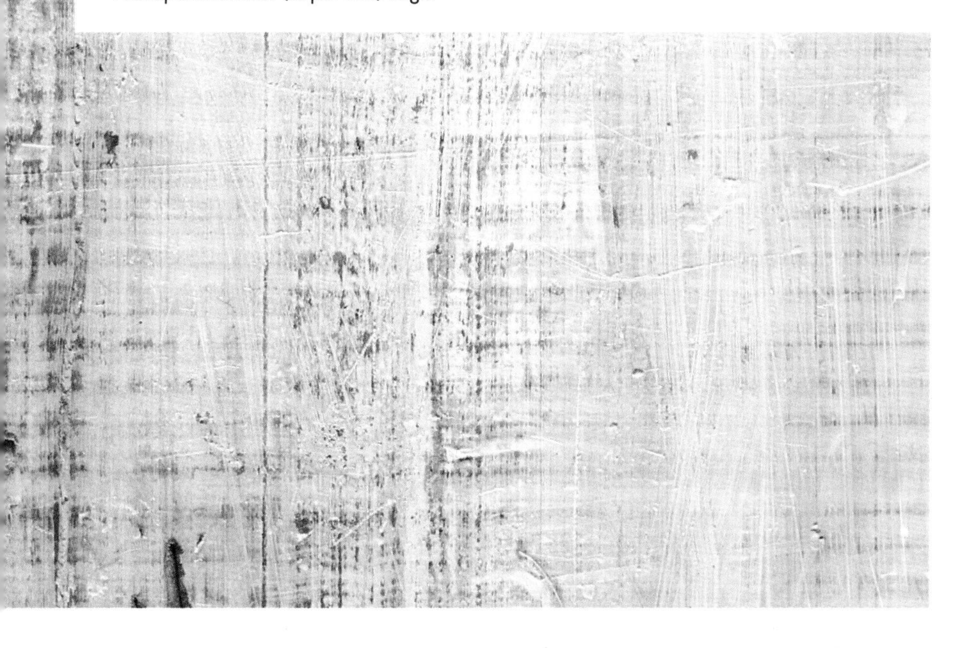

AVANT-GARDE

IN THE VANGUARD

The culinary sweet spot between the familiar and the interesting

SLOW-ROASTED SHOULDER OF LAMB, SMOKED POTATOES AND MINT SAUCE

STEAK DIANE, CHARRED ONION, POTATO FONDANT, PEPPERCORN AND BONE MARROW CROQUETTES

COD, PEA PURÉE AND CRAB

MARBLED CALOTTE, SHISO DRESSING AND WASABI

DEXTER BEEF SIRLOIN, SNAIL PERSILLADE, TRUFFLE CREAMED POTATO AND SCORCHED ONIONS

SALT-BAKED SALMON

CELERIAC, ROSEMARY AND PINE NUT CAPPELLETTI, BOTTARGA AND PINE TREE OIL

45-DAY DRY-AGED BEEF, SWEET ONIONS, PICKLED CHERRIES, FETA AND COLATURA

CHICKEN BAKED IN HAY WITH CHICKEN FAT RICE

BRAISED VEAL NECK, PUMPKIN AND SMOKED RICOTTA

SADDLE OF RABBIT WITH SHOULDER AND LEG COTTAGE PIE

SLOW-ROASTED SHOULDER OF LAMB, SMOKED POTATOES AND MINT SAUCE

CHEF: SHAUN KELLY

SERVES 6

2 kg (4 lb 8 oz) lamb shoulder, bone in
2 tablespoons olive oil
organic hay, for roasting

SMOKED POTATOES

1 kg (2 lb 4 oz) small potatoes
1–3 tablespoons butter

MINT SAUCE

80 g (2¾ oz/1 bunch) mint, leaves picked, stalks reserved
100 ml (3½ fl oz) cider vinegar
50 g (1¾ oz) sugar

Preheat the oven to 160°C (315°F/Gas 2–3).

Rub the lamb with the olive oil and season with salt and pepper. Lay a couple of handfuls of hay in a roasting tin, cover with a layer of muslin (cheesecloth) or a wire rack and put the seasoned lamb on top. Roast in the oven for 5 hours, basting the lamb with the juices as it cooks.

Boil the potatoes in salted water until just cooked, then strain. To smoke them, you will need a large saucepan or tray with a fitted lid, and a wire rack or metal steamer basket that fits inside but is raised from the base of the saucepan. Place the saucepan over high heat and add a handful of hay. Once it begins to smoke, ignite it with a match, quickly put the wire rack on top and add the potatoes, then cover with the lid to snuff out the flames. Place outside for 20 minutes to allow the potatoes to absorb the smoke.

Meanwhile, put the mint stalks in a medium saucepan and add the vinegar, 100 ml (3½ fl oz) of water, the sugar and a pinch of salt. Bring to a light simmer and infuse for 20 minutes then allow to cool. Strain. Finely chop the mint leaves and add to the infused liquid.

Toss the smoked potatoes with butter, and season with salt and pepper. Serve the lamb and potatoes with the roasting juices and the mint sauce separately in a small pot.

STEAK DIANE, CHARRED ONION, POTATO FONDANT, PEPPERCORN AND BONE MARROW CROQUETTES

CHEF: LEE COOPER

SERVES 4

4 brown onions
grapeseed oil, for frying
680 g (1 lb 8 oz) aged beef tenderloin, at room temperature

BONE MARROW CROQUETTES

2 large veal bones, cut lengthways
2 tablespoons finely chopped flat-leaf (Italian) parsley
70 g (2½ oz/½ cup) plain (all-purpose) flour
1 egg, lightly beaten
110 g (3¾ oz/1 cup) dry breadcrumbs, to coat
vegetable oil, for frying

POTATO FONDANT

225 g (8 oz) unsalted butter
4 kennebec potatoes, peeled, trimmed into four rectangular blocks

RED WINE SAUCE

1 tablespoon chopped shallots
1 tablespoon black pepper, freshly cracked
1 tablespoon pink peppercorns, freshly cracked
30 ml (1 fl oz) brandy
120 ml (4 fl oz/½ cup) red wine
60 ml (2 fl oz/¼ cup) thick (double) cream

Preheat the oven to 200°C (400°F/Gas 6). Season the veal bones generously with salt and pepper. Place on a baking tray and roast for 10–20 minutes or until the marrow is golden and cooked. Set aside to cool. Once cooled, remove the marrow and combine with the parsley in a small bowl. Form the mixture into 4 uniform balls, cover and chill in the refrigerator until firm.

Put the flour, egg and breadcrumbs in separate bowls. Lightly coat the marrow croquettes in the flour, then in the egg and finally in the breadcrumbs. Put the croquettes on a baking tray lined with baking paper and place in the refrigerator.

Put the onions in their skins on a baking tray and cook in the oven for 30 minutes or until completely cooked through. Peel the onions and cut in half. Put a heavy-based ovenproof frying pan over medium heat and add a small amount of grapeseed oil. Cook the onions, cut side down, until lightly charred. Set aside.

Meanwhile, for the potato fondant, heat a frying pan over medium heat. Add the butter and cook until foaming. Add the potatoes and season generously with salt. Increase the temperature until the butter foams around the potatoes, and adjust the heat as necessary to maintain this foam. Cook the potatoes on all sides until crisp and golden. Remove the pan from heat, add the charred onions and allow the potatoes and onions to stand in the hot butter until ready to serve.

Reduce the oven temperature to 150°C (300°F/Gas 2). Using the same frying pan that you used for the onions, season the tenderloin and sear it on all sides, then put the pan into the oven for 10 minutes or until cooked to your liking. Remove the tenderloin from the pan and set aside to rest.

Add the shallots and combined cracked pepper to the meat drippings and flambé with the brandy and wine, then cook over low heat until reduced. Strain through a fine sieve into a clean saucepan, return to the pan and add the cream.

Preheat the vegetable oil in a deep-fryer or large, heavy-based saucepan to 180°C (350°F) or until a cube of bread dropped into the oil turns brown in 15 seconds. Carefully fry the croquettes for 2–3 minutes or until golden. Remove the potatoes and charred onions from the warm butter and drain on paper towel, separating the onions into their petals.

Carefully slice and plate the tenderloin with the potato fondant and a bone marrow croquette, scatter with the charred onion and carefully spoon the red wine sauce over the beef. Serve immediately.

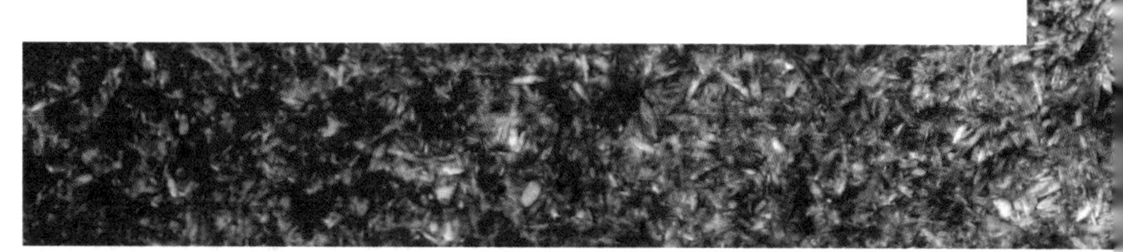

COD, PEA PUREE AND CRAB

CHEF: MATT LAMBERT

SERVES 4

You will need to begin this recipe five days ahead.

4 tablespoons butter
4 fresh cod fillets, 150 g (5½ oz) each
1 lemon
butter, extra, to monte with the crab and pea sauce
black mint, dill, bronze fennel and fava flowers, to serve

PICKLED MUSSELS
875 ml (30 fl oz/3½ cups) cider vinegar
220 g (7¾ oz/1 cup) caster (superfine) sugar
500 ml (17 fl oz/2 cups) dry white wine
10 peppercorns
2 tablespoons salt
4 tarragon stalks
6 bay leaves
900 g (2 lb) steamed mussels

PEA PURÉE
310 g (11 oz/2 cups) fresh peas, blanched
1 teaspoon salt
1 tablespoon unsalted butter, softened
1 cup thickened (whipping) cream, hot

CRAB AND PEA SAUCE
4 tablespoons freshly picked crabmeat
270 g (9½ oz/1¾ cups) fresh peas, blanched
3 tablespoons pickling liquid (from the mussels)
2 tablespoons dry white wine
1 teaspoon finely chopped chives
1 teaspoon finely chopped coriander (cilantro) leaves

To make the pickled mussels, put the vinegar, sugar, wine, peppercorns, salt and herbs into a large saucepan over medium heat and cook until the sugar and salt have completely dissolved, adjusting the sugar to taste. Let cool, then add the mussels, cover and stand in the refrigerator for 5 days.

To make the pea purée, put all the ingredients except the cream into a blender. Blend on high speed, slowly adding the hot cream to ensure the purée is as smooth and silky as possible. Keep warm.

To make the crab and pea sauce, gently warm all the ingredients in a saucepan over low heat, stirring constantly to ensure the mixture doesn't split. Monte with butter just before serving.

To cook the cod, heat the butter in a large non-stick frying pan over medium-high heat. Season the fish with salt and pepper and place it in the pan skin side down. Cook, pressing lightly so the skin cooks evenly, 4–6 minutes until crisp and golden. Turn, add butter to pan and cook for 3–4 minutes until just cooked through. Remove from the heat and squeeze lemon juice over.

To plate, smear the pea purée on the base of each plate. Put the fish on top and carefully place a dollop of crab and pea sauce adjacent to the fish. Place one pickled mussel per serve, garnish with black mint, dill, bronze fennel and fava flowers and serve.

MARBLED CALOTTE, SHISO DRESSING AND WASABI

CHEF: RYAN SQUIRES

SERVES 4

500g (1 lb 2 oz) calotte (rib eye cap), at room temperature
freshly grated wasabi, to serve
baby mustard, radish leaves, or spicy peppery leaves in season, to serve

SHISO DRESSING

2 large bunches shiso (perilla) leaves
small handful bonito flakes
1 garlic clove, crushed
4 cm (1½ inch) piece ginger, peeled and crushed
1 star anise, toasted
1 teaspoon sesame oil
50 ml (1½ fl oz) Japanese soy sauce (bonito flavour)
1 g (1/32 oz) 1% xanthan gum

Prepare the shiso dressing by combining the shiso, bonito flakes, garlic, ginger, star anise, sesame oil and soy sauce in a large saucepan. Set aside to steep for 4 hours in a warm environment. Strain into a bowl. Add the xanthan gum to thicken and stir until incorporated. Set aside.

To cook the calotte over coal, place coal pieces on a gas stove and ignite for at least 20 minutes or until the coal pieces turn white with a red-hot glow in the centre. Working quickly and carefully, place the coal in a barbecue set up with a fine mesh rack roughly 5–8 cm (2–3¼ inches) above the coal. Allow the rack to heat through thoroughly, at least 10 minutes.

Place the beef on the hottest part of the grill and cook for 3–5 minutes on one side, until it is a rich golden brown and almost burnt and charred in appearance. Flip the beef over and repeat on the other side. When cooked to your liking, set aside to rest in a warm place, uncovered, for 15 minutes.

Just before serving, place the beef back on the hot spot of the coal and season generously with salt. Slice the beef in serving slices, place on plates then douse liberally with shiso dressing, add freshly grated wasabi and scatter with spicy leaves to serve.

DEXTER BEEF SIRLOIN, SNAIL PERSILLADE, TRUFFLE CREAMED POTATO AND SCORCHED ONIONS

CHEF: ADAM BYATT

SERVES 4

4 dexter beef sirloin steaks, 250g (9 oz) each
1 tablespoon unsalted butter
1 rosemary stalk
1 garlic clove

SCORCHED ONION PETALS
2 white onions, unpeeled
olive oil, for frying
1 tablespoon butter

SNAIL PERSILLADE
250 g (9 oz) snails, blanched
500 ml (17 fl oz/2 cups) red wine
1 garlic bulb, cloves finely chopped, plus 1 clove extra
1 bouquet garni
4 white onions, diced
175 g (6 oz) butter
150 g (5½ oz/1 bunch) flat-leaf (Italian) parsley

PARSLEY PURÉE
300 g (10½ oz/3 bunches) curly parsley
50 ml (1½ fl oz) vegetable oil

RED WINE SAUCE
800 ml (28 fl oz) brown chicken stock
200 ml (7 fl oz) red wine
200 ml (7 fl oz) Port (tawny)
1 French shallot
1 bouquet garni
1 garlic clove
1 peppercorn
1 star anise
1 tablespoon Cabernet Sauvignon vinegar

PARSLEY CRUMB
100 g (3½ oz/1 bunch) curly parsley
100 g (3½ oz) panko breadcrumbs
40 g (1½ oz) parmesan cheese, to serve

TRUFFLE MASH
500 g (1 lb 2 oz) desiree potatoes
200 ml (7 fl oz) thick (double) cream
200 g (7 oz) unsalted butter
truffle oil, to taste
10 g (¼ oz) fresh Périgord truffle

To make the scorched onion petals, cut the onions into quarters, leaving the skin on. Cover the base of a frying pan with olive oil and place over high heat until smoking. Add the onion quarters and fry until coloured on all sides. Remove from the heat, add the butter, season with salt and pepper and allow to cool in the pan.

To make the snail persillade, put the snails, red wine, garlic and bouquet garni in a casserole and cook over high heat quickly until the wine has completely reduced, then stand in the refrigerator to chill quickly. Discard the bouquet garni. Put the onions and butter in a frying pan with a large pinch of salt and heat over low to medium heat. Sweat until soft, without allowing the onions to colour. Chop the snails and the parsley; mix with the onions and use a microplane to grate the extra clove of garlic into the mix. Set aside until ready to serve.

To make the parsley purée, blanch the parsley in a medium saucepan in heavily salted boiling water for 8 minutes. Refresh in iced water. Squeeze dry and blend with the vegetable oil and a small amount of water for 4 minutes. Pass through a drum sieve and chill to retain colour.

To make the red wine sauce, put the chicken stock in a medium saucepan over medium heat and reduce to a sauce consistency, approximately 200 ml (7 fl oz). Meanwhile, in another medium saucepan over medium heat, put the remaining ingredients for the sauce and reduce by half. Strain and combine with the chicken stock. Pass through a fine sieve into a clean container. Cover with plastic wrap to prevent a skin forming.

To make the parsley crumb, blend the parsley and breadcumbs together, seasoning with a little salt. If the mixture is too moist, add more breadcrumbs.

To make the truffle mash, cut the potatoes in quarters, put them in a large saucepan with cold salted water to cover and bring to the boil over high heat. Cook for 12–15 minutes until the potatoes are just tender when pierced with a small sharp knife. Drain the water, return to the heat and dry out in the pan. Pass through a drum sieve. In a saucepan, season the cream with salt and pepper, add the butter and bring to the boil. Add the potato and work with a spatula over low heat until the cream and butter mixture is incorporated. Finish with the truffle oil to taste.

Season each beef sirloin well. In a very hot frying pan, colour both sides of the meat, ensuring you colour and render the fat. Add butter, rosemary and garlic to the pan. Baste for 1 minute, then remove the beef from the pan to rest for 6–7 minutes.

Once rested, slice the beef into 2 cm (¾ inch)slices and cover the top with the snail persillade. Sprinkle the parsley crumb on top with some grated parmesan. Cook for 1–2 minutes under a grill (broiler) until the crumb is just golden in colour.

To serve, spoon a portion of truffle mash on the side of a plate using a tablespoon and grate the Perigord truffle over the top. Make a well in the middle and fill with the red wine sauce. Place petals of scorched onion beside the mash and top with the beef sirloin. Pipe dots of parsley purée into each petal. Serve immediately.

Note: Make bouquet garni with thyme, rosemary and bay leaf tied with kitchen string.

SALT-BAKED SALMON

CHEF: LEE COOPER

SERVES 8

3 kg (6 lb 12 oz) whole salmon, gutted and scaled
2 eggwhites
780 g (1 lb 11 oz/6 cups) sea salt or volcanic grey salt
extra virgin olive oil, to rub
1 lemon, sliced
25 g (1 oz/1 bunch) dill
1 fennel bulb, thinly sliced
1 white onion, thinly sliced
1 teaspoon black pepper, coarsely cracked
lemon wedges, to serve
good quality olive oil, to serve

Preheat the oven to 230°C (450°F/Gas 8). Line a large baking tray (or a baking dish large enough to hold the fish) with baking paper and set aside.

Whip the eggwhites and mix with the grey salt in a large bowl until well combined. Add a little water if it seems too dry: you are looking for a paste consistency.

Rub the salmon with the olive oil and stuff the cavity with the lemon slices, dill, fennel, onion and pepper. Spread a layer of the salt mix on the baking tray, slightly larger than the fish and place the stuffed fish on top of the salt. Cover the fish with the remaining salt mixture, ensuring you make a complete seal all the way around the fish. Bake in the oven for 25 minutes or until cooked to your liking.

Remove from the oven and allow to rest for 10 minutes. Break open the crust and gently remove fillets from the fish. Serve with lemon wedges and a drizzle of good quality olive oil.

CELERIAC, ROSEMARY AND PINE NUT CAPPELLETTI, BOTTARGA AND PINE TREE OIL

CHEF: GIOVANNI PASSERINI
SERVES 4

You will need to begin this recipe one day ahead.

400 g (14 oz/2⅔ cups) 00 (pastry) flour, sifted
100 g (3 ½ oz/½ cup) fine semolina
10 egg yolks
olive oil, extra, for frying
garlic, crushed, for frying
12 slices bottarga (dried mullet roe)
lemon juice, to season
pine tree oil (see *Accompagnement* for recipe), to serve
12 chickweed leaves

FILLING
2 celeriac, peeled
50 g (1¾ oz) butter
1 rosemary stalk
150 g (5½ oz/1 cup) pine nuts, lightly toasted
50 g (1¾ oz/⅓ cup) finely grated parmesan cheese
1 bunch lovage
½ lemon, peel zested
2 teaspoons dashi stock, reduced by half (see *Accompagnement* for recipe)

Prepare the pasta dough 1 day ahead. Put the flour and semolina in a bowl and make a well in the centre. Add the egg yolks in the well, then mix with a fork until a dough starts to form. Gradually add cold water as needed. Turn the dough onto a lightly floured surface and knead for up to 25 minutes until the dough is smooth and elastic. Wrap in plastic wrap and set aside to rest.

Dice one celeriac into very small cubes (brunoise). Put it into a medium saucepan with the butter over low heat. Add enough water to just submerge the celeriac, and cook, covered, for 25 minutes. Remove the cover and continue to cook until the liquid has evaporated.

Preheat the oven to 100°C (200°F/Gas ½). Put the rosemary on a baking tray and dry in the oven for 15 minutes. Pull the leaves and grind them to a fine powder using a spice grinder. Pass through a sieve to remove any large pieces.

Put the pine nuts in a blender and blend to a powder. Work quickly to ensure that the pine nuts do not heat up and turn into a fatty cream: you want a powder consistency.

Put the cooked celeriac, pine nut powder, rosemary powder, parmesan, lovage and lemon zest into a large bowl. Stir to combine, season generously with salt and pepper. Pour into a piping (icing) bag and place in the refrigerator until ready to use.

Juice the remaining celeriac, reserving the juice and the pulp, and put both juice and pulp in a large saucepan, adding 1 litre (35 fl oz/4 cups) of cold water. Cook for 2 hours and then strain through a sieve line with muslin (cheesecloth). Check the flavour and, if the liquid appears slightly watery, return to the saucepan to reduce. Add the reduced dashi stock and stir to combine.

To make the pasta, divide the dough into three and, working with one piece at a time, feed and roll it through the rollers of a pasta machine at the widest setting until the dough is smooth and silky, then fold and roll, reducing the settings notch by notch, until the dough is 3–5 mm (⅛–¼ inch) thick. Lay each pasta sheet on a floured surface as you repeat with the remaining dough.

Cut 16 small rounds of pasta (about 8 cm or 3¼ inches diameter) and pipe approximately a teaspoon of filling into the centre of each. Take a round in your hands, fold it in half like a half moon, pressing the stuffing to the middle. Bring together the two opposite points to make a cappelletto. Repeat with the remaining rounds and filling.

Line a baking tray with baking paper and dust with semolina to prevent sticking. Place the cappelletti on the tray and put them in the refrigerator (close to the fan). The cappelletti should be slightly dry before cooking.

Bring a large saucepan of water to a rolling boil over high heat. Add the cappelletti and cook for 40 seconds. Strain. Put olive oil and garlic in a large frying pan over high heat, add the cappelletti and cook for 30 seconds or until coated and fragrant.

To serve, put the cappelletti in soup bowls and add a few spoons of the celeriac broth, three slices of bottarga and lemon juice to season. Finish with a few drops of pine tree oil and three chickweed leaves. Serve immediately.

45-DAY DRY-AGED BEEF, SWEET ONIONS, PICKLED CHERRIES, FETA AND COLATURA

CHEF: GREGORY MARCHAND
SERVES 4

500 g (1 lb 2 oz) 45-day dry-aged grass-fed sirloin of beef, trimmed
1 tablespoon grapeseed oil
15 g (½ oz) butter
1 thyme sprig
1 rosemary sprig
1 garlic clove, crushed
colatura (anchovy essence), to season
beef jus, to serve
fleur de sel, to serve
80 g (2¾ oz) feta cheese, to serve
mignonette and samphire, to serve

PICKLED CHERRIES
10 cherries, halved and pitted
125 ml (4 fl oz/½ cup) white wine
125 ml (4 fl oz/½ cup) sherry vinegar
125 g (4½ oz) sugar

ONION PURÉE
100 g (3½ oz) butter
500 g (1 lb 2 oz) onions, peeled, thinly sliced on a mandolin
1 thyme sprig
lemon juice, to season
pickled ginger juice, to season

CARAMELISED BABY ONIONS
1 bunch baby onions
½ tablespoon olive oil
½ tablespoon butter
fleur de sel, to season
1 tablespoon lemon juice
1 tablespoon colatura (anchovy essence)
1 tablespoon pickled ginger juice

To make the pickled cherries, put the cherry halves in a sous-vide bag with the remaining ingredients and cook in a water bath at 64°C (147°F) for 20 minutes. Put the bag in an ice bath immediately after cooking, then set aside until ready to plate.

To make the onion purée, put the butter in a medium frying pan over low heat. When melted and lightly foaming, add the onion and thyme and sweat over very low heat, until the onions are soft, ensuring there is no colouration. Purée in a blender until you have a very smooth white purée. Season to taste with the salt, lemon juice and pickled ginger juice.

To make the caramelised baby onions, cut away the green stem and peel the first layer of skin, ensuring that you leave the roots attached. Cut each baby onion in half. Put the olive oil and butter in a frying pan over medium heat. Sear the onions, sliced side down, charring them until they are golden black. Season heavily with fleur de sel. Make a dressing with the lemon juice, colatura and pickled ginger juice. Marinate the onions in the dressing at room temperature.

Season the beef generously with salt and pepper. Heat a frying pan over medium heat, add the grapeseed oil and sear the beef on all sides. Add the butter, thyme, rosemary and garlic and baste the beef until cooked to rare. Let the meat rest for 15 minutes before slicing. Season the beef with colatura.

To serve, reheat the onion purée and put a smear of purée on each plate with a slice of sirloin on top. Add a few pickled cherries and caramelised onions with some of the marinade. Coat the beef with the jus, season with fleur de sel, sprinkle with crumbled feta and finish with a few sprigs of samphire and mignonette.

CHICKEN BAKED IN HAY WITH CHICKEN FAT RICE

CHEF: MICHAEL CABALLO

SERVES 4

1.5 kg (3 lb 5 oz) organic free-range chicken, at room temperature
chicken fat or butter to coat
6–8 generous sprigs of thyme, parsley and sage
2 fresh bay leaves
five 5 cm (2 inch) pieces of green garlic (or substitute 5 whole garlic cloves)
5 wild leek bulbs
2 generous handfuls of hay
500 ml (17 fl oz/2 cups) chicken stock
125 ml (4 fl oz/½ cup) alcoholic cider (ideally Spanish or French)

CHICKEN FAT RICE

1 fresh bay leaf
15 g (½ oz) salt
200 g (7 oz/1 scant cup) bomba rice (or substitute arborio)
3 tablespoons chicken fat
2 tablespoons finely chopped green garlic (or 1 garlic clove, minced)

Preheat the oven to 150°C (300°F/Gas 2). Rub the chicken generously in chicken fat or butter and season with salt, including the cavity. Fill the cavity with the fresh herbs and bay leaves and truss the chicken with kitchen string. Spread the garlic and leek bulbs in the base of a large, ovenproof casserole with a tight-fitting lid, large enough to accommodate the chicken. Add a layer of washed hay and pour in the chicken stock and cider. Place the chicken on top and cover with the remaining hay. Cover with the lid and cook in the oven for 1–1½ hours or until just pink at the thigh joint. Remove from the oven and rest the chicken for 15 minutes.

Strain the cooking liquid into a small saucepan and place over medium heat. Cook for 15–20 minutes or until reduced by a third, seasoning with salt if necessary.

While the chicken is resting, prepare the chicken fat rice: bring 2 litres (70 fl oz/8 cups) of water to the boil in a large saucepan with the bay leaf and salt. Add the rice and boil for 13 minutes. Strain. In a large frying pan over medium heat, put the chicken fat and green garlic and sweat until soft, but do not allow to colour. Add the rice, stirring to combine and ensuring it is thoroughly coated in chicken fat. Season with salt.

To serve, carve the chicken. Pour the seasoned juices over the carved chicken and serve immediately with the chicken fat rice.

Note: If you are using a fresh chicken from a trusted source, there is no problem with a bird that is still pink, says Michael Caballo: 'This is how we serve it at the restaurant.'

LE VIN

One thing will never change. Food and wine need each other. Restaurants have always been more than simply a place where we go to eat, and hunger is only ever a small part of the equation. We are seeking the total experience: of food, of people, and of wine.

For bistronomy chefs and restaurateurs it is an obvious and necessary synergy to marry food and wine in unexpected and exciting ways. If bistronomy shakes up the ossified world of French *haute cuisine*, then it makes sense that its approach to wine breaks down the ferocious expense and acrid snobbery that often goes with its selection and drinking. It presents another opportunity to take diners on an adventure: to disarm any preconceptions and introduce them to pairings of food and wine to which most other menus or wine lists would not lead them.

Bistronomy promotes the power of food and wine and the capacity of each to strengthen and enrich the other, to create an inimitable sensory experience. The approach is based on an understanding that the overall taste of a dish is more important than its constituent parts and that finding the right balance in a dish, and the right balance between a plate of food and the most appropriate glass of wine, is more exciting than anything else. It places an emphasis on establishing personal connections and a strong sense of place through the dishes the chefs plate and the wines they source, while seeking to establish an easy, coherent balance of flavour and texture.

With the exception of a few grape chasers, the bistronomy wine list is by and large seen as a tool to be used, not an *oeuvre* to be admired. Like the food menu, the wine lists are short, sharp and approachable; yet they still parlay

'At the table, for me, wine defines a meal as much as what is on the plate. It guides my seasoning and vision for a dish, and it helps me bring all the elements of cooking together. I love it.'

LUKE BURGESS

the philosophical approach with spirit and concision. They're not necessarily about pure harmony between wine and food: there is significant focus on their combined forces and capacity to create something of a discourse about food and wine matches designed to both challenge and excite. The objective is to offer a range of wines that are much wider in geography and style than those offered by other restaurants. Any restrictions are self-imposed and physical rather than geographical, so the choice is broad and deep. Collections are often eclectic and built on the clean, the unusual, the vanguard and wines distinctly grounded in *terroir*. There are controversial choices that might split the room. The wines are stylistically unique, ranging from big boisterous flavours, hugs rather than a tickle, to light delicate varietals tasting of refined English garden parties and freshly mown grass lawns.

It is a natural progression, from understanding and caring about where food comes from to learning how grapes are grown, taking an interest in soil health, and all the flow on effects this has for the marriage of food and wine. Much has evolved in the way winegrowers manage their land. Organics, and even the more philosophically evolved practice of farm management, is no longer regarded as fringe. Bistronomy tends to celebrate wines that challenge. From those made following ancient winemaking traditions to those that follow a 'whole bunch' philosophy (where the winemaker includes all the grape stems in the fermentation as well as the berries). The openness enables listings of microvineyard selections, not just single vineyards but wines from rows within blocks. There are orange wines, biodynamic wines and wines based on wild yeast fermentation — where great attention is placed on when the grapes are harvested to maintain natural acidity — natural selection theory and a preference for the natural wine movement. It offers a design and pace that realises wines go in and out of style; that our tastes fluctuate; and that it is important to be aware of and open to new sensory experiences. Taste shouldn't stop.

The wine list echoes the economic sensibility of bistronomy, working with the food to help create environments rather than 'temples of gastronomy' with lists and price points that don't act as if they are trying to pat you down for cash. They are broad, bold and unafraid to challenge the more pedestrian palate. There is a serious and genuine concern to correct the misconceptions many harbour about wine; such as price, vigneron, and the role of the sommelier. The wine list is no longer there to intimidate, but rather to delight: it's about giving people the confidence to state their opinions and feel free enough to do that. It should be entertaining, not intimidating; fun, not fraught with indecision; all the while directing guests towards a pairing of food and wine that is as close to ideal as possible. In reality, it is so much more than this.

The bistronomy wine list places the unusual in a digestible narrative, one that is sharp, humane and always progressive. The relaxed nature of this approach to wine and the fun that it can create for the diner appeals to the growing number of people who know about wine and the even greater number who want to learn more about it. It meets the swelling ranks of those who might crave the differences in each vintage, celebrate nuance and desire wines that make them think, laugh and feel. It is an interconnection between the kitchen, the floor of the restaurant and the customer. It is crucial. And exactly what we need to ensure restaurants are humming with humankind.

BRAISED VEAL NECK, PUMPKIN AND SMOKED RICOTTA

CHEF: WESLEY YOUNG

SERVES 8

You will need to begin this recipe two days ahead.

20 g (¾ oz) caster (superfine) sugar
45 g (1½ oz) salt
2 bay leaves
1 tablespoon white peppercorns
2.5 kg (5 lb 8 oz) veal neck, halved lengthways, deboned, bones reserved
4 litres (140 fl oz/16 cups) homogenised milk
pumpkin seeds (pepitas), toasted, to serve

PUMPKIN RIBBONS

1.5 kg (3 lb 5 oz) Japanese pumpkin (winter squash)
1 tonka bean
1 clove
½ cinnamon stick
25 ml (¾ fl oz) apple cider vinegar

VEAL GLAZE

2 large onions, peeled, halved
500 g (1 lb 2 oz) carrots
500 g (1 lb 2 oz) celery stalks, leaves removed
500 ml (17 fl oz/2 cups) dry white wine
50 g (1 ¾ oz) foie gras fat
10 g (¼ oz) lactose (milk) powder, toasted

PUMPKIN JAM

3.5 kg (7 lb 14 oz) Japanese pumpkin (winter squash), peeled, deseeded, cut into 6 cm (2½ inch) cubes
2 tablespoons grapeseed oil
3 teaspoons apple cider vinegar

SMOKED RICOTTA

1.75 litres (60 fl oz/7 cups) milk
250 ml (9 fl oz/1 cup) thick (double/heavy) cream
250 ml (9 fl oz/1 cup) buttermilk
½ lemon, juice
wood chips, for smoking

Prepare a brine for the veal with the sugar, salt, bay leaves, peppercorns and 8 litres (280 fl oz/32 cups) of water in a large, heavy-based saucepan over medium heat. Bring to a simmer for 10 minutes. Remove from the heat and chill completely. Place the veal neck in the brining solution, cover and refrigerate for 12 hours.

Meanwhile, make the pumpkin ribbons. Peel and seed the pumpkin, then use a vegetable peeler or a slicer to make approximately 2 cups of thin pumpkin 'ribbons'. Juice the remaining pumpkin to yield 500 ml (17 fl oz/2 cups) of liquid. Put the liquid in a large saucepan over medium heat with the tonka bean, clove and cinnamon and simmer for 10 minutes. Skim and strain the juice mixture and season with the apple cider vinegar and salt. Allow to cool. Lay the pumpkin ribbons flat in a sous-vide bag, add the cooled pumpkin juice mixture and vacuum seal, then set aside for 10 hours.

Preheat the oven to 150°C (300°F/Gas 2). Remove the veal neck from the brine and rinse under cold running water. Char the veal neck on a charcoal barbecue to impart a smokiness to the meat. Put the neck into a large, deep-sided ovenproof pan and cover with the milk. Put the pan on the stovetop over medium heat and bring the contents to a boil, then remove from heat. Cover the contents with parchment paper and a lid then transfer to the oven and braise for 5 hours.

To make the veal glaze, preheat the oven to 220°C (425°F/Gas 7). Chop the reserved neck bones into 5 cm (2 inch) segments. Place in a roasting tin and roast in the oven for 40 minutes, turning them with a spoon until evenly browned. Remove from the oven and transfer the entire contents of the tin to a large stockpot. Put the vegetables into the roasting tin and sweat until caramelised. Deglaze the pan with the wine. Reduce by half, then pour the mixture into the stockpot with the bones. Cover with cold water, bring to a boil, then reduce the heat and simmer for 12 hours, skimming regularly. Strain the liquid into a clean saucepan, return to the heat and reduce by half or until the glaze coats the back of a spoon. Remove from the heat, and monte with the fois gras fat and toasted lactose powder. Cover with plastic wrap to prevent a skin from forming and set aside.

To make the pumpkin jam, toss the pumpkin pieces in the grapeseed oil and put them in a single layer in a wide, heavy-based saucepan or rondeau over medium heat and lightly caramelise the pumpkin on all sides. You want to cook the pumpkin to medium-rare; retaining a raw core with the exterior yielding to the touch. Remove from the heat and put the pumpkin in a blender. Purée to a thick chunky consistency. Season with salt and apple cider vinegar to taste.

To make the smoked ricotta, combine all the ingredients in a large saucepan and season lightly with salt. Bring to a simmer and cook until it is completely curdled, about 45 minutes. Line a colander with muslin (cheesecloth), set it over a bowl and pour the liquid through to strain out the curds. Leave the curds in the colander overnight in the refrigerator to extract even more moisture.

Preheat a coal-bedded kettle barbecue to low heat and set up for indirect grilling using the top rack. Add half of the wood chips around the coals and cook until smoke appears (3–4 minutes). It is very important for cold smoking to have your coal base well established and glowing before adding the wood chips. Once smoking turn off the heat. Lay the cheese curds on smoking trays and cold smoke for 30 minutes.

To assemble the dish, cut the pressed veal neck into 110 g (3¾ oz) portions and reheat in the glaze. Warm the pumpkin jam and place a large dollop onto each plate. Add 35 g (1¼ oz) of the smoked ricotta. Place a portion of veal neck beside the jam. Add the marinated pumpkin ribbons on top and garnish with toasted pumpkin seeds.

SADDLE OF RABBIT WITH SHOULDER AND LEG COTTAGE PIE

CHEF: ANTHONY DEMETRE

SERVES 4

You will need to begin this recipe two days ahead.

1 large tame rabbit (or 2 fat wild rabbits)
2 large pieces pig's caul
4 tablespoons olive oil
2 tablespoons butter
1 large carrot, diced
1 celery stalk, diced
1 brown onion, diced
4 garlic cloves, split in half
100 ml (3½ fl oz) white wine vinegar
300 ml (10½ fl oz) white wine
1.25 litres (44 fl oz/5 cups) chicken stock
6 tomatoes, blanched, peeled, chopped
1 bay leaf
1 rosemary stalk
1 tablespoon chopped tarragon
1 tablespoon chopped parsley
dehydrated blueberries, to serve
fresh Provençal almonds, to serve
honey glazed salsify, to serve
bee pollen, to serve
Tokyo turnip, raw ribbons, to serve
wilted lettuce, to serve

POTATO PURÉE

3 sebago potatoes, approximately 750 g (1 lb 10 oz)
180 g (6¼ oz) butter, cubed
50 ml (1¾ fl oz) milk, warm

To prepare the rabbit, remove the front and back legs, then remove the head and separate the thorax from the loins without piercing the skin. The two loins of meat should remain joined. Set aside. Remove the livers and kidneys and set aside. Reserve the bones for later use. Season the loins with salt and pepper. Put the liver and kidneys down the centre between the loin meat and roll the saddle, encasing the offal. Lay the pig's caul on a flat surface, place the rolled saddle at one edge and wrap the rabbit in the caul so it is completely encased. Tie with butcher's string to secure. Cover and leave to chill in the refrigerator.

To make the cottage pie, put 1 tablespoon of butter in a saucepan over medium heat with 3 tablespoons of olive oil and heat until foaming. Add the remaining rabbit pieces including the legs, head and backbone. Season generously and cook until golden. Remove the meat from the pan and set aside.

Add the remaining butter and olive oil and cook the carrot, celery, onion and garlic until they are just coloured. Return the rabbit pieces to the pan. Add the vinegar and reduce almost completely (about 1-2 minutes) then add the wine and reduce by two-thirds. Add the chicken stock, tomatoes, bay leaf and rosemary, bring to the boil and skim, then gently simmer for about 2 hours until the meat is tender.

Meanwhile, make the potato purée. Put the potatoes in a saucepan of cold salted water, simmer for 35–40 minutes until very tender. Drain and set aside in the saucepan to steam for 1–2 minutes, then press through a ricer or mouli grater back into the saucepan. Beat in the butter with a spatula, one cube at a time, stirring constantly over low heat (if mixture begins to split, add a little milk). Season to taste and keep warm.

Preheat the oven to 170°C (325°F/Gas 3). Lift the rabbit pieces out of the stock and set aside, then reduce the stock to a sauce consistency. Strain the sauce, reserving the vegetables for the pie. Pull the meat from the bones and combine with the vegetables and chopped herbs. Taste and season with salt and pepper. Place the mixture in four individual pie dishes with a few tablespoons of the sauce and a drizzle of olive oil. Top this with the potato purée. Sprinkle the pie with tarragon and parsley. Reserve the remaining sauce for the finished dish.

Take the saddle from the refrigerator 30 minutes before roasting and bring to room temperature to prevent the exterior becoming overcooked and tough. Bake the cottage pies in the oven for 40 minutes. Meanwhile, season the saddle with salt and pepper, colour it lightly in a frying pan then roast in the oven for about 10–15 minutes. Rest for 8 minutes, then carve it into slices.

To serve, place a piece of saddle on the plate. Loosely scatter the blueberries, almonds, salsify and bee pollen. Add a few turnip ribbons and pieces of wilted lettuce. Drizzle with the reserved sauce and serve with the cottage pie and potato puree to the side.

STAUB

LA POÉSIE COMESTIBLE

EDIBLE POETRY

The intersection of skill, restraint and first-line produce

RICOTTA, PLUMS AND LAVENDER

BURNT KUNZEA BLOSSOM CREAM

ICED LEMON PARFAIT, CONFIT FENNEL AND RASPBERRIES

FROZEN CURD, MANDARIN AND FENNEL

TONKA BEAN ICE CREAM, HAZELNUT CHOCOLATE, COOKIES AND BRITTLE

WARM PEAR CAKE AND LICORICE ICE CREAM

POOR KNIGHTS OF WINDSOR

RHUBARB MADELEINES

SWEET CORN AND APRICOT CUSTARD, APRICOTS, CORN CAKE AND SALTED ALMOND TOFFEE

SPICED DOUGHNUTS, BLOOD ORANGE CURD AND WHEY BUTTERSCOTCH

PANDAN ICE CREAM, TOASTED MILK AND MALT

QUINCE AND EARL GREY

SUMMER CHAMOMILE SEMIFREDDO, LICORICE ICE CREAM AND LEMON BALM MERINGUE

FRENCH TOAST, PRUNES AND FERMENTED MILK ICE CREAM

FENNEL STRAWBERRIES, STRAWBERRY GRANITA AND SOUR CREAM

LEMON AND YUZU CURD, COCONUT SORBET AND SPICED RUM

CARAMELISED PINEAPPLE, PINE NEEDLE SYRUP AND PINE NUT BRITTLE

CARROT CAKE, HONEYCOMB AND CARDAMOM CARAMEL CREAM

PEAR, CHOCOLATE AND CELERY

Olives
Almonds
Saucisson
Jambon bigorre
Fromages

RICOTTA, PLUMS AND LAVENDER

CHEF: SHAUN KELLY

SERVES 2

250 g (9 oz) excellent quality fresh ricotta
1 tablespoon icing (confectioners') sugar
100 g (3½ oz) caster (superfine) sugar
5 lavender stalks, including flower heads
12 mirabelle plums or 6 small plums, halved, stoned
1 teaspoon caster (superfine) sugar, extra
fruity olive oil (optional), to serve
edible flowers, to serve

Place the ricotta and icing sugar in a bowl and stir to combine. You may add more to taste but you don't want the ricotta to be overly sweet. Combine 125 ml (4 fl oz/½ cup) of water and the caster sugar in a medium saucepan. Add the lavender stalks and bring the mixture to the boil over low–medium heat. Simmer, then set aside to cool and allow the flavours to infuse. Strain into a clean bowl, reserving the flowers for serving. (You will have more syrup than you need, and can keep what's left over in an airtight container in the refrigerator for future use.)

Dust the cut side of the plum halves with the extra caster sugar. Put the plums in a large non-stick frying pan, cut side down, over medium heat to caramelise. Alternatively, use a blowtorch to caramelise the sugar to achieve a brûlée effect.

To serve, place a large dollop of the ricotta in the centre of each plate. Strew with the plum halves. Drizzle with the lavender syrup and decorate with the reserved lavender stalks. Sprinkle with a few drops of fruity olive oil, if using, and scatter with edible flowers.

Note: You can use dried lavender if fresh flowers are unavailable.

BURNT KUNZEA BLOSSOM CREAM

CHEF: LUKE BURGESS
SERVES 6

You will need to begin this recipe one day ahead.

1 litre (35 fl oz/4 cups) thin (pouring) cream
40 g (1½ oz) Kunzea blossoms
4 eggwhites
75 g (2½ oz/⅓ cup) sugar

JERUSALEM ARTICHOKE GRANITA
500 ml (17 fl oz/2 cups) jerusalem artichoke juice, from approximately 1 kg (2 lb 4 oz) jerusalem artichokes
200 ml (7 fl oz) sugar syrup
500 ml (17 fl oz/2 cups) still mineral water
2 g (1/16 oz) ascorbic acid
2 ml (1/16 fl oz) lemon juice

SABLÉ
140 g (5 oz) butter
55 g (2 oz/¼ cup) caster (superfine) sugar
3 egg yolks
160 g (5½ oz) plain (all-purpose) flour, sifted
90 g (3¼ oz) butter, extra, for the beurre noisette

Put the cream and Kunzea blossoms in a bowl and place in the refrigerator overnight for the flavour to infuse.

Meanwhile, combine the jerusalem artichoke juice, sugar syrup, mineral water, ascorbic acid and lemon juice in a freezer tray and put it in the freezer until firm and frozen. Scrape into ice crystals with a fork every couple of hours until a uniform granita is produced. Stand in the freezer for 4–6 hours, preferably overnight.

Preheat the oven to 180°C (350°F/Gas 4). To make the sablé, cream the butter and sugar until light and pale. Add the egg yolks, one at a time, until well combined. Gently fold the flour into the mixture until a dough forms. Cover and rest for 30 minutes. Roll the dough out between sheets of baking paper to 2 cm (¾ inch) thickness. Bake on a baking tray in the oven until golden brown.

To make the beurre noisette, put a frying pan over medium heat until hot. Add the butter and cook, swirling constantly, until it turns a nut-brown colour. Break the sablé into pieces and put it in a food processor. Purée on high speed, then reduce the speed to low and slowly add the warm beurre noisette until combined. Pour the liquid sablé into a 10 cm (4 inch) square freezerproof container lined with plastic wrap. Place in the freezer until set, preferably overnight.

Preheat the oven to 90°C (195°F/Gas ½). Strain the blossom cream through a fine sieve into a large bowl and add the eggwhites and sugar. Whisk gently until incorporated. Strain the cream and egg mixture through a fine sieve into a shallow ovenproof dish. Place the dish in a roasting tin, fill the tin with enough cold water to come almost to the top of the side of the dish. Bake for 35–45 minutes or until just set to the consistency of a crème brûlée. Remove the dish from the roasting tin, cool to room temperature, then cover and refrigerate for 3–3½ hours until completely chilled.

To serve, take a scoop of the Kunzea blossom cream and place it on a plate. Use a blowtorch to gently caramelise the top of the cream. Spoon some of the granita over the top of the cream. Remove the sablé from the freezer and use a mandolin to shave scrapings of sablé into a cold bowl — it should look like wood shavings. Scatter shavings onto the plate and serve immediately.

ICED LEMON PARFAIT, CONFIT FENNEL AND RASPBERRIES

CHEF: ANTHONY DEMETRE

SERVES 10

You will need to begin this recipe one day ahead.

160 ml (5¼ fl oz) lemon juice
150 g (5½ oz/⅔ cup) caster (superfine) sugar
160 g (5¾ oz) egg yolks
20 ml (½ fl oz) limoncello
½ sheet bronze-strength gelatine, bloomed
250 g (9 oz) thickened (whipping) cream
crushed meringue, to serve
fresh and dried raspberries, to serve
edible flowers and microgreens, to garnish

CONFIT FENNEL

5 small fennel bulbs
150 ml (5 fl oz) lemon juice
150 g (5½ oz/⅔ cup) caster (superfine) sugar

Put the lemon juice in a saucepan over medium heat and reduce the juice by half.

Mix 50 ml (1¾ fl oz) of water and the sugar in a saucepan over medium heat and cook to 118°C (244°F) using a sugar thermometer. Pour the syrup onto the egg yolks in a blender and blend at high speed for 5 minutes.

Put the reduced lemon juice and limoncello in a saucepan and gently warm over low heat. Add the bloomed gelatine and stir until dissolved.

Whip the cream to soft peaks and gently fold through the yolk mixture, then add the lemon juice mixture, folding until just incorporated. Spoon mixture into a piping bag then pipe into spherical moulds and freeze for at least 6 hours, preferably overnight.

To make the confit fennel, use a small knife to carefully trim the fennel bulbs and expose the central stalk, reserving the rest of the bulb for another use. Cut the stalks into 5 cm (2 inch) lengths. In a saucepan, combine the lemon juice and sugar. Bring to a simmer, stirring to dissolve the sugar. Remove from the heat and add the fennel stalks. Set aside to steep for 2 hours then strain, reserving the fennel pieces.

To serve, lay the fennel pieces in the centre of the serving bowls. Put the crushed meringue into a wide flat bowl. Dip the lemon parfait moulds in a bowl of hot water for 2 seconds (take care not to get any water in the parfait), slip a blunt knife down the inside of each mould to release the parfait, then turn out into the meringue and, working quickly, coat the parfait in the meringue before turning onto the confit fennel. Scatter with fresh and dried raspberries and garnish with edible flowers and microgreens. Serve immediately.

FROZEN CURD, MANDARIN AND FENNEL

CHEF: JOSH MURPHY

SERVES 4

330 g (11½ oz/1½ cups) caster (superfine) sugar
80 g (2¾ oz) glucose
5 g (1/8 oz)] sheets gold-strength gelatine, bloomed
80 g (2¾ oz) lemon juice
600 g (1 lb 5 oz) fromage frais
100 g (3½ oz) pumpkin seeds (pepitas)
50 g (1¾ oz) glucose, extra
½ teaspoon salt
1 ripe mandarin
4 freeze-dried mandarin segments, to serve

MANDARIN CURD

2 teaspoons cornflour (cornstarch)
300 ml (10½ fl oz) mandarin juice
3 mandarins, zest
250 g (9 oz) caster (superfine) sugar
1½ sheets gold-strength gelatine, bloomed
100 g (3½ oz) butter, cold, cubed

MACERATED FENNEL

250 g (9 oz) caster (superfine) sugar
1 fennel bulb

CRYSTALLISED FENNEL FRONDS

1 eggwhite
12 small fennel fronds
caster (superfine) sugar, to coat

To make the frozen curd, combine the sugar, glucose, gelatine, lemon juice and fromage frais with 600 ml (21 fl oz) of water in a bowl until well incorporated. Divide between Pacojet canisters and freeze then churn, or churn in an ice-cream machine according to the manufacturer's instructions. Keep in the freezer until ready to serve.

To make the mandarin curd, mix the cornflour with 60 ml (2 fl oz/¼ cup) of mandarin juice. Combine the remaining juice, mandarin zest and sugar with the cornflour mixture in a heatproof bowl over a saucepan of simmering water, stirring continuously until the mixture begins to thicken. Add gelatine and combine thoroughly. Whisk the butter into the mixture cube by cube until it is all incorporated. Transfer to an airtight container and set aside until ready to serve.

To make the macerated fennel, combine the sugar with 300 ml (10½ fl oz) of water in a heavy-based saucepan and bring to a simmer. Once the sugar has completely dissolved, remove from the heat. Discard any unsuitable outer pieces of fennel, then halve the fennel bulb and remove the core with a sharp knife. Slice the fennel very thinly with a mandolin. Lay the fennel in a plastic dish with 5 cm (2 inch) high sides and pour the warm sugar syrup over. Leave to cool in the dish.

Preheat the oven to 160°C (315°F/Gas 2–3). Spread the pumpkin seeds on a baking tray and warm in the oven for 3 minutes. Remove from the oven and put the seeds in a bowl with the glucose and salt, stirring to coat. Line a baking tray with baking paper and spread the coated pumpkin seeds evenly on the tray. Bake in the oven for 18 minutes until golden.

To make the crystallised fennel fronds, whisk the eggwhite. Gently coat each fennel frond in eggwhite. Coat each side of the frond in caster sugar and dehydrate in a dehydrator or oven at 55°C (130°F) for 6 hours.

Peel the mandarin and separate the segments. Using a small sharp knife, scrape away the pith from each mandarin segment. Dip each segment in clean, cold water and lay on a clean cloth to dry.

Place a tablespoon of mandarin curd in each bowl. Scatter some pumpkin seeds and mandarin segments in the bowls. Drain the macerated fennel and lay three pieces per serve over the curd and pumpkin seeds. Put 3 pieces of crystallised fennel frond on each plate, and crush a small spoonful of freeze-dried mandarin segments over the garnishes. Finish each plate with a large scoop of the frozen curd.

TONKA BEAN ICE CREAM, HAZELNUT CHOCOLATE, COOKIES AND BRITTLE

CHEF: WESLEY YOUNG

SERVES 6–8

You will need to begin this recipe one day ahead.

12 egg yolks
150 g (5½ oz) sugar
300 ml (10½ fl oz) milk
700 ml (24 fl oz) thin (pouring) cream
1 tonka bean (grated)

CHOCOLATE COOKIES

225 g (8 oz/1½ cups) plain (all-purpose) flour
80 g (2¾ oz/¾ cup) cocoa powder
220 g (7¾ oz/1 cup) caster (superfine) sugar
¼ teaspoon salt
¼ teaspoon bicarbonate of soda (baking soda)
200 g (7 oz) butter, cubed, softened
3 teaspoons milk
1 vanilla bean, seeds scraped

HAZELNUT CHOCOLATE CREAM

80 g (2¾ oz) caster sugar
400 g (14 oz) double (heavy) cream
200 g (7 oz) hazelnuts, toasted
175 g (6 oz) dark chocolate, finely chopped

HAZELNUT BRITTLE

vegetable oil, for greasing
220 g (7¾ oz/1 cup) caster sugar
60 g (2¼ oz) butter
50 ml (1½ fl oz) rice syrup
225 g (8 oz) hazelnuts, roasted, roughly chopped

Using an electric mixer, whisk the egg yolks and sugar for 2–3 minutes on high speed until pale. Combine the milk, cream and tonka bean in a heavy-based saucepan, bring to the boil over medium heat, then pour in the egg yolk mixture, whisking to combine. Strain into a clean saucepan and cook over low heat, stirring constantly until the mixture coats the back of a spoon. Strain into a bowl placed over an ice bath, then stir occasionally until chilled. Freeze in an ice-cream machine according to the manufacturer's instructions. Freeze for 6 hours or overnight.

Preheat the oven to 175°C (345°F/Gas 3–4). Mix all the dry ingredients for the chocolate cookies in a large bowl. Incorporate the butter then add the milk and vanilla seeds, stirring until well combined. Turn out the mixture onto a large sheet of plastic wrap and roll into a 5 cm (2 inch) diameter log. Wrap tightly and refrigerate for 2 hours. Thinly slice into 3 cm (1¼ inch) slices. Lay the slices on a large baking tray lined with baking paper and bake for about 10–15 minutes, or until just cooked through.

To make the hazelnut chocolate cream, put the sugar in a saucepan with 1 tablespoon of water and place over medium heat. Heat until the sugar dissolves, bring to the boil and cook for 4–5 minutes until caramelised. Add the cream (be careful, hot caramel will spit) and whisk to combine. Working quickly, add the hazelnuts, then pour the mixture into a blender and blend until smooth. Pour the warm mixture over the chopped dark chocolate in a bowl, and stir until the chocolate has melted and the ingredients are thoroughly combined.

To make the brittle, brush a baking tray with vegetable oil and set aside. Combine the sugar, butter, rice syrup and 75 ml (2¼ fl oz) of water in a saucepan over high heat and cook for 20–30 minutes until golden and caramelised, stirring occasionally to prevent the caramel from sticking to the base. Add the hazelnuts, stir to combine and pour onto the prepared tray. Set aside in a cool, dark place for 1 hour to cool and set. When set, break into pieces and set aside until serving. Brittle will keep in an airtight container in a cool, dry, dark place for 2–3 days.

To assemble, thickly smear the hazelnut chocolate cream on a serving plate. Scoop generous quenelles of the tonka bean ice cream on top. Scatter with pieces of the hazelnut brittle and crumble chocolate cookies over the top.

WARM PEAR CAKE AND LICORICE ICE CREAM

CHEF: JAMES KNAPPETT

SERVES 8

You will need to begin this recipe one day ahead.

250 g (9 oz) unsalted butter
300 g (10½ oz) sugar
4 eggs
3 tablespoons milk
300 g (10½ oz/2 cups) plain (all-purpose) flour, sifted
2 teaspoons baking powder
3 taylor's gold pears (or best in season) peeled, cored
2 tablespoons brown sugar
1 bunch sweet cicely or fresh licorice herb, leaves picked, to serve

LICORICE ICE CREAM

500 ml (17 fl oz/2 cups) milk
500 ml (17 fl oz/2 cups) cream
125 g (4½ oz) licorice, chopped
250 g (9 oz) egg yolks
200 g (7 oz) caster (superfine) sugar
25 ml (1 fl oz) Sambuca (anise-flavoured liqueur)

LICORICE POWDER

250 g (9 oz) licorice sticks

To make the licorice ice cream, gently heat the milk, cream and licorice in a large saucepan until boiling. Add to a blender and purée until smooth. Place the egg yolks and sugar in a bowl and whisk until thick and pale. Pour the licorice mixture and Sambuca into the yolk mixture and whisk to combine. Strain the mixture into a large saucepan and place over low heat. Stir constantly until the mixture thickly coats the back of a spoon. Strain into a clean bowl and refrigerate until chilled. Freeze in an ice-cream machine according to the manufacturer's instructions, then transfer to a container and freeze until required.

To make the licorice powder, line a baking tray with baking paper, put the licorice sticks on the tray and bake overnight in the oven at 65°C (145°F). Alternatively dry out in a dehydrator for 4–6 hours. Depending on the type of licorice used, dehydrating times may vary. Put the dried licorice in a spice grinder and grind to a powder consistency. Set aside until ready to serve.

To make the pear cake, preheat the oven to 180°C (350°F/Gas 4), grease and line a 20 cm (8 inch) square cake tin with baking paper and set aside. Beat the butter and sugar using an electric mixer until pale and creamy. Add the eggs one at a time until incorporated, then add the milk. Sift in the combined flour and baking powder. Mix slowly. Once combined, pour the cake mixture into the prepared tin, ensuring the mixture is distributed evenly. Cut 2 of the pears into small chunks and press into the mix. Sprinkle the brown sugar on the top and bake for 40–50 minutes or until golden on top and a skewer inserted in the centre comes out clean.

To assemble, place pieces of cake slightly off-centre in bowls and lean two slivers of the remaining pear against the cake. Place one scoop of licorice ice cream next to the cake and sprinkle the entire dish with licorice powder. To finish, garnish with sweet cicely or licorice herb.

POOR KNIGHTS OF WINDSOR

CHEF: SHAUN KELLY

SERVES 6

You will need to begin this recipe one day ahead.

VANILLA BEAN ICE CREAM

2 vanilla beans
375 ml (13 fl oz/1½ cups) milk
450 ml (16 fl oz) thin (pouring) cream
5 egg yolks
150 g (5½ oz) caster (superfine) sugar

BRIOCHE

300 g (12 oz/2⅓ cups) plain (all-purpose) flour, sifted, plus extra for dusting
15 g (½ oz) fresh yeast
125 ml (4 fl oz/½ cup) tepid milk
5 egg yolks, at room temperature, lightly whisked
30 g (1 oz) brown sugar
30 g (1 oz) caster (superfine) sugar
150 g (5½ oz) butter, cubed, at room temperature, plus extra for greasing
25 ml (¾ fl oz) milk, whisked with 1 egg yolk, for egg wash
100 g (3½ oz) butter, extra, to serve
icing (confectioners') sugar, for dusting (optional)

CUSTARD

1 vanilla bean
250 ml (9 fl oz/1 cup) milk
250 ml (9 fl oz/1 cup) thin (pouring) cream
6 egg yolks
150 g (5½ oz) caster (superfine) sugar

To make the ice cream, scrape the seeds from the vanilla beans into a saucepan and add the milk and cream. Put the saucepan over medium heat and bring to a simmer. Whisk the egg yolks and sugar together in a bowl before gradually pouring the hot cream mix over, whisking constantly to combine. Strain the mixture into a clean saucepan and cook over low heat until the mixture coats the back of a wooden spoon. Refrigerate until cool before churning in an ice-cream machine according to the manufacturer's instructions. Freeze overnight.

To make the brioche, combine the flour and a pinch of salt in a large bowl. In another bowl, whisk the yeast, 125 ml (4 fl oz/½ cup) of water, the tepid milk, egg yolks, brown sugar and caster sugar until well combined. Set aside until bubbles appear on the surface (up to 10 minutes). Add this to the flour mixture and combine with your hands until the dough is a sticky consistency and just comes together. Cover with plastic wrap and set aside in a warm place for 20 minutes.

Turn the dough out onto a lightly floured flat surface and knead for 15–20 minutes, adding the butter a few cubes at a time, making sure each piece is fully incorporated before adding more. The dough should appear smooth and shiny. Lightly flour the dough and return to the bowl. Cover with plastic wrap and refrigerate for 1 hour.

Take the dough out of the refrigerator, shape it into a loaf approximately 25 x 15 cm (10 x 6 inches) and place it seam side down in a greased and lined 500 g (1 lb 2 oz) loaf (bar) tin. Set aside, covered, to rest for 1 hour or return to the refrigerator to rest for 1 hour, ensuring that it is removed from the refrigerator and rested at room temperature for at least 30 minutes before baking.

Preheat the oven to 220°C (425°F/Gas 7). Brush the dough with egg wash. Turn the oven down to 180°C (350°F/Gas 4) and bake for 35–40 minutes, being careful not to burn the top. Remove from the oven and allow to cool in the tin before turning out onto a wire rack to cool completely. Thickly slice the brioche.

On the day of serving, make the custard. Scrape the seeds from the vanilla bean into a saucepan and add the milk and cream. Put the saucepan over medium heat and bring to a simmer. Whisk the egg yolks with the sugar in a bowl and pour in the hot cream mixture while continuing to whisk, then transfer to a clean saucepan. Cook, stirring constantly, over low-medium heat until the mixture is thick enough to coat the back of a wooden spoon. Strain into a deep-sided tray, add the slices of brioche and stand in the refrigerator for 1 hour, turning once to ensure the brioche has been properly submerged in the custard.

Heat one-third of the extra butter in a frying pan over medium-high heat until foaming, add 2 soaked brioche slices and cook, turning once, until golden (2–3 minutes each side), then transfer to a baking tray. Repeat with the remaining butter and brioche slices, wiping the frying pan clean between batches. Warm in the oven for 5 minutes, then serve, dusted with icing sugar, if using, with a scoop of the vanilla bean ice cream.

THE FOOD

Good food is good food and in our ambulance-chasing need for what's new and what's next, we often lose sight of that.

But the food of bistronomy, with its beguiling proposition of minimal intervention, multiple styles and cleverly handled ingredients, makes its supposedly casual dining a serious proposition.

Bistronomy is a culinary mutt. There is no genre or formula to the food. It is an intriguing culmination of bits, bobs and chef's whims filtered through a range of dishes that are casual but precise, embrace boisterous flavours, while keeping them clean and sharp. The background is often French but the muse is sensible modernism where newness is not necessarily the important thing. Dishes traverse between rib-sticking simplicity and obscurity on the plate and back again. The food isn't easy or expected. At times there is an almost incongruous dichotomy of subtle and slap-in-the-face flavour profiles in dishes that regularly incorporate frugality and creativity; or of high and low where street-food-inspired lobster rolls might sit alongside dishes involving consommés, mousses and the sort of soufflés that would make Escoffier cry.

Sometimes they are sophisticated and not particularly obvious flavours. The chefs go off-piste, paring outwardly opposing flavours and techniques with stunning results. They present us with a fascinating collection of unpredictable dishes in a food language you can taste and feel. Offcuts, offal and unusual cuts are celebrated on the bistronomy menu, which features those parts of animals too often discarded. This approach is consistent with the bistronomy style, of utilising everything and maximising flavour; it is also a nod to the thriftiness necessary for the chef–proprietor model and ensuring they maintain affordable price points. There might be seared scallops with a carpaccio of pig's head, a salted chicory root iced mousse with vanilla rice pudding, a crisp lamb breast with delightfully old-fashioned mint sauce or potatoes doused in beurre noisette, air-dried tuna and coffee. And onwards it goes.

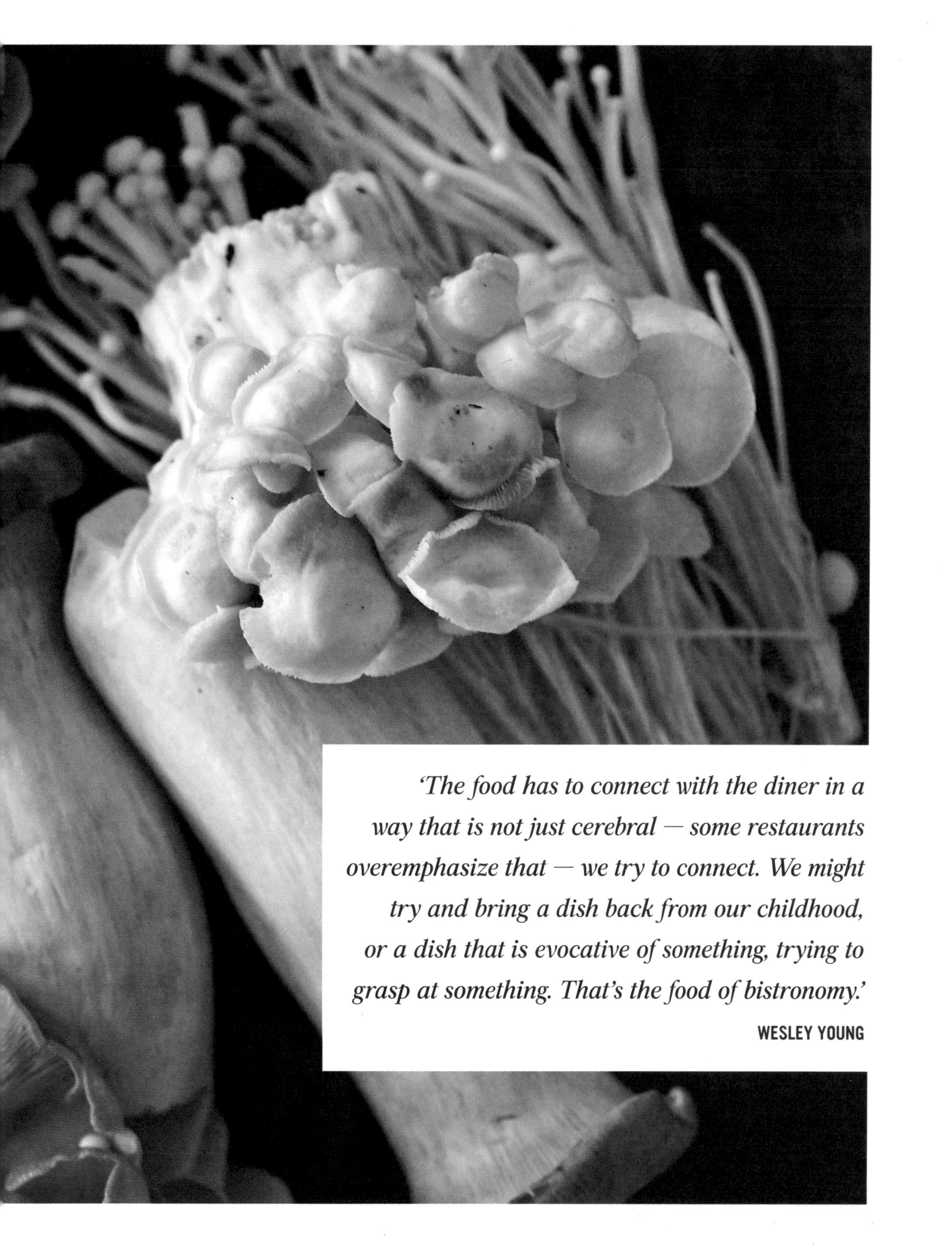

'The food has to connect with the diner in a way that is not just cerebral — some restaurants overemphasize that — we try to connect. We might try and bring a dish back from our childhood, or a dish that is evocative of something, trying to grasp at something. That's the food of bistronomy.'

WESLEY YOUNG

'It's like a dirty love triangle of foraged ingredients, earthy flavours executed with some serious technique and delicious food memories; all seasoned with heaping spoonfuls of nostalgia.'

DAN PEARSON

There is a definite balance between simplicity and technique at play where, in the hands of a great chef, the worked food appears to be intrinsically humble on the plate. At times the dishes may not win beauty pageants but their sometimes oafish looks belie the beauty of their taste and the technique in their construction; or the chef may pull out the tweezers to create a dish of portraitlike perfection. Nothing is constant and the rules continually change. It is these complications and contradictions that work together to build a marvelous sense of harmony and a stunning visual feat on the plate.

The food of bistronomy is the kind of eating experience that makes you a partner in an imminent adventure; part spice detective; part ingredient evangelist; part pusher of rare and esoteric flavors. It's lip-smacking stuff and every bite makes you a believer as potential meets skill and anything seems possible. The tasting plates are an exercise in miniaturisation, a series of shaped intense meals of tiny tastes where the flavours punch and kick and punch again. It is big-fisted stuff. The food of bistronomy is sexy, refined, rustic and filled with soul; the experience of eating it joyful, funny, unexpected and life affirming. It's the stuff of life.

You get to embrace that rabbit-out-of-a-hat flash; tasting the precise Houdini moment when a chef seems to pull together an unexpected dish or flavour combination only to discover that it works perfectly. It's food that makes you think, not just about your own dining habits, but about flavour combinations, textures, and, most importantly, the act of eating. It's unique. And it works.

RHUBARB MADELEINES

CHEF: DAN PEARSON
MAKES: 25 LARGE OR 40 SMALL MADELEINES

You will need to begin this recipe one day ahead.

500 g (1 lb 2 oz) rhubarb
1 orange, zest and juice
3 heaped tablespoons raw (demerara) sugar
20 g (¾ oz) fresh ginger
300 g (10½ oz) caster (superfine) sugar
300 g (10½ oz) eggwhites (approximately 10 eggs)
120 g (4¼ oz) cake flour, sifted
120 g (4¼ oz) almond meal, sifted
300 g (10½ oz) butter
icing (confectioners') sugar, to dust

Put the rhubarb, orange zest and juice, raw sugar and ginger in a bowl. Cover tightly with plastic wrap to seal and leave overnight in the refrigerator to marinate. Remove the rhubarb, discard the marinating liquid, dice the rhubarb into 2 cm (¾ inch) cubes and set aside.

Preheat the oven to 180°C (350°F/Gas 4), grease the madeleine moulds and set aside.

Make a beurre noisette by heating a frying pan over medium heat until hot, add the butter and cook, swirling constantly, until it turns a nut-brown colour. Mix the caster sugar and eggwhites in an electric mixer until soft peaks form. Add the sifted flour and almond meal a little at a time to prevent the mixture from clumping. Fold the beurre noisette gently through the madeleine mixture. Transfer the mixture to a piping (icing) bag and place in the refrigerator until firm (about 2 hours before use). Pipe the madeleine mixture into the moulds until they are three-quarters full. Gently place a piece of marinated rhubarb in the centre of each madeleine and bake in the oven for 10–12 minutes or until they are golden brown and spring back lightly to the touch. Turn out to cool on a wire rack. Dust with icing sugar before serving.

SWEET CORN AND APRICOT CUSTARD, APRICOTS, CORN CAKE AND SALTED ALMOND TOFFEE

CHEF: MICHAEL CABALLO

SERVES 4

4 apricots, halved, stones removed and reserved
100 g (3½ oz) caster (superfine) sugar
1 tablespoon Lillet Blanc
1 lemon, zest
5 pineapple sage leaves
125 ml (4 fl oz/½ cup) milk
125 ml (4 fl oz/½ cup) thin (pouring) cream
70 g (2½ oz) honey
60 g (2¼ oz) corn kernels
½ vanilla bean, split
2 eggs
½ lemon, juice
4 pineapple sage leaves, extra, rolled, thinly sliced

CORN CAKE

60 g (2¼ oz) butter
55 g (2 oz/¼ cup) caster (superfine) sugar
90 g (3¼ oz/¼ cup) honey
1 teaspoon finely grated lemon zest
½ vanilla bean, seeds scraped
1 egg
75 g (2½ oz/½ cup) plain (all-purpose) flour
50 g (1¾ oz/¼ cup) cornmeal (polenta)
1 teaspoon baking powder
⅛ teaspoon bicarbonate of soda (baking soda)
½ teaspoon salt
60 ml (2 fl oz/¼ cup) buttermilk
100g (3½ oz/½ cup) corn kernels

SALTED ALMOND TOFFEE

olive oil, for greasing
125 g (4½ oz/1 cup) slivered almonds, toasted
120 g (4¼ oz) caster (superfine) sugar
40 g (1½ oz) brown sugar
1 teaspoon sea salt
60 g (2¼ oz) butter
¼ teaspoon bicarbonate of soda (baking soda)

Preheat the oven to 175°C (345°F/Gas 3–4). Place the apricot halves in a single layer in the base of a high-sided baking dish. Combine 200 ml (7 fl oz) of water, the sugar, Lillet Blanc, half the lemon zest and the pineapple sage in a saucepan. Bring just to a simmer and cook for 5 minutes to combine the flavours and dissolve the sugar. Turn off the heat and allow to infuse for 10 minutes. Return to a simmer, then immediately pour over the apricots. Let the apricots cool completely in the liquid.

To make the custard, spread the reserved apricot stones on a baking tray and bake for 10 minutes. Allow to cool, then crack each stone in half with a nutcracker or meat mallet. Remove the kernels and discard the stone carcass. Combine the apricot kernels with the milk, cream, honey, corn, vanilla bean, remaining lemon zest and a tiny pinch of salt in a saucepan over medium heat and bring to a simmer for 2 minutes. Remove from the heat, cover and allow the flavour to infuse for 10 minutes. Strain and reserve. In a large bowl, whisk the eggs until smooth, then slowly add the strained milk mixture until combined. Pour into a 20 cm (8 inch) square baking dish, so the liquid comes roughly 2.5 cm (1 inch) up the sides. Bake, uncovered, for 45–60 minutes or until completely set and the centre barely trembles. The objective is to cook through rather than having a slightly runny centre as you might with a crème brûlée. Allow the custard to cool to room temperature, then pour into a blender and blend until smooth. Cover and refrigerate to cool.

To make the corn cake, grease and line a 20 cm (8 inch) round cake tin. Beat the butter and sugar in bowl of an electric mixer until light and fluffy. Add the honey, lemon zest and vanilla seeds and beat until smooth. Add the egg and beat until smooth.

Sift the dry ingredients into a bowl and stir to combine. Add half of the flour mix to the cake batter, alternating with the buttermilk, until all the ingredients are just combined. Gently fold in the corn kernels and pour the batter into the prepared cake tin, spreading it out evenly. Bake for 20 minutes or until a skewer inserted in the centre comes out clean, the top is lightly golden, and the sides begin to pull away from tin. Allow to cool in the tin on a wire rack, then remove from the tin and cut into four wedges.

To make the salted almond toffee, grease a small baking sheet with olive oil and spread the toasted almonds in a single layer. In a small saucepan over low heat, combine the sugar, brown sugar, salt and butter, stirring until completely dissolved. Increase the heat until the mixture becomes light caramel in colour and measures 150°C (300°F) on a sugar thermometer. Immediately remove from the heat, stir in the bicarbonate of soda, and pour over the toasted almonds. Allow to cool, then break into pieces. Put the broken pieces in a food processor and pulse in short bursts until the toffee forms soft crumbs.

When ready to serve dessert, heat a frying pan over medium–high heat. Butter all sides of the corn cake wedges and toast in the frying pan until golden on all sides. Spoon the custard into shallow bowls. Top with toasted corn cake and poached apricots. Sprinkle with almond toffee crumbs and thinly sliced sage leaves.

SPICED DOUGHNUTS, BLOOD ORANGE CURD AND WHEY BUTTERSCOTCH

CHEF: MATT GERMANCHIS

MAKES 40 DOUGHNUTS

45 g (1½ oz) fresh yeast (or 22 g/¾ oz dried yeast)
180 g (6¼ oz) butter
1.5 kg (3 lb 5 oz/10 cups) strong flour
750 ml (26 fl oz/3 cups) milk
120 g (4¼ oz) caster (superfine) sugar
30 g (1 oz) salt
6 eggs
vegetable oil, for deep-frying
whipped cream, to serve

BLOOD ORANGE CURD

6 blood oranges, peeled
200 g (7 oz) butter
caster (superfine) sugar, to taste

SPICED SUGAR

2 blood oranges, zest dried
1 vanilla bean, seeds scraped
10 g (¼ oz) dried mint leaves
2 star anise
100 g (3½ oz) caster (superfine) sugar

WHEY BUTTERSCOTCH

500 ml (17 fl oz/2 cups) buttermilk or yoghurt
150 g (5½ oz) caster (superfine) sugar
150 g (5½ oz) sour cream
40 g (1½ oz) butter

To make the blood orange curd, preheat the oven to 160°C (315°F/Gas 2–3). Wrap the blood oranges and 100 g (3½ oz) of the butter in baking paper, tie with butcher's string to seal and cook for 4 hours or until soft. Put the orange mixture, remaining butter and the sugar into a blender and purée until smooth. Strain and refrigerate.

To make the doughnut batter, put the yeast, butter and flour in the bowl of a food processor and rub together. Add the milk, caster sugar, salt and eggs and mix on low to medium speed, using the dough hook, until a dough forms. Increase the speed to high and continue to mix for about 10 minutes until smooth and shiny. Form into 60 g (2¼ oz) balls for large doughnuts or 20 g (¾ oz) balls for small doughnuts. Set aside to prove for about 1–1½ hours until they have doubled in size. Cover the balls with a tea towel (dish towel) or plastic wrap to prevent a crust forming on the outside.

Prepare the spiced sugar by putting the orange zest, vanilla seeds, mint and star anise in a spice grinder and pulsing until they become powder. Pour into a bowl, add the sugar and stir to combine.

To make the whey butterscotch, heat the buttermilk or yoghurt in a medium saucepan over very low heat and gradually bring to 90°C (195°F) using a sugar thermometer or until you begin to see the mixture split into curds and whey. Remove from the heat and strain through a fine sieve. Reserve 100 ml (3½ fl oz) of the whey (liquid) and set aside.

Place the sugar in a stainless steel saucepan and cook over medium heat until it begins to caramelise. Add 100 ml (3½ fl oz) of whey and continue to heat gently for a further 5 minutes until the mixture reaches soft-ball stage or 110°C (225°F) on a sugar thermometer. Add the sour cream and reduce for 5 minutes, stirring constantly. Remove from the heat, then gradually whisk in the butter.

Heat the vegetable oil in a large, heavy-based saucepan or deep-fryer to 175°C (345°F) or until a cube of bread dropped into the oil turns brown in 15–20 seconds. Deep-fry the doughnuts in batches, turning occasionally, until golden and puffed (3–4 minutes on each side). Take care, as the hot oil will spit. Drain on paper towel. Roll each doughnut in the spiced sugar then, while still warm, pierce a hole in one end and pipe blood orange curd into the centre.

To serve, place the doughnuts in serving bowls and spoon the whey butterscotch over. Add a quenelle of whipped cream dusted with spiced sugar.

PANDAN ICE CREAM, TOASTED MILK AND MALT

CHEF: KARL FIRLA

SERVES 6–8

You will need to begin this recipe one day ahead.

10 ribbons pandan leaf
1.25 litres (44 fl oz/5 cups) milk
500 ml (17 fl oz/2 cups) cream
6 egg yolks
130 g (4¾ oz) caster (superfine) sugar
100 g (3½ oz) popped popcorn, to serve
100 g (3½ oz) rye breadcrumbs, toasted, to serve

MALT GEL

1 teaspoon dark malt powder
2 g (1/16 oz) agar-agar
1 tablespoon brown sugar

MILK JAM

395 g (14 oz) tin condensed milk

TOASTED MILK

250 ml (9 fl oz/1 cup) milk
50 ml (1¾ fl oz) milk, extra

To make the ice cream, put the pandan leaf, milk and cream in a large saucepan over medium heat. Bring to a simmer then remove from the heat, cover and refrigerate overnight to allow the flavours to infuse. Remove the pandan leaves. Put the egg yolks and sugar in the bowl of an electric mixer and beat until pale and fluffy. Add the mixture to the saucepan of infused milk and place over medium heat. Bring the mixture to 85°C (185°F) then allow to cool completely. Churn in an ice-cream machine according to the manufacturer's instructions. Freeze overnight.

To make the malt gel, put all the ingredients in a saucepan with 100 ml (3½ fl oz) of cold water. Place over low to medium heat and bring to a simmer. Set aside to cool until the mixture becomes quite solid. Break up into pieces, add to a bowl and purée with a stick blender until a toothpaste-like consistency is achieved. Set aside.

To make the milk jam, preheat the oven to 220°C (425°F/Gas 7). Pour the condensed milk into a heatproof baking dish. Place the dish in a roasting tin. Pour water into the tin to come halfway up the side of the baking dish. Cover the tin with foil and bake, refilling with water if necessary, for 1¾ hours or until the milk is dark golden. Season with salt and whisk until smooth.

For the toasted milk, heat the milk in an ovenproof frying pan over medium heat. When the milk comes to a simmer, place in the oven at 190°C (375°F/Gas 5) and allow a skin to form (about 5 minutes). Remove the skin carefully from the pan and set aside on a plate. Add extra milk to the pan and repeat the process. The skin will be ready when it appears crustlike and takes on a golden appearance.

To serve, drag a spoonful of milk jam across the base of each plate. Scatter with the popped popcorn and rye breadcrumbs. Dollop 1–2 teaspoons of malt gel on the plate. Add 1–2 spoonfuls of pandan ice cream and gently place toasted milk pieces on top.

QUINCE AND EARL GREY

CHEF: SCOTT PICKETT
SERVES 4

You will need to begin this recipe four days ahead.

1 quince
500 ml (17 fl oz/2 cups) red wine
200 ml (7 fl oz) Port (tawny)
1 clove
1 cinnamon stick
1 star anise
½ bay leaf
½ vanilla bean, seeds scraped
1 orange, peel, juice
50 ml (1¾ fl oz) red wine vinegar
100 g (3½ oz) caster (superfine) sugar
freeze-dried mandarin segments, to serve
red-veined sorrel cress, to serve

EARL GREY ICE CREAM
250 ml (9 fl oz/1 cup) milk
250 ml (9 fl oz/1 cup) thin (pouring) cream
10 g (¼ oz) Earl Grey tea leaves
8 egg yolks
100 g (3½ oz) caster (superfine) sugar

PAIN D'ÉPICES
3 eggs, separated
50 g (1¾ oz) caster (superfine) sugar
125 g (4½ oz) treacle or molasses
125 g (4½ oz) honey
125 ml (4 fl oz/½ cup) milk
1 lemon, juice
½ vanilla bean, seeds scraped
250 g (9 oz) rye flour
20 g (¾ oz) baking powder
2 teaspoons mixed spice
1 teaspoon ground ginger

ORANGE GEL
500 ml (17 fl oz/2 cups) orange juice, freshly squeezed
5 g (⅛ oz) agar-agar

Peel the quince and leave uncovered to dry overnight in the refrigerator. Cut into quarters and remove the core. Put the red wine, port, spices, bay leaf, vanilla bean, orange peel, vinegar and caster sugar in a saucepan and bring to a gentle boil, then remove from the heat and allow to cool. Add the quince, cover and marinate for 2 days in the refrigerator. Seal the mixture in a sous-vide bag and cook in a waterbath at 75°C (165°F) for 12–16 hours. Strain, reserving the quince and the liquid in separate containers.

Make the Earl Grey ice cream by putting the milk, cream and tea leaves in a saucepan and gently warming over low heat to allow the flavours to infuse. Remove, cover and place in the refrigerator overnight to steep. Strain into a clean saucepan and warm over low heat. Beat the egg yolks and sugar together until thick and creamy, then slowly add to the milk mixture in the saucepan, stirring constantly. Cook until it reaches the consistency of custard and coats the back of a spoon, stirring constantly so it doesn't catch. Strain into a large bowl and place over an ice bath to chill. Churn in an ice-cream machine according to the manufacturer's instructions and freeze overnight.

Preheat the oven to 160°C (315°F/Gas 2–3). Grease and line a loaf (bar) tin and set aside. To make the pain d'épices, put the egg yolks and sugar in the bowl of an electric mixer and beat until pale and thick. Add the remaining wet ingredients, stirring gently to incorporate. Slowly incorporate the dry ingredients until well combined. Pour into the loaf tin and bake for 30-45 minutes or until it is golden and springs back lightly to the touch. Allow to cool completely before breaking into a crumb. Place in a dehydrator or oven at 80°C (175°F/Gas ¼–½) for 6 hours or until hard.

To make the orange gel, combine the juice and agar-agar in a saucepan over low to medium heat and slowly bring to the boil. Pour the liquid into a tray and leave to set. When it has hardened, cut it into rough pieces. Put the pieces in a blender and blend until a purée forms, adding a tablespoon of orange juice to loosen if needed.

To serve, warm the quince quarters in the poaching liquid in a saucepan over low heat. Cut each quarter of quince into 3 pieces. Arrange pieces of quince on a serving plate and scatter generously with the pain d'épices crumb. Pipe dots of orange gel purée beside the quince pieces. Add 3 pieces of broken mandarin and a scoop of Earl Grey ice cream. Scatter with sprigs of sorrel cress. Serve with a small jug of the poaching liquid on the side.

SUMMER CHAMOMILE SEMIFREDDO, LICORICE ICE CREAM AND LEMON BALM MERINGUE

CHEF: ARI TAYMOR

SERVES 10

You will need to begin this recipe three days ahead.

400 ml (14 fl oz) cream
20 g (¾ oz) fresh chamomile flowers, substitute dried if not available
125 ml (4 fl oz/½ cup) milk
150 g (5½ oz) caster (superfine) sugar
150 g (5½ oz) egg yolk
1½ sheets silver-strength gelatine, bloomed
65 g (2¼ oz) eggwhite
110 g (3¾ oz/½ cup) caster (superfine) sugar, extra
flowering herbs, such as chamomile, fennel, tarragon, to garnish

LICORICE ICE CREAM

650 ml (22½ fl oz) milk
100 g (3½ oz) caster (superfine) sugar
100 g (3½ oz) honey
10 g (¼ oz) licorice powder
30 g (1 oz) fennel seeds, toasted
5 g (⅛ oz) iota carrageenan
250 g (9 oz) egg yolk

LEMON BALM MERINGUE

100 g (3½ oz) lemon balm leaves
200 g (7 oz) caster (superfine) sugar
30 g (1 oz) eggwhite powder
1 eggwhite

SORREL SAUCE

150 g (5½ oz) sorrel leaves
40 g (1½ oz) sugar
1 g (1/32 oz) citric acid
xanthan gum, to thicken

Steep chamomile flowers in cream overnight. Strain, chill and whip the cream to firm peaks.

In a saucepan over low heat, mix 50 g of the chamomile cream with the milk and caster sugar. Gradually add the egg yolk, stirring constantly, and cook gently until thick. Remove from the heat. Squeeze the excess water from the gelatine, add to the mix and stir until dissolved. Cool completely. Whip the eggwhite and extra caster sugar to firm peaks. Gently fold together with the custard gently using a spatula. Spread 3–5 cm (1¼–2 inches) thick on a tray and freeze for at least 6–8 hours.

To make the licorice ice cream, mix the remaining chamomile cream in a large saucepan with milk, sugar, honey, licorice powder, fennel seeds and iota carrageenan. Gradually add the egg yolk, stirring constantly and cook gently until thick and the mixture coats the back of a spoon. Cool and allow to steep overnight. Strain and churn the mixture in an ice-cream machine according to the manufacturer's instructions. Freeze overnight.

To make the lemon balm meringue, purée the lemon balm leaves with 70 ml (2¼ fl oz) of water, then strain to make a thin purée weighing 170 g (6 oz). Combine the purée with the sugar, eggwhite powder and eggwhite in an electric mixer and whisk to stiff peaks. Spread a layer 2 cm (¾ inch) thick on a baking tray lined with a non-stick baking mat and dehydrate for 10 hours in a dehydrator. Alternatively, dehydrate overnight in a 50°C (120°F) oven. Break into shards.

To make the sorrel sauce, put the sorrel leaves, sugar and citric acid in a blender with 70 ml (2¼ fl oz) of water and purée until smooth. Add xanthan gum a little at a time until the liquid is no longer runny. Strain and reserve.

To assemble, place a pool of sorrel sauce on a plate. Add 2 small meringue shards. With a spoon, cut out a small circle of semifreddo and place on the shards. Add a small quenelle of licorice ice cream. Place a larger shard of meringue on top and garnish with fresh flowering herbs.

FRENCH TOAST, PRUNES AND FERMENTED MILK ICE CREAM

CHEF: GIOVANNI PASSERINI

SERVES 4

You will need to begin this recipe one day ahead.

butter, to serve
brown sugar, to serve
coriander (cilantro) flowers, to serve

FERMENTED MILK ICE CREAM

375 ml (13 fl oz/1½ cups) thickened (whipping) cream
25 g (1 oz) glucose
190 g (6¾ oz) caster (superfine) sugar
1.3 litres (44 fl oz/5 cups) fermented milk (such as Yakult)

BRIOCHE

42 g (1½ oz) fresh yeast
480 g (1 lb 1 oz/3¼ cups) plain (all-purpose) flour, sifted
5 eggs
80 g (2¾ oz) caster (superfine) sugar
1 teaspoon salt
170 g (6 oz) unsalted butter, softened, cubed
1 litre (35 fl oz/4 cups) milk, for soaking
6 eggs, lightly whisked, for soaking
40 g (1½ oz) sugar, for soaking

PRUNES ESCABECHE

100 g (3½ oz/½ cup) prunes, pitted, skins removed
100 g (3½ oz) caster (superfine) sugar
45 g (1½ oz/½ bunch) coriander (cilantro)
Japanese Umeboshi plum vinegar

CARAMELISED PECANS

125 g (4½ oz) sugar
25 g (1 oz/¼ cup) pecans

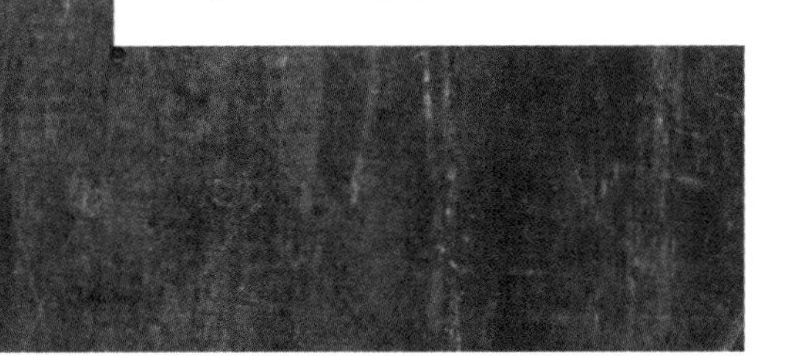

To make the fermented milk ice cream, slightly warm half of the cream in a saucepan over low heat. Add the glucose and mix using a stick blender. Add the remaining cream and the sugar and mix again. Warm the mixture to 70°C (150°F), before removing from the heat and adding the fermented milk. Mix well to combine. Refrigerate until cool before churning in an ice-cream machine according to the manufacturer's instructions.

Make the brioche by dissolving the yeast in 120 ml (4 fl oz) of warm water, and adding it to a bowl with 240 g (8½ oz) of the flour. Knead the dough lightly then let it rest, covered, in a warm and dry place for 1½–2 hours, until it doubles in size. Place the dough in a food processor and, using the whisk attachment, start mixing on low, adding the eggs one at a time. Once the eggs are incorporated, add the remaining flour, the sugar and the salt. Set the food processor to high and add the butter, little by little, continuing to mix until most of the dough begins to clump on the whisk. Set aside, covered in a cool, dry place to rest for 30–60 minutes, until doubled in size again. Shape the dough into two loaves, 15 x 25 cm (6 x 10 inches).

Meanwhile, preheat the oven to 170°C (325°F/Gas 3). Transfer the loaves into two buttered and lightly floured bread-baking tins and allow to rest for an additional 10 minutes. Bake for 35–40 minutes, checking after 20 minutes, until the brioche is cooked and golden. Remove and set aside until ready to serve. As older bread achieves a better result with French toast, it's a good idea to make the brioche a day ahead along with the ice cream.

To make the prune escabeche, put the prunes and sugar into a medium saucepan with 310 ml (10¾ fl oz/1¼ cups) water and boil over medium heat for 10–15 minutes until pulpy. Remove the pulp and set aside for plating. Add the coriander to the prune liquid and set aside for the flavours to infuse until the mixture has cooled. Strain, then mix with the Japanese vinegar at 3 parts of the filtered syrup to 2 parts Japanese vinegar.

To make the caramelised pecans, put 125 ml (4 fl oz/½ cup) of water, the sugar and pecans into a saucepan and place over medium heat. Boil until the mixture is shiny and syrupy in consistency. Pour onto a baking tray lined with baking paper and place in the oven at 170°C (325°F/Gas 3) until caramelised. Set aside until ready to serve.

Combine the milk, eggs and sugar for the soaking bath in a large, high-sided dish, ensuring they are well combined. Cut the brioche into bite-size cubes and soak in the bath for at least 10 minutes before draining on paper towel.

To serve, caramelise each side of the brioche cubes with butter and brown sugar in a heavy-based frying pan over medium heat. Place 3 mounds of prune pulp on each plate in a triangular shape. Place one piece of caramelised pecan and a coriander flower on each mound. Pour 10 ml of prune escabeche over, then place the French toast and quenelles of ice cream in the triangle. Add some additional fresh coriander flowers and serve.

FENNEL STRAWBERRIES, STRAWBERRY GRANITA AND SOUR CREAM

CHEFS: DAN PUSKAS, JAMES PARRY
SERVES 6–8

You will need to begin this recipe one day ahead.

30 g (1 oz) caster (superfine) sugar
1½ tablespoons fennel seeds, toasted
600 g (1 lb 5 oz) strawberries, hulled
100 g (3½ oz) icing (confectioners') sugar
fennel fronds and flowers, to garnish

STRAWBERRY GRANITA
600 g (1 lb 5 oz) strawberries, hulled
100 g (3½ oz) icing (confectioners') sugar

SOUR CREAM
250 ml (9 fl oz/1 cup) thin (pouring) cream
30 ml (1 fl oz) buttermilk

To make the granita, marinate the strawberries in the icing sugar for 3 hours. Purée the strawberry mixture in a blender then strain and pour the juice into a sealable freezerproof container and freeze until solid, stirring and scraping occasionally with a fork until crystals form and granita is frozen (preferably overnight).

Prepare the sour cream by bringing the cream to 82°C (180°F) in a Thermomix and holding that temperature for 30 minutes. Reduce the temperature to 21°C (70°F), add the buttermilk then pour into a large jar. Stand in a cool dry spot for 18 hours with the lid slightly loosened. Refrigerate for 6 hours before use.

Prepare the fennel strawberries by making a simple sugar syrup: combine 90 ml (3 fl oz) of water with the caster sugar in a medium saucepan over low heat until the sugar has dissolved. Increase the heat and bring the syrup to the boil. Remove from the heat, add the toasted fennel seeds and set aside for 1 hour for the flavour to infuse. Strain the syrup and reserve, discarding the seeds.

Combine the strawberries and icing sugar in a heatproof bowl. Place over a saucepan of boiling water and cook until the strawberries have released all their juices. Strain the strawberry liquid into a bowl and add the fennel syrup to taste. You want to achieve a slight anise flavour.

To serve, lightly whip a small amount of the sour cream and place a heaped tablespoon in each bowl, then add a tablespoon of the fennel and strawberry syrup before covering completely with the granita. Garnish with fennel fronds and flowers.

Note: You can use 275 g (9½ oz) of good quality sour cream instead of making your own.

LEMON AND YUZU CURD, COCONUT SORBET AND SPICED RUM

CHEF: DAVE VERHEUL

SERVES 4

You will need to begin this recipe one day ahead.

135 ml (4½ fl oz) lemon juice, approximately 3 lemons
20 ml (¾ fl oz) yuzu juice
150 g (5½ oz) eggs
110 g (3¾ oz/½ cup) caster (superfine) sugar
1 sheet gold-strength gelatine, bloomed
150 g (5½ oz) unsalted butter, diced
100 g (3½ oz) white chocolate

BURNT COCONUT STREUSEL
1 coconut husk
100 g (3½ oz) unsalted butter
110 g (3¾ oz/½ cup) caster (superfine) sugar
60 g (2¼ oz) almond meal
140 g (5 oz) plain (all-purpose) flour
5 g (⅛ oz) sea salt

COCONUT SORBET
60 g (2¼ oz) caster (superfine) sugar
1 g (1/32 oz) pectin NH
150 ml (5 fl oz) coconut water
250 g (9 oz) coconut cream
75 g (2½ g) glucose
sea salt

MERINGUE TUBES
50 g (1¾ oz) eggwhite
80 g (2¾ oz) caster (superfine) sugar

SPICED RUM JELLY
1 cinnamon stick
2 star anise
10 cardamom pods
90 ml (3 fl oz) rum
40 g (1½ oz) caster (superfine) sugar
1 sheet titanium-strength gelatine, bloomed

COCONUT POWDER
50 g (1¾ oz) desiccated coconut
15 g (½ oz) maltodextrin
30 g (1 oz) icing (confectioners') sugar

To make the burnt coconut streusel, dry the coconut husk overnight in a 50°C (120°F) oven. Use a blowtorch to burn the husk, then reserve 25 g (1 oz) of the ash powder. Combine the butter and sugar in the bowl of an electric mixer fitted with a paddle attachment, and beat until smooth and pale. Add the almond meal, flour, reserved ash and salt. Mix slowly until you get a crumbly texture. Bake this mix at 140°C (275°F/Gas 1) in a high-sided baking tray lined with baking paper until dry.

To make the sorbet, combine the sugar and pectin in a saucepan, add 115 ml (3¾ fl oz) of water and bring to the boil, then cool. Mix all of the remaining ingredients together and churn in an ice-cream machine according to the manufacturer's instructions. When churned, transfer the sorbet to a piping (icing) bag and freeze overnight.

To make the meringue tubes, put the eggwhite and a pinch of salt into the bowl of an electric mixer fitted with the whisk attachment, and whisk on low speed. Heat the sugar and 2 tablespoons of water to 117°C (235°F) measured on a sugar thermometer. Turn to high speed, slowly add the sugar and whisk until the mixture reaches body temperature and is smooth and dense in appearance. Cut 10 pieces of acetate, 9 x 10 cm (3½ x 4 inches), and 10 pieces of adhesive tape. Spread meringue over the acetate, roll up to form a tube then use adhesive tape to secure. Dry in a dehydrator at 55°C (130°F) overnight, and store in an airtight container until ready to use.

To make the curd, combine the lemon and yuzu juice, eggs and sugar in a Thermomix. Set the temperature to 80°C (175°F), blend on high speed for 10 seconds then turn down to low and cook until the mixture reaches 72°C (160°F), then turn the heat off. Squeeze excess water from the gelatine and add it to the curd mixture, then slowly add the butter until the mixture is emulsified. Strain into a container, cover with a circle of baking paper and chill to set.

To make the spiced rum jelly, lightly toast the cinnamon stick, star anise and cardamom in a dry frying pan. Mix the rum and sugar with 110 ml (3¾ fl oz) of water and warm in a saucepan over medium heat. Remove from the heat, add the spices, cover and infuse for 20 minutes. Return to the heat and bring the temperature of the rum mixture to 90°C (195°F). Squeeze the excess water from the bloomed gelatine and add it to the rum mixture, strain into a container and chill to set. When totally set, turn out onto a chopping board and cut into 5 mm (¼ inch) dice.

Combine the ingredients for the coconut powder in a blender on high speed until the coconut breaks down. Pass through a fine sieve and store in an airtight container.

Melt the white chocolate and spread very thinly on a chilled marble slab. When it is almost set, scrape to form irregular shavings. Store the shavings in the freezer until ready to serve.

To serve, scoop some yuzu curd onto each plate and make a small flat spot on top. Place rum jelly in the flat spot. Stand the white chocolate shavings upright in the curd. Sprinkle with alternating layers of the burnt coconut streusel and coconut powder. Fill the meringue tubes with coconut sorbet and place gently on top to serve.

CARAMELISED PINEAPPLE, PINE NEEDLE SYRUP AND PINE NUT BRITTLE

CHEF: BEAU VINCENT
SERVES 6

You will need to begin this recipe one day ahead.

200 g (7 oz) caster (superfine) sugar
200 g (7 oz) pine needles
1 pineapple, peeled, cored, cut into rings

TONKA BEAN AND COCONUT SORBET
160 g (5½ oz) caster (superfine) sugar
40 g (1½ oz) glucose
700 ml (24 fl oz) coconut cream
3 tonka beans, grated with a microplane

PINE NEEDLE SUGAR
200 g (7 oz) pine needles
400 g (14 oz) caster (superfine) sugar

PINE NUT BRITTLE
90 g (3¼ oz) butter
120 g (4¼ oz) isomalt powder
50 g (1¾ oz) caster (superfine) sugar
4 g (⅛ oz) bicarbonate of soda (baking soda)
200 g (7 oz/1⅓ cups) pine nuts, toasted

Put the caster sugar and pine needles in a saucepan with 800 ml (28 fl oz) of water. Put over low heat and simmer for 30 minutes to allow the flavours to infuse. Set aside to cool then strain the liquid into a large bowl and submerge the pineapple pieces. Cover and refrigerate overnight to intensify the flavour.

To make the sorbet, put 200 ml (7 fl oz) of water, the sugar and glucose in a saucepan over medium heat and cook, stirring constantly until the sugar has dissolved. Turn the heat to low and add the coconut cream, grated tonka beans and an extra 100 ml (3½ fl oz) of water. Simmer for 2 minutes until well combined and set aside to cool and allow flavours to infuse. Strain and chill until cold then pour into an ice-cream machine and churn according to the manufacturer's instructions. Freeze overnight.

To make the pine needle sugar, dry the pine needles in a 50°C (120°F) oven for 4–6 hours then blend in a spice grinder until a fragrant green powder is formed. Alternatively, blend the needles on high in a Thermomix set to 40°C (105°F). Add the sugar and mix to combine. Remove from the grinder and set aside.

To make the pine nut brittle, line a baking tray with baking paper. Heat the butter, isomalt powder, sugar and a pinch of salt in a small saucepan over high heat until caramelised, stirring to prevent catching. Add the bicarbonate of soda and toasted pine nuts, stir to combine then pour onto the prepared baking tray. Once the brittle has set, cut or break it into bite-size pieces.

To finish, place the pineapple on a heatproof tray and spoon enough pine needle sugar over the surface of the pineapple to cover it. Use a blowtorch to brûlée the surface of the pineapple until the sugar has set and is dark golden. Place a ring of pineapple on each plate, spoon on additional sugar to add gloss then arrange pieces of brittle on top. Finish with a quenelle of the sorbet.

CARROT CAKE, HONEYCOMB AND CARDAMOM CARAMEL CREAM

CHEF: OWEN CLARK

SERVES 6–8

You will need to begin this recipe one day ahead.

5 green cardamom pods
10 cloves
½ cinnamon stick
1 teaspoon coriander seeds
1 teaspoon freshly grated nutmeg
pinch of salt
160 g (5¾ oz) cake flour
75 g (2½ oz) almond meal
10 g (¼ oz) baking powder
3 eggs
155 g (5½ oz) caster sugar
150 ml (5 fl oz) grapeseed oil
125 ml (4 fl oz) milk
200 g (7 oz) carrots, blanched and puréed

MILK AND HONEY SORBET

160 g (5¾ oz/¾ cup) caster (superfine) sugar
40 g (1½ oz) glucose
500 ml (17 fl oz/2 cups) milk
200 g (7 oz) thick (double) cream
100 g (3½ oz) raw honey, plus 1 tablespoon extra
1 sheet silver-strength gelatine, bloomed

CARDAMOM CARAMEL CREAM

225 g (8 oz/1 cup) caster (superfine) sugar
1 litre (35 fl oz/4 cups) thick (double) cream
25 g (1 oz) cardamom pods, bruised
7 g (¼ oz) kappa carrageenan

CARAMELISED HONEYCOMB

25 g (1 oz) honey
160 g (5¾ oz/¾ cup) sugar
60 g (2¼ oz) liquid glucose
7 g (¼ oz) bicarbonate of soda (baking soda)

CARROT CURD

500 ml (17 fl oz/2 cups) carrot juice
270 g (9½ oz) eggs
270 g (9½ oz/1¼ cups) caster (superfine) sugar
4 g (⅛ oz) agar-agar
350 g (12 oz) unsalted butter, cubed

CARROT GARNISH

1 tablespoon sugar
1 tablespoon water
1 tablespoon cider vinegar
multicoloured carrots, shaved
edible flowers

To make the sorbet, combine 200 ml (7 fl oz) of water with the sugar and glucose in a saucepan and bring to a simmer, then allow to cool. Add the honey to the sugar syrup and bring to the boil. Remove from the heat, add the drained, bloomed gelatine to the hot syrup and whisk until incorporated. In a blender, combine the milk and cream, then add the warm syrup to the milk mixture and blend on high for a minute to make sure everything is incorporated. Place in the refrigerator until completely cool. Pour into an ice-cream machine and churn according to the manufacturer's instructions. Freeze overnight.

Preheat the oven to 190°C (375°F/Gas 5) and grease and line a 20 x 30 cm (8 x 12 inch) cake tin. To make the carrot cake, lightly toast the cardamom pods, cloves, cinnamon stick, coriander seeds, nutmeg and salt, then grind them very finely using a spice grinder. Sift the flour, almond meal, baking powder and ground spices into a large bowl. Whisk the eggs and sugar together in an electric mixer, using the whisk attachment, until tripled in volume and fluffy. Add the grapeseed oil, milk and carrot purée, then quickly incorporate the sifted dry ingredients gently with a rubber spatula, making sure there are no lumps. Pour into the cake tin and bake for 30 minutes. Allow to cool in the tin, then transfer to a wire rack to cool completely.

To make the cardamom caramel cream, put the sugar in a saucepan with a splash of water over medium heat. Cook for 4–6 minutes until it is a medium dark caramel. Slowly add the cream. Let the mixture simmer until the sugar is completely dissolved, then steep the cardamom pods. Cool the mixture down completely, then strain into a clean saucepan and add the carrageenan. Bring to the boil while stirring constantly, then pour into a container and chill. When the gel is firm and cool, purée in a blender until smooth. Set aside until serving.

To make the caramelised honeycomb, combine the honey, sugar and glucose in a saucepan and cook to a light caramel colour. Separately combine 1½ tablespoons of water and bicarbonate of soda in a bowl, stirring to combine. Bring the caramel mixture to 166°C (331°F) using a sugar thermometer, then add the bicarbonate of soda mixture, taking care to whisk constantly so the mixture doesn't catch and burn. Pour the honeycomb onto a tray lined with baking paper to cool. Break into pieces and set aside.

To make the carrot curd, reduce the carrot juice in a saucepan over medium heat until you have 270 ml (9½ fl oz) with an intense carrot flavour. Whisk the eggs and sugar together in a bowl. Put the reduced carrot juice and agar-agar in a medium saucepan and bring to the boil over medium heat, whisking constantly. Remove from the heat and add the egg mixture, whisking until incorporated. Heat the combined mixture gently until the eggs begin to thicken the mixture, then pour into a blender. Blend on a low setting and start adding the butter slowly so that it emulsifies, but not so slowly that the mixture cools and collapses. When all the butter has been incorporated, pour the mixture onto a tray that you can unmold the curd from when cool.

To make the carrot garnish, warm the sugar, water and vinegar in a saucepan over low heat until dissolved. Marinate the shaved carrots in the dressing until ready to serve.

To finish, swipe some cardamom caramel cream on a plate and add a strip of carrot curd, bookended by hand-torn pieces of carrot cake. Place crumbled and whole pieces of honeycomb on the cake and curd, then add the marinated carrot garnish, edible flowers and finally a quenelle of milk and honey sorbet.

PEAR, CHOCOLATE AND CELERY

CHEF: KARL FIRLA

SERVES 6

You will need to begin this recipe one day ahead.

200 g (7 oz) caster (superfine) sugar
45 ml (1½ fl oz) Poire William liqueur
4 star anise
½ cinnamon stick
3 josephine pears (or best in season)

CELERY SORBET

30 g (1 oz) liquid glucose
70 g (2½ oz) caster (superfine) sugar
½ bunch of celery, juiced, approximately 350 ml (12 fl oz)

CHOCOLATE CHANTILLY

110 g (3¾ oz) chocolate (62% cocoa minimum)
60 ml (2 fl oz/¼ cup) hot water
45 ml (1½ fl oz) cocoa liqueur
sea salt

CHOCOLATE GLASS

75 g (2½ oz) liquid glucose
50 g (1¾ oz) fondant
50 g (1¾ oz) chocolate (62% cocoa minimum)

To make the sorbet, gently heat the glucose, caster sugar and 2½ tablespoons of water in a saucepan over low to medium heat until the sugar has dissolved. Allow to cool and add to the celery juice. Churn in an ice-cream machine according to the manufacturer's instructions. Freeze overnight.

To make the poached pear, put 500 ml (17 fl oz/2 cups) of water, the sugar, pear liqueur, star anise and cinnamon stick in a medium saucepan and bring to a simmer over medium heat. Allow to stand for 1 hour for flavours to infuse. Peel and core the pears. Slice into 1 cm (3/8 inch) discs and gently poach the slices for 5 minutes in the spiced liquor. You want the pear to be just cooked, it needs to retain some bite. Remove from the heat and cool in the poaching liquor in the refrigerator.

To make the chocolate chantilly, ensure your ingredients are very precisely measured as any change in measurements may result in the chantilly collapsing. Melt chocolate in a heatproof bowl placed over a saucepan of simmering water, then remove the bowl from the saucepan. Add the water, liqueur and a pinch of sea salt and whisk until light and airy.

To make the chocolate glass, line a baking tray with baking paper and set aside. Heat the glucose, 100 ml (3½ fl oz) of water and the fondant in a saucepan until it reaches 160°C (315°F) on a sugar thermometer. Add the chocolate then take off the heat and stir constantly for 1–2 minutes until the mixture emulsifies. Pour the mixture onto the lined baking tray and allow to set. Break into large bite-size pieces. Heat the oven to 150°C (300°F/Gas 2) and place one or two pieces in the oven to soften for up to a minute. Remove, place between two sheets of baking paper and roll flat using a rolling pin. Allow to cool, remove the top piece of baking paper, return to the oven to soften for 30 seconds before removing and carefully cutting strips off with a paring knife. You can pull at these strips and the mixture should behave like caramel.

To serve, place some poached pear on the base of each plate with 2 tablespoons poaching liquid. Top with a quenelle of chocolate chantilly and a quenelle of celery sorbet. Finish with a piece of chocolate glass.

ACCOMPAGNEMENT
SIDE NOTES

KETCHUP

SMOKED VEGETABLE HOT SAUCE

HAZELNUT OIL

PINE TREE OIL

BAY LEAF OIL

GREEN ALMOND ESSENCE

DASHI STOCK

CHICKEN JUS

BEEF JUS

DATE JAM

PICKLES

BUCKWHEAT NOODLES

GREENS WITH HORSERADISH CRÈME FRAÎCHE DRESSING

CARROT, BEET, PERSIMMON SALAD

BLACK GARLIC PURÉE

KETCHUP

CHEF: RYAN SQUIRES

2 kg (4 lb 8 oz) tomatoes on the vine, very ripe
3 star anise, toasted
20 juniper berries, toasted
1 garlic bulb, cloves separated
5 cloves
small handful of dried bonito flakes
2 sheets of kombu, roughly 15 cm (6 inches) square
50 ml (1½ fl oz) fish sauce
2 tablespoons aged chardonnay vinegar
4 tablespoons caster (superfine) sugar

Score a shallow cross in the base of the tomatoes, then blanch in boiling water and refresh in an ice bath. Drain and peel the tomatoes, reserving the skins in the same bowl. Quarter the tomatoes, scooping out the seeds and inner pulp into the bowl. Place the remaining tomato flesh in a large, deep frying pan. Put the pulp, skin and seeds in an upright blender and purée until liquid. Strain the liquid through a chinois or fine sieve into the frying pan with the tomato flesh.

Cut two large 30 cm (12 inch) squares of muslin (cheesecloth) and lay them flat. Divide the toasted spices, garlic, cloves and bonito flakes between the two pieces and tie using butcher's string to make 2 flavour sachets. Smash the sachets gently with a rolling pin to bruise the berries and garlic then add to the tomato mix. Place the frying pan over medium heat and bring to a simmer. Add the sheets of kombu. After 20 minutes of light simmering, remove the kombu and discard. Continue to cook the tomato mix over low heat until reduced by half, stirring continuously. Remove the flavour sachets and pass the tomato mixture through a sieve into a clean frying pan or large, heavy-based saucepan and continue to reduce until any liquid has evaporated and the tomato mixture is thick. Season with the fish sauce, vinegar and sugar. Taste and adjust the seasoning to your liking: you want to achieve a balance of sweetness, saltiness and tartness.

Store the ketchup in screwtop jars in the refrigerator for up to 6 months.

SMOKED VEGETABLE HOT SAUCE

CHEF: JOSÉ CARLES

150 g (5½ oz) roma (plum) tomatoes, quartered lengthways
100 g (3½ oz) brown onions, peeled, sliced
50 g (1¾ oz) red capsicum (pepper)
15 g (½ oz) garlic
30 g (1 oz) aji dulce (cachucha pepper)
1½ habañero chillies
hickory wood smoking chips
2 tablespoons tomato paste (concentrated purée)
3 tablespoons sherry vinegar

Smoke the tomato, onion, capsicum, garlic, aji dulce and chilli slowly in a smoker using hickory wood smoking chips for 50 minutes. Alternatively, you can use a barbecue grill to smoke the vegetables: put charcoal and hickory wood chips on one side of the grill with a pan of water on top to create humidity. Make a wall beside the charcoal with foil so that the charcoal doesn't cook the vegetables directly and smoke the vegetables on the other side of the grill.

Put the smoked vegetables in an upright blender with the tomato paste and vinegar, season with salt and blend to a thin purée consistency.

Store the sauce in airtight containers in the refrigerator for up to 6 months.

HAZELNUT OIL
CHEF: MICHAEL CABALLO

50 g (1¾ oz/⅓ cup) hazelnuts, blanched
100 ml (3½ fl oz) grapeseed oil
pinch of fine sea salt
pinch of sugar

oast the hazelnuts in the oven at 180°C (350°F/Gas 4) for 10 minutes or until nicely browned. Combine toasted hazelnuts with remaining ingredients in a blender and purée until smooth. Strain through a chinois or fine sieve. Store in an airtight container.

PINE TREE OIL
CHEF: GIOVANNI PASSERINI

250 ml (9 fl oz/1 cup) olive oil
pine tree essential oil

Fill a glass, or a jar with a screwtop lid, with the olive oil. Add about 4 drops of pine tree essential oil, tasting after each drop as the intensity of oils can vary. Set aside to infuse. Store in an airtight container.

BAY LEAF OIL
CHEF: LUKE BURGESS

20 fresh bay leaves, blanched
750ml (26 fl oz/3 cups) grapeseed oil

Process the bay leaves and grapeseed oil in a blender. Set aside overnight to infuse. Alternatively use a Thermomix set on high speed at 60°C (140°F) for 12 minutes. Allow the sediment to separate before decanting the oil into a separate container with a lid. Store at room temperature until ready to use.

GREEN ALMOND ESSENCE
CHEF: LUKE BURGESS

500 g (1 lb 2 oz) green almond husks
500 g (1 lb 2 oz) caster (superfine) sugar

Evenly prick the green almond husks with a fork and coat in the sugar in a non-reactive plastic container, then cover and refrigerate for 5 months. After the 5 months, gently strain into a sealable container and reserve in the refrigerator.

The syrup can be kept for up to 1 year and can be used as a condiment across a broad range of dishes. Green almonds are available in spring.

DASHI STOCK

CHEF: WESLEY YOUNG

15–20 cm (6–8 inch) square sheet of dried kombu
4 litres (140 fl oz/16 cups) distilled water
1 cup bonito flakes

Brush any dirt or sandy bits off the dried kombu, being careful to keep the white 'bloom' that you might see on the surface. Soak the kombu in the distilled water for 8 hours or overnight.

Transfer the water and the kombu to a large saucepan and bring it to a simmer. Add the bonito flakes and keep the temperature at a low simmer. When the bonito sinks halfway down the liquid after about 5–10 minutes, strain the liquid through a fine sieve and allow the liquid to cool.

Store in a clean jar or airtight container in the refrigerator, or freeze for later use.

CHICKEN JUS

CHEF: DAVE VERHEUL

1.5 kg (3 lb 5 oz) chicken bones
1 onion, roughly chopped
3 celery stalks, roughly chopped
2 garlic bulbs, halved crossways
half a pork trotter
2 bay leaves
2½ tablespoons thyme leaves

To make chicken jus, chop the chicken bones into even-size pieces and roast in a 200°C (400°F/Gas 6) oven until golden brown. In a stockpot or very large ovenproof saucepan, caramelise the onion, celery and garlic. Add the trotter and roasted chicken bones to the pan, cover with water, bring to the boil and skim well. Add the herbs, cover tightly and cook in a 140°C (275°F/Gas 1) oven for 10 hours. Strain the stock into a saucepan, put it over medium-high heat and reduce to a sauce consistency.

Store covered in the refrigerator until ready to use, or freeze for later use.

BEEF JUS

CHEF: KATRINA MEYNINK

2 kg (4 lb 8 oz) beef shin bones
3 carrots, roughly chopped
3 celery stalks, roughly chopped
1 onion, peeled, cut in half
1 garlic bulb, cut in half crossways
1 teaspoon black peppercorns
4 bay leaves
10 g (¼ oz/½ bunch) thyme
1 pig's trotter, about 350 g (12 oz)

Preheat oven to 200°C (400°F/Gas 6). Roast beef bones in 2 large roasting tins for 1 hour or until golden. Remove from oven and combine in one roasting tin. Strain rendered fat from the empty tin, add vegetables and roast for 30 minutes or until golden. Transfer bones and vegetables to a stockpot, add peppercorns, bay leaves, thyme, pig's trotter and enough water to cover. Bring to the boil over high heat, then simmer, occasionally skimming any scum from surface, over very low heat for 7 hours. Strain through a fine sieve, then strain again through a fine sieve lined with muslin (cheesecloth). Cool, then refrigerate for 2–3 hours or until the fat has separated from the stock, then skim solidified fat from the top and discard. Strain the stock into a saucepan, put it over medium-high heat and reduce the stock to sauce consistency, about 20–30 minutes.

Store, covered, in the refrigerator until ready to use, or freeze for later use.

DATE JAM

CHEF: ARI TAYMOR

- 225 g (8 oz) medjool dates, pitted, chopped
- 2 tablespoons sherry vinegar or red wine vinegar
- 2 tablespoons sugar

Put the dates, vinegar, sugar, and 125 ml (4 fl oz/½ cup) of water in a small saucepan, bring to the boil then reduce the heat and simmer, stirring occasionally, for 6–8 minutes until the dates are very soft. Allow to cool slightly, then transfer the mixture to an upright blender and purée until smooth. Press the jam through a fine sieve into a small bowl, discarding any solids.

Store in an airtight container in the refrigerator.

PICKLES

CHEF: RYAN SQUIRES

- 200 g (7 oz/1½ cups) sea salt
- 10 Lebanese (short) cucumbers, washed
- 500 ml (17 fl oz/2 cups) aged chardonnay vinegar
- 2–5 tablespoons caster (superfine) sugar
- 2–3 teaspoons mustard seeds, toasted
- 3 dill sprigs

Put 2 litres (70 fl oz/8 cups) of water and the salt in a large saucepan and stir until the salt has dissolved. Add the cucumbers, ensuring they are fully submerged. If you need to add more brine, the ratio is 10 per cent salt to water. Cover and refrigerate for 60 hours.

Combine the remaining ingredients in a saucepan over medium heat, stir to dissolve the sugar and simmer for 2–3 minutes, then cool to room temperature. Remove the cucumbers from the brine solution and put them in a bowl with the vinegar mixture, stir to combine, then transfer to sterilised jars. Seal and refrigerate for 60 hours to pickle before using. Consume within 2 weeks.

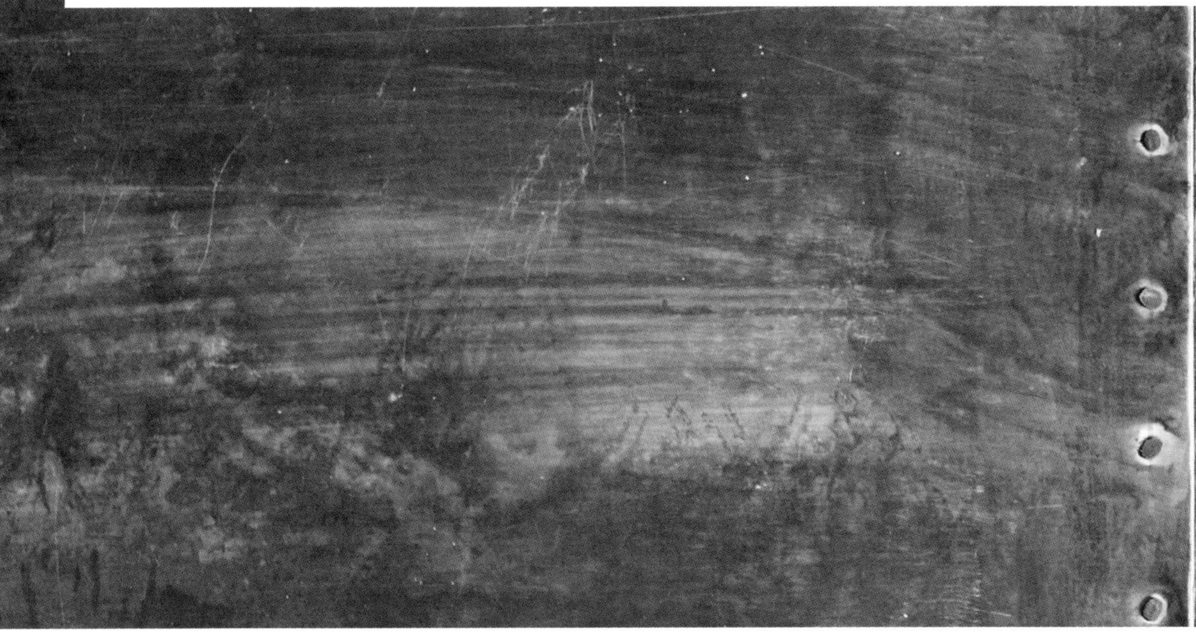

BUCKWHEAT NOODLES

CHEF: RYAN SQUIRES

400 g (14 oz) good quality buckwheat flour, sifted
100 g (3½ oz/⅔ cup) 00 (pastry) flour, sifted, plus extra for dusting

SEASONING

1 tablespoon sesame oil
2 teaspoons rice vinegar
2 teaspoons Japanese soy sauce (bonito flavour)
1 tablespoon sesame seeds, toasted
1 tablespoon finely chopped chives
chilli oil

Pour about 350 ml (12 fl oz) of water into a saucepan and bring to a simmer over medium heat. Pour the water into the bowl of an electric mixer fitted with the whisk attachment, add the combined flours and turn it onto medium speed to incorporate. Add 50 ml (1½ fl oz/2½ tablespoons) of water at a time, mixing continuously. When you are roughly halfway through the process, your dough should look like tiny grey pebbles. At this stage, change the whisk attachment to the dough hook, continue adding the water and work slowly for 7–10 minutes. Please note that doughs can be temperamental with variations in humidity, temperature, air draughts and different batches of flour, so adding the water slowly helps you control these variations. When all the water is incorporated, the dough should nearly stick to your fingers when you touch it. Turn onto a lightly floured cold marble surface or a wooden pasta board.

Cut the dough into 3 portions and cover two of the pieces with a just-damp cloth. Roll out the dough, using flour to dust your rolling pin.

Roll to an even 1–2 mm (1/16 inch) thickness and about the same shape as an A4 (letter) sheet of paper. Gently fold the dough over to make it easier to slice: fold three or four times in one direction. Slice firmly and precisely with a sharp knife: a meat cleaver works best. Fluff the noodles gently with your fingertips coated with flour to separate the initial cut.

Put the noodles in a large saucepan of boiling water and stir gently to make sure the noodles aren't sticking together. Simmer for approximately 3 minutes until the noodles are al dente. While the noodles are cooking, prepare a bath of ice and water in a large bowl. Place the cooked noodles directly in the ice bath. Once completely cold, place on a clean tea towel (dish towel) and gently dry with another.

Combine the seasoning ingredients in a large bowl, adjusting the chilli oil to taste. Add the noodles, tossing to coat. Place the noodles in serving bowls and serve cold.

Note: Makes about 4–5 servings as a side dish.

GREENS WITH HORSERADISH CREME FRAICHE DRESSING

CHEF: ARI TAYMOR

1 tablespoon linseeds (flaxseeds), golden or brown
1 tablespoon amaranth seeds
3 tablespoons crème fraîche
2 tablespoons freshly grated horseradish or 1 tablespoon prepared horseradish
1 tablespoon Champagne vinegar or white wine vinegar
sea salt flakes and freshly ground black pepper, to season
8 cups young bitter greens (such as watercress or miner's lettuce)
radish flowers or sprouts (optional)

Toast linseeds in a large, dry frying pan over medium heat, tossing often, for about 2 minutes until fragrant. Transfer to a small bowl. Toast the amaranth seeds in the same pan for about 2 minutes until fragrant. Combine with the linseeds and set aside to cool.

Put the crème fraîche, horseradish and vinegar in a large bowl and whisk to combine. Thin with a little water, if needed, and season with salt and pepper. Add the greens and radish flowers, if using, and toss to coat. Serve sprinkled with the linseeds and amaranth seeds.

CARROT, BEET, PERSIMMON SALAD

CHEF: DAN PEARSON

1 persimmon, thinly sliced
1 purple carrot, thinly sliced
1 orange beetroot, thinly sliced
50 g (1¾ oz/⅓ cup) pistachio nuts, toasted, crushed
100 g (3½ oz) orange segments
50 g (1¾ oz) nasturtium leaves and petals
20 g (¾ oz) wild radish flowers
olive oil, to serve
sea salt, to season

MANDARIN VINEGAR
250 ml (9 fl oz/1 cup) chardonnay vinegar
250 ml (9 fl oz/1 cup) chardonnay
250 g (9 oz) raw (demerara) sugar
500 g (1 lb 2 oz) mandarins, peeled, pith removed

BOUQUET GARNI
1 bay leaf
1 teaspoon mustard seeds
1 teaspoon juniper berries
20 g (¾ oz) thyme

To make the mandarin vinegar, bring the vinegar, wine and sugar to the boil in a saucepan over medium heat, stirring until the sugar has dissolved. Cut the mandarins in half and put them in a sous-vide bag or resealable plastic bag with the bouquet garni. Pour in the vinegar mixture and seal. Leave to cool at room temperature then set aside to infuse for at least 1 week.

Open the bag and press all the ingredients through a fine sieve. Strain again, then store in a bottle at room temperature for no more than 2 months.

To assemble the salad, mix all the ingredients with a little splash of the mandarin vinegar and olive oil. Season with sea salt and place on the plate.

BLACK GARLIC PUREE

CHEF: MATT AITA

6 g (⅛ oz) agar-agar
4 g (⅛ oz) salt
140 g (5 oz) black garlic

To make the black garlic puree, place the agar-agar, salt and 400 ml (14 fl oz) of water in a saucepan. Put it over medium heat and bring to the boil. Boil for 45 seconds, stirring constantly, then pour into a container to set. Once set, blend 300 g (10½ oz) of the gel with the black garlic until very smooth.

THE CHEFS

If the bistronomy menu changes every day, progressively, particularly with the arrival of new seasonal raw ingredients, so too can the chef. In their quest for flavour and la cuisine radicale, *chefs are always on the move, seeking new experiences. At the time of printing these are the restaurant kitchens and spaces they call home.*

MATT AITA
ON THE PASS: LE PHILOSOPHE, NEW YORK CITY, USA
Matt Aita started working at the tender age of 16 as a restaurant cashier. Realising that he preferred to cook for people rather than talk to them, Matt quickly moved into the cockroach-ridden kitchens of Philadelphia under hardcore old-school chefs in dodgy cafés and pubs before making a slow migration to New York. Free labour and stages under some of the city's best chefs led to jobs as sous chef at db bistro moderne, Jean-Georges and Nougatine as well as stints at Jim Lahey's Sullivan Street Bakery, before taking on his role as head chef at Le Philosophe. Here Matt Aita, backed by years working for Daniel Boulud and Jean-Georges Vongerichten, is cooking from the French canon with style.

INAKI AIZPITARTE
ON THE PASS: LE CHATEAUBRIAND, LE DAUPHIN, PARIS, FRANCE
The youngest of five children, Inaki Aizpitarte was born in Besançon from Spanish parents fleeing from the Franco dictatorship in Spain. French-Basque Aizpitarte set out as a landscape designer, only to discover cooking in Israel while washing dishes for a Serbian chef in Tel Aviv who taught him the basics of cooking. Floating from job to job, from Latin America to Paris, he began working his way through the city's kitchens: Café des Délices then La Famille in Montmartre and Le Transversal at the MAC/VAL museum before opening Le Chateaubriand in Belleville with his friend, Frédéric Peneau, in 2006. He quickly overtook Joël Robuchon on the S.Pellegrino World's 50 Best Restaurants list and has been awarded the coveted Chevalier de l'Ordre des Arts et des Lettres.

LUKE BURGESS
OWNER-CHEF: GARAGISTES, HOBART, AUSTRALIA
Luke Burgess began cooking in Sydney in 1994, finishing his apprenticeship with two years at Tetsuya's. Luke travelled through Europe, returning to Australia with a new career in food and travel photography. In 2006, Luke moved to Tasmania to open his first restaurant, Pecora Café, with a menu inspired by produce from small gardeners, farmers and fishermen in the area. In 2009 Luke staged at Noma in Copenhagen, which inspired a new connection to food and wine. In 2010, Luke and his two business partners opened Garagistes, Hobart. Their aim is to maintain a casual, communal environment where dishes — inspired by high-quality raw ingredients and influenced by many different cultures — can be enjoyed with a glass or bottle of natural wine. In early 2012, Luke and the team opened a small wine bar, Sidecar, serving house-made charcuterie and natural wines.

ADAM BYATT
OWNER-CHEF: TRINITY & BISTRO UNION, LONDON, UK
Cooking is in Adam Byatt's blood. Not only was his grandfather a cook in the army, but his mother is also a professional chef, so from an early age he was immersed in the world of the kitchen. At 16, he apprenticed at Claridge's while training at the Royal Academy of Culinary Arts. After a brief stint at The Berkeley, Adam joined Phil Howard's Mayfair restaurant, The Square, and was sous chef when the restaurant was awarded its second Michelin star. In 2001 Adam opened his first restaurant, Thyme, in Clapham. He closed it after four years and opened Trinity in Clapham Old Town, which has held three AA rosettes for five years and been voted among the top 10 restaurants in London in 2010, 2011 and 2012 by both Harden's and Zagat. Adam opened Bistro Union in 2012, a relaxed neighbourhood affair serving British classics while remaining faithful to Adam's love of seasonal British produce. Adam regularly appears on BBC One's *Saturday Kitchen* and has appeared on *Market Kitchen* and *Celebrity Masterchef*. Adam published *How to Eat In* (Bantam Press, 2010). Adam is joint chair of the Kitchen category for their annual Awards of Excellence of the Royal Academy of Culinary Arts.

MICHAEL CABALLO
OWNER-CHEF: EDULIS, TORONTO, CANADA

Michael completed his culinary training at the Northern Alberta Institute of Technology and was apprenticed at the Sheraton Hotel until 2002 when he accepted a position as chef de partie at Avalon Restaurant, Toronto. He staged at the two-star Mugaritz in Spain and worked as second cook at the two-star La Broche in Madrid before returning to Canada to work as chef de partie for three years at Niagara Street Café. He returned to Europe, working at La Petraia in Chianti, Italy, before returning to Canada in 2010 as executive chef at the West Coast Fishing Club. In 2012 Michael became executive chef and co-owner of Edulis Restaurant, where he brings his passion for wild foods, mushroom foraging, and influences from his Spanish heritage as well as inspiration from roaming the kitchens, forests, and dining rooms of Canada, Panama, France, Italy and Spain.

YVES CAMDEBORDE
OWNER-CHEF: LE COMPTOIR DU RELAIS, PARIS, FRANCE

Yves Camdeborde has worked in the most prestigious houses in Paris including the Ritz, La Tour d'Argent and Hôtel de Crillon with his mentor, chef Christian Constant. In 1992 he opened La Régalade in the 14th arrondissement of Paris where he cooked for 10 years, offering traditional cooking influenced by his upbringing in south-western France. He then took over Le Relais Saint Germain and its restaurant, Le Comptoir du Relais, as well as Le Comptoir Bar where he continues his cooking philosophy — high-quality accessible ingredients to feed anyone from the mailman to the movie star — with a warm and casual atmosphere. Yves Camdeborde appears regularly on French television, including as a judge on *Masterchef*, and has published nine cookbooks.

JOSÉ CARLES
OWNER-CHEF: DONDE JOSÉ, PANAMA CITY, PANAMA

José began his culinary studies at the age of 22, at the Interamerican University in Panama, and completed them in Australia with a Diplôme de Cuisine from Le Cordon Bleu. While in Australia, he worked at Icebergs Dining Room and Bar, Lucio's and Attica under Ben Shewry. His experience, particularly at Attica, taught him the value of developing long-forgotten and little-known local ingredients to bring new ideas to traditional local fare. José returned to Panama and opened Artisan Workshop, a pop-up restaurant focused on Panamanian cuisine. In December 2013 he opened Donde José, a 16-seat fine-dining restaurant offering his take on new Panamanian cuisine.

OWEN CLARK
AT LARGE AT THE TIME OF PRINTING

Starting his culinary career in a family-style Italian restaurant, Owen entered a culinary program in Boulder, Colorado, at the Culinary School of the Rockies. He apprenticed at the elite two-Michelin-starred Oustau de Baumanière in Les Baux-de-Provence, France. Owen was then apprenticed at The Fat Duck in Bray, UK. From there he was invited to cook at wd~50 on New York City's Lower East Side. He spent two years rising through the ranks and learning more than he ever thought possible about flavour pairing, technique, and modern styles of cuisine. After leaving wd~50, Owen worked at Blue Hill restaurant, with Dan Barber, a James Beard Foundation award winner and one of *Time* magazine's 100 influential people in 2009. Owen started as sous chef on the opening team of Gwynnett St., moved to the position of executive chef and now freelances as a chef across New York City and beyond.

LEE COOPER
COOWNER-CHEF: L'ABATTOIR, VANCOUVER, CANADA

Lee Cooper had an early introduction to the restaurant business, earning his pocket money in the kitchens of his father's A&W franchises and watching his uncle, chef Bernard Casavant, a highly regarded chef in Vancouver. He completed a one-year culinary program at Malaspina College before working at restaurants on Vancouver Island, in Whistler, and in the Okanagan. After working at the Fat Duck, Lee returned to Canada, met business partner Paul Grunberg while on staff at Jean-Georges' Market and together they opened L'Abattoir in 2010. Cooper has earned high praise from critics for his food: *Western Living* has ranked him among its top 40 Foodies Under 40, and *The Vancouver Sun* named him as a chef to watch, saying his cuisine is 'casual and refined with an ease in orchestrating flavours, textures, presentation and technique.'

ANTHONY DEMETRE
COOWNER-CHEF: WILD HONEY, ARBUTUS, LES DEUX SALONS, LONDON, UK

Anthony spent his adolescent years watching and helping his grandmother in the kitchen, yet he started his culinary career pretty late by chef's standards. Initially he pursued a life in the Royal Navy before injury set his sights on the kitchen. Having learnt his craft working in some of the world's leading restaurants alongside renowned chefs, Anthony garnered experience in both Michelin-starred establishments and modern bistros. In 1999, Anthony was appointed chef-director of Putney Bridge restaurant and ,within a year of opening, the team were awarded a Michelin star followed by four AA rosettes for food and service. In 2006, Anthony opened his first restaurant with business partner Will Smith: Arbutus, which received countless awards including a Michelin star in its first year. In 2007 they opened Wild Honey, which also garnered a Michelin star within a year of opening. Their third restaurant Les Deux Salons, opened in 2010. Anthony has written a cookbook, *Today's Special* (Quadrille Publishing Ltd, 2008) and has appeared on the BBC's *Great British Menu* series and *Saturday Kitchen* with James Martin.

KARL FIRLA
OWNER-CHEF: OSCILLATE WILDLY, SYDNEY, AUSTRALIA

Karl completed his apprenticeship with Salvatore Pepe at Cibo Ristorante, Adelaide, before taking on a position at the Bridgewater Mill restaurant under Le Tu Thai; here he developed the culinary skills to combine French techniques with an Asian influence. After three years he took a position as pastry chef at Marque Restaurant under Mark Best before moving on to become sous chef at est.. After two years he became head chef at Oscillate Wildly before taking over as owner and chef. Here Karl tries to push the boundaries commercially, professionally and personally, using it as an opportunity to constantly experiment, learn and develop as a chef and businessman.

MATT GERMANCHIS
COOKING AT: PEI MODERN, MELBOURNE, AUSTRALIA

Matthew's culinary career began with an apprenticeship at Guy Grossi's Caffe Grossi in Melbourne. The experience and his passion prompted him to start his first restaurant in the Yarra Valley, The Riberry. In 2002 he sold The Riberry and travelled extensively before settling in the UK to further his culinary knowledge at Heston Blumenthal's The Hinds Head and The Fat Duck. He spent the next two years working with Heston, developing his iconic 'historical' dishes. From there he worked with Rowley Leigh, the renowned pioneer of modern Anglo-French cuisine. Moving back to Melbourne Matt worked with Frank Camorra at MoVida, where he remained until the opportunity arose to run his own kitchen at Pandora's Box and then in 2012 at Pei Modern with revered chef Mark Best.

BERTRAND GRÉBAUT
OWNER-CHEF: SEPTIME AND CLAMATO, PARIS, FRANCE

After training at one of France's top culinary schools Bertrand worked at Marius et Jeannette, La Table de Joël Robuchon, and finally at L'Arpège under Alain Passard in 2006. During his employment there, the restaurant won its first Michelin star. Bertrand departed in 2011 to open Septime a year later: since then he's been listed in the S.Pellegrino World's 50 Best Restaurants and being awarded a Michelin star. Creative, progressive and seasonal, the menu changes every day depending on the fresh ingredients available. Bertrand has since opened Septime La Cave, a wine bar, and Clamato, an oyster bar.

JAMES HENRY
OWNER-CHEF: BONES, PARIS

James Henry has always enjoyed food and grew up surrounded by cookbooks but didn't seriously consider working in the kitchen until his twenties. At 21, he moved from washing dishes at James Street Bistro, Brisbane, into the kitchen. He worked under the guidance of highly regarded Australian chef Andrew McConnell, who helped James turned his raw talent to honed craft. After working as a chef for five years, James set his sights on Paris, securing gigs at Spring as well as at Au Passage for the first year of the restaurant's existence. He is now head chef and owner at Bones where he combines on the best produce in simple dishes, focusing on minimalist, produce-driven small plates as well as a set market-driven menu.

STEPHANE JEGO
OWNER-CHEF: L'AMI JEAN, PARIS, FRANCE

Stephane Jego left school at the age of 14 to complete his cooking apprenticeship. After 12 months in the army, Stephane handed his CV to everyone he could and was hired by Hédiard, place de la Madeleine, until Christian Constant — head chef at the Hôtel de Crillon — found Stephane's CV in a wastepaper bin and gave it to Yves Camdeborde, who turned him into a real chef. Stephane worked under Camdeborde, winning a contest for young chefs in 1994. He continued to work with Camdeborde at La Régalade until he opened l'Ami Jean in 2002.

SHAUN KELLY
ON THE PASS: YARD, PARIS, FRANCE

Before an interest in cooking took hold, Shaun was an art student. Changing the brush for a knife, he started working at The London Club, Brisbane, with Nick Stapleton before moving to Spirit House in Yandina, Queensland, working with Thai cooking stalwarts Helen Brierty and Annette Fear. A move to Melbourne soon followed and Shaun worked at Pearl with Geoff Lindsay before cooking stints at Cumulus Inc. with Andrew McConnell and Coda with Adam D'Sylva. He moved to London, cooking for two years at St. John under Fergus Henderson. A holiday to Paris turned into permanent residency and after a brief time at Saturne, he took over the hotplates at Au Passage.

JAMES KNAPPETT
OWNER-CHEF: BUBBLEDOGS AND KITCHEN TABLE, LONDON, UK

James Knappett has worked at some of the world's most highly regarded restaurants, cooking in the kitchens of The Ledbury (two Michelin stars), Marcus Wareing at The Berkeley (two stars), Restaurant Gordon Ramsay at Royal Hospital Road (three stars) and Rick Stein's The Seafood Restaurant in Padstow. James has also spent time in the kitchens at Noma (two stars) and Thomas Keller's New York City restaurant, Per Se (three stars). James was also part of the team that brought Keller's The French Laundry to Harrods for two weeks in 2012. James opened Kitchen Table at the back of Bubbledogs Champagne bar in October 2012, an intimate chef's table dining room seating just 19. Taking inspiration from his time at Noma and Per Se, James serves seasonal tasting menus, with a focus on British traditions, ingredients and flavours.

MATT LAMBERT
OWNER-CHEF: THE MUSKET ROOM, NEW YORK CITY, USA

Lambert knew from a young age that he wanted to be a chef. At 16, he apprenticed with New Zealand restaurateur Garry Bates, then completed the culinary program at Auckland Insitute of Technology. In 1999, Lambert relocated to Wellington, New Zealand, where he worked in various restaurants while studying. After graduating from Whitireia Community Polytechnic, Lambert opened a café called Sun Seair. Wanting to learn more, Lambert returned to Auckland to work at Red, and then with chef Michael Meredith at The Grove, where he developed a passion for combining classical techniques with Asian flavours. Lambert moved to the USA and became sous chef at John's Café in Woodbury, Connecticut. After two years, he secured a position at PUBLIC, a one-star Michelin-rated restaurant owned by the AvroKO group. He was promoted to sous chef at their sister restaurant Double Crown and then chef de cuisine at PUBLIC and Saxon + Parole in 2011. During this time Lambert competed on *Chopped* on the Food Network, and took on a consulting position with Nestlé, where he helps with their efforts to provide safe and healthy food to families across the USA. He is now owner-chef at The Musket Room.

GREGORY MARCHAND
OWNER-CHEF: FRENCHIE, PARIS, FRANCE

Originally from Nantes, Gregory Marchand left France after finishing cooking school. With his knives as his steady companions, he travelled to New York, London, Spain and Hong Kong. While working at the Gramercy Tavern in New York, his wife received some exciting and fortunate news and the future family returned to Paris, France, where Gregory opened Frenchie; a restaurant that reflected his personality, his trips abroad and his culinary identity.

JOSH MURPHY
OWNER-CHEF: MOON UNDER WATER, MELBOURNE, AUSTRALIA

Born and raised in Tasmania, Josh moved to Melbourne at the age of 18 to begin his cooking career. After a stint at The Palace Hotel in South Melbourne, Josh moved to the three-hatted Circa, The Prince, at St Kilda where he began his long-standing working relationship with Andrew McConnell. At Circa, Josh was introduced to an approach to cooking that is both restrained and considered and where the produce itself is championed. In 2006 Josh was part of the opening team of Three, One, Two restaurant in Carlton where he progressed to the position of head chef. In 2008, Josh headed the kitchen team of the lauded Cumulus Inc. and was awarded Young Chef of the Year by *The Age Good Food Guide* 2012. In April 2012 Josh became part owner of the Builders Arms Hotel and head chef of its dining room Moon Under Water, which was named the hottest restaurant in Victoria in *The Australian* Hot 50 restaurant awards 2012.

JAMES PARRY
OWNER-CHEF: SIXPENNY, SYDNEY, AUSTRALIA

James Parry has diverse experience working at restaurants in Australia and overseas. While working alongside Dan Puskas at Oscillate Wildly, James won the 2009 Josephine Pignolet Young Chef of the Year award. This provided an opportunity for James to travel internationally and spend time in the kitchens at Mugaritz, Noma, and Blue Hill at Stone Barns. Inspired by the produce garden at Mugaritz and the farm at Stone Barns, James helped build sixpenny's very own garden, otherwise known as The Patch, in the Southern Highlands of New South Wales.

GIOVANNI PASSERINI
AT LARGE AT THE TIME OF PRINTING

Passerini's impressive training (he previously worked at l'Arpège, Le Chateaubriand and La Gazzetta) and innovative instincts mean that culinary missteps are rare: he has an innate sense for how to make seasonal produce shine in dishes that draw on tradition but play up surprises. Giovanni was chef and owner of Rino, Paris, for four years and was looking to secure a new location at the time of writing.

DAN PEARSON

AT LARGE AT THE TIME OF PRINTING

Burger van, sausage-making factory, factory canteen, greasy spoon, supermarket, pub, horrible pub, okay pub. Moved to the UK's Chicago Rock Café nightclub then the Hilton, Northampton, followed by the Ambassador in Scarborough and a Best Western hotel in Jersey, UK. Started as an apprentice pastry chef at Chapter 2 and Nico Ladenis's Deca; then spent four and a half years at the Mandarin Oriental's Foliage, working his way to junior sous while sacrificing everything in life including health, love-life and sanity. Moved to New Zealand to work in alleged 'best restaurant'. Lasted one month. Took a job on eight hectares in the sticks and was fired for knocking out a chef with a 7 kg (15½ lb) hapuka. Started the pop-up restaurant Egg & Spoon in Auckland.

PASI PETANEN

OWNER-CHEF: CAFE PACI, SYDNEY, AUSTRALIA

After finishing his culinary training in Finland, Pasi spent four years developing his skills in numerous Finnish restaurants before moving to London to work as chef de partie at The Lowndes Hotel then the three-starred Chez Nico. In 2001, Pasi worked at Sydney's Quay before moving to Marque as pastry chef and then sous chef, as well as doing consulting work in Finland. He worked at The Four in Hand for a year before returning to Marque in 2004 as head chef. In 2013 Pasi opened Café Paci, a pop-up restaurant. How, why and what are common questions with every dish; Pierre Gagnaire's mad hatter's approach of uncommon pairings, unusual ingredients and use of modern techniques, combined with the flavours of his Finnish childhood are huge influences on his food.

SCOTT PICKETT

OWNER-CHEF: ESTELLE BAR & KITCHEN, SAINT CRISPIN, MELBOURNE, AUSTRALIA

Aged 18, Scott entered the Salon Culinaire competition, securing three gold medals and recognition as 'one to watch' by judge Bruno Cerdan. Scott then worked for his mentor Philipe Mouchel at Restaurant Paul Bocuse, before following him to Langton's Restaurant and Wine Bar and The Brasserie by Phillipe Mouchel. A stint at Melbourne's three-hatted restaurant Ondine working under Donovan Cooke, then three years as junior sous chef to Phil Howard at two-Michelin-star restaurant The Square, London. In 2005 Scott represented Australia at the prestigious Bocuse d'Or competition and achieved fourteenth place, Australia's best-ever result at the time. Scott returned to Australia, working at The Point Albert Park Lake, which was named Best Steak Restaurant 2010 by Restaurant & Catering Victoria. In 2011, Scott opened his first restaurant venture, The Estelle Bar & Kitchen in Northcote. In 2013 he received a chef's hat from *The Age Good Food Guide* — an accolade maintained in 2014 — and was nominated for Best New Restaurant. He launched his second restaurant, Saint Crispin, which was awarded one hat and named the Best New Restaurant in *The Age Good Food Guide* 2014.

DAN PUSKAS

OWNER-CHEF: SIXPENNY, SYDNEY, AUSTRALIA

Daniel Puskas began his cooking career with an apprenticeship at Tetsuya's in 2002. Since then he has worked with some of Australia's and the USA's best chefs and won the prestigious Josephine Pignolet Young Chef of the Year award in 2006. After some travel Dan became head chef at Oscillate Wildly, where he received acclaim for his progressive and unusual menu, earning his first chef's hat.After leaving Oscillate, Dan worked with chef Martin Benn at Sepia before leaving to open his own restaurant, sixpenny, with fellow chef and business partner James Parry. Passionate about his cooking, Dan takes inspiration from progressive chefs and techniques from around the world as well as everyday experiences.

RYAN SQUIRES

OWNER-CHEF: ESQUIRE, BRISBANE, AUSTRALIA

After finishing his apprenticeship Ryan opened his first bistro, Terra Sana, with five friends in Marbella, Spain. Moved to Olten, Switzerland, one year later, working at Château Mosimann, then transferred to Mosimann's Club, a private restaurant in Belgrave Square, London. Twelve months later, a 3 am phone call and visa approval saw him cook for the opening of Per Se, New York, then The French Laundry in the Napa Valley for two years before working as a private chef in Hamilton, Bermuda. After six years, Ryan moved back to Brisbane to work at Urbane; but after being fired he moved to Roses, Spain, working at elBulli and staging at wd~50, New York, and Providence, Los Angeles. He was appointed head chef at The Buffalo Club, Brisbane, receiving *The Courier-Mail* chef of the year award in 2009 and the *Australian Gourmet Traveller* 2010 gong for best new talent. From here, he staged at Noma, Copenhagen, before returning to Brisbane to open Esquire, achieving three hats and restaurant of the year in the *brisbanetimes.com.au Good Food Guide* in 2012 and 2013. Ryan is a boating enthusiast and single at the time of printing.

ARI TAYMOR
OWNER-CHEF: ALMA, LOS ANGELES, USA

Ari Taymor started cooking during his university years in Sydney, Australia. After he graduated, Ari worked in the USA for a year, staging in numerous restaurants. With this experience under his belt, Taymor was on the opening team at James Beard Foundation award-nominated flour + water in San Francisco. Ari then spent a season at Armand Arnal's one-starred La Chassagnette in Arles, France, both cooking and working in the garden. Returning to San Francisco he worked at the iconic Mission District restaurant Bar Tartine and was on Kim Alter's opening team at Plate Shop. Ari relocated to Los Angeles where he opened Alma, first as a pop-up restaurant moving around the city and, finally, in its current home downtown. Alma was recently named *bon appétit*'s Best New Restaurant in America 2013.

DAVE VERHEUL
OWNER-CHEF: THE TOWN MOUSE, MELBOURNE, AUSTRALIA

Dave discovered his culinary calling while studying for a degree in psychology at the University of Otago, New Zealand, and working as a chef at a seaside fine-dining establishment in Auckland. He moved to London and from 2004 he worked at the starred Savoy Grill under Marcus Wareing. He supplemented his experience with extended stages at various Michelin-starred restaurants, including The Fat Duck. In 2007 he moved to Sydney to take up a role with culinary mentor, Brent Savage: co-owner of Sydney's hatted Bentley Restaurant and Bar. He then headed the kitchen of New Zealand culinary institution Matterhorn, receiving critical recognition both locally and internationally for his food. Moving to Melbourne in 2013, he opened The Town Mouse with his business partner. Since then the restaurant has secured places in *Australian Gourmet Traveller*'s Top 100, *The Australian* Hot 50 restaurant awards and *The Age Good Food Guide*'s 10 hottest new restaurants 2014 list.

BEAU VINCENT
OWNER-CHEF: SUBO, NEWCASTLE, AUSTRALIA

Beau Vincent began cooking at the age of 16 in a small pub near his parents' farm in Walcha, New South Wales. He learnt the basics of running a small pub kitchen but craved more and completed an apprenticeship under the tutelage of Tetsuya Wakuda in Sydney. Beau then worked at Guillaume at Bennelong, where he spent three years exploring French cuisine, before joining Warren Turnbull at Restaurant Assiette. His awards include the Lexus Young Chef of the Year 2006 and was part of a team who won third place in the San Pellegrino Cooking Cup in Venice, Italy, 2007. Returning to Guillaume at Bennelong as sous chef, Beau learnt the intricacies of running a large kitchen, and accepted the head chef position at Melbourne's Bistro Guillaume, which earned one chef's hat from *The Age Good Food Guide* in his first year. Beau now runs Subo, where he is both head chef and owner.

WESLEY YOUNG
COOKING AT: WILDEBEEST, VANCOUVER, CANADA

Chef Wesley Young is famous for his daring whole-animal cookery with the utmost integrity: his cooking mentality is 'the odd bits rule'. Young, who has worked at Wildebeest since it opened in August 2012, previously cooked at West and C restaurants in Vancouver, 357c in Montreal and Tom Aikens Restaurant in London.

COME IN
for good times

GLOSSARY

EQUIPMENT

ESPUMA GUN Espuma (foam) is made using a cream whipper, also known as a siphon, using nitrous oxide cartridges to incorporate air and create a dense mousse-type foam.

HANDHELD FOOD SMOKER The Smoking Gun is an alternative to traditional smoking methods. It is a smoking chamber, operated with batteries. Similar to traditional smoking it burns a variety of woodchips to create the smokey flavour.

MOULI GRATER This is a hand-operated kitchen utensil designed for grating or puréeing small quantities of food. It consists of a small metal drum with holes that grate the food and a handle for turning the drum.

INGREDIENTS

AMARANTH (CHINESE SPINACH) SEEDS An especially high-quality source of plant protein including two essential amino acids, lysine and methionine. Amaranth is packed with iron and calcium, and its fiber content is triple that of wheat. The leaves of this plant are also used.

BANYULS WINE VINEGAR Aged sweet vinegar.

BLACK GARLIC Caramelised fermented garlic.

BOTTARGA Salted, cured fish roe.

CAMELINA OIL Replace with flax oil if unavailable.

LARDO DI COLONNATA Cured pork backfat from Colonnata, Italy.

LILLET BLANC A French aperitif wine, blending 85 per cent Bordeaux wines with citrus liqueur.

MATCHA Powdered green tea.

SALTBUSH *Atriplex nummularia* is an Australian native that is used in cooking as a savoury herb and flavourful green vegetable.

SAMPHIRE (SEABEAN) *Sarcocornia quinqueflora* has vibrant green stalks, similar to baby asparagus, with a distinctively crisp and salty taste. It can be used raw in salad, though it tends to be very salty so it is more often boiled or steamed for a few minutes.

SHIO KOJI Fermented rice.

TASAJO Beef jerky.

WAKAME Edible brown seaweed.

YUZUKOSHO A type of Japanese seasoning. It is a paste made from chilli peppers, yuzu peel and salt, which is then allowed to ferment before being used.

SEASONINGS

AJI DULCE (CACHUCHA PEPPER) A small green and sweet capsicum (pepper). It is mild in heat.

ALEPPO PEPPER A variety of capsicum that is used in Mediterranean cooking. It starts as pods which ripen to a burgundy colour and are then semi-dried, deseeded and crushed or coarsely ground.

BLACK LAVA SALT This has an earthy flavour and smoky top note from the blending of salt with activated charcoal, distinguishing itself from many other finishing salts.

ESPELETTE PEPPER Piment d'Espelette is a chilli plant that originated in Mexico, now cultivated widely in the Pyrénées. Espelette pepper is mild in heat, but rich in its sweet, fruity fragrance: reminiscent of tomatoes and roasted capsicum.

FLEUR DE SEL 'Flower of salt' is considered the gold standard of salts. The famous thin layer of fine crystal salt that forms on the marshes of the Île de Ré is prized for its delicate flavour and beautiful crystalline appearance.

KAMPOT PEPPER A pepper grown in Cambodi, popular in cooking and seasoning for its delicacy and sweetness.

SHICHIMI TOGARASHI Called seven spice (shichi is 'seven' in Japanese). It works well with fatty foods such as unagi (broiled eel), tempura, shabu shabu (small bits of food cooked in rich broth), noodle dishes, and yakitori (grilled dishes).

SETTING AGENTS

AGAR-AGAR Considered the king of gelling agents. It is an excellent thickening agent. Agar-agar is derived from *Gracilaria* and *Gelidium* species of red algae.

CARRAGEENAN Food-grade carrageenan is a purified extract from red algae (*Chondrus crispus*). It is used as a thickener and stabiliser in a wide range of food products including ice cream. Carrageenan is a naturally sourced material with little taste or odour and a long history of safe use in food products. **Iota** dissolves in cold water and is heated for a soft gel that does not form while the mixture is stirred. **Kappa** will mix while cold and its rapid setting allows the user to cover ingredients. Once set it can withstand temperatures of up to 60°C (140°F). **Lambda** is non-gelling, high viscosity and cold-soluble.

GELATINE Gelatine is a colourless, odourless substance made from collagen derived from animal byproducts. Throughout this book, leaf gelatine has been used. Leaf gelatine is sold at specialty food stores and delis. Gelatine sheets are available in different strengths and weights: titanium (5 g), bronze (3.3 g), silver (2.5 g), gold (2 g) and platinum (1.7 g). One sheet of gelatine will set 100 ml (3½ fl oz) of liquid to a firm (mouldable) jelly, or 125 ml (4 fl oz/½ cup) to a soft jelly.

XANTHAN GUM Made from fermented cornflour (cornstarch) and widely used as a thickener, it's gluten free and available from health food stores and some supermarkets.

CHEF INDEX

INDEX

Page numbers in *italics* refer to photographs.

ACKNOWLEDGMENTS

Books are huge, overwhelming, life-encompassing beasts. And this one, which started as a dream on the streets of Paris, is now alive in our hands thanks to a multitude of people who cared as deeply as I did about bringing it to fruition. To each and every one of you I am thankful.

First and foremost the chefs. The hardworking foot soldiers of our culinary world who found an email from me in their inbox one day and so willingly responded with their time, talent and patience. One email turned to many, which turned into phone calls and, where geographically possible, coffees, meals and some of the most exciting and heated discussions about food and culinary trends I am ever likely to have. I will forever treasure this process.

Julia Child for the enduring legacy of sharing food at the table, and her ongoing generosity through scholarships and research funding; without it ideas and stories about food like this are a little less likely. Bon appétit.

Diana Hill, Sue Hines, Hugh Ford, Claire Grady, Melody Lord and the Murdoch Books/Allen & Unwin family. Thank you for your relentless patience, fortitude and enthusiasm, and for shaping and moulding this monster into what it now is. I am always flabbergasted by the editing and design process and the depth and quality it can bring to an idea when translating it to paper.

TS for putting up with me flitting off to Paris at every opportunity researching for this book, and always being my number one supporter, friend and believer.

Luke Burgess, a man of many talents. Thank you for your beautiful photographs, for teaching me how to shuck abalone, for your relentless enthusiasm and making sure everything is 'just so'. You have created a visual feast.

My family and friends for putting up with the insufferable. For the reading, rereading, taste testing and enduring the psychotic angst that came with each and every one of my deadlines.

Also a special thank you to a few people who really went above and beyond in helping get this project off the ground: thank you, Dan Pearson, Wendy Lyn, Pasi Petanen and to Sébastien Villeneuve who tragically passed away while this book was being written.

Published in 2014 by Murdoch Books, an imprint of Allen & Unwin.

Murdoch Books Australia
83 Alexander Street
Crows Nest NSW 2065
Phone: +61 (0) 2 8425 0100
Fax: +61 (0) 2 9906 2218
www.murdochbooks.com.au
info@murdochbooks.com.au

Murdoch Books UK
Erico House, 6th Floor
93–99 Upper Richmond Road
Putney, London SW15 2TG
Phone: +44 (0) 20 8785 5995
Fax: +44 (0) 20 8785 5985
www.murdochbooks.co.uk
info@murdochbooks.co.uk

For Corporate Orders & Custom Publishing contact
Noel Hammond, National Business Development Manager, Murdoch Books Australia

Publisher: Diana Hill
Designers: Jay Ryves at Future Classic and Hugh Ford
Photographer: Luke Burgess
Editor: Melody Lord
Editorial Managers: Claire Grady and Barbara McClenahan
Production Manager: Mary Bjelobrk

All photography by Luke Burgess except for the following.

7 David Lanthan Reamer; 8 David Lanthan Reamer; 16 Tyson Sutton; 21 Dean Cambray; 27 Gilles Jacob; 38 courtesy of Yves Camdeborde; 49 Tyson Sutton; 53 Tyson Sutton; 59 Sarah Anderson; 66 Tyson Sutton; 69 Tyson Sutton; 70 Tyson Sutton; 73 Tyson Sutton; 74 courtesy of Septime Restaurant; 99 Gilles Jacob; 104 Tyson Sutton; 105 Katrina Meynink; 150 Phoebe Glasfurd; 189 Rob Whitrow; 197 Rob Whitrow; 203 Tyson Sutton; 207 Gilles Jacob; 219 Dean Cambray; 233 Rob Whitrow; 248–9 Chef portraits by Luke Burgess, Dean Cambray, Saul Germaine, Daniel Krieger, Damien Lafargue, Laura Leyshon, Katrina Meynink, Tyson Sutton, Josh Vincent and Lauren Volo, or courtesy of the chef.

A cataloguing-in-publication entry is available from the catalogue of the National Library of Australia at www.nla.gov.au.

A catalogue record for this book is available from the British Library.

Printed by 1010 Printing International Limited, China

IMPORTANT: Those who might be at risk from the effects of salmonella poisoning (the elderly, pregnant women, young children and those suffering from immune deficiency diseases) should consult their doctor with any concerns about eating raw eggs.

OVEN GUIDE: You may find cooking times vary depending on the oven you are using. For fan-forced ovens, as a general rule, set the oven temperature to 20°C (35°F) lower than indicated in the recipe.

MEASURES GUIDE: We have used 20 ml (4 teaspoon) tablespoon measures. If you are using a 15 ml (3 teaspoon) tablespoon add an extra teaspoon of the ingredient for each tablespoon specified.

Sage by Heston Blumenthal appliances supplied by Breville.